Poetry of Our Time

Poetry of Our Time

AN INTRODUCTION TO
TWENTIETH-CENTURY POETRY

INCLUDING
MODERN CANADIAN POETRY

Edited by Louis Dudek

TORONTO

THE MACMILLAN COMPANY

OF CANADA LIMITED

Acknowledgments

(Page v-xi constitute an extension of the copyright page.)

The editors are grateful to those publishers, agents, and individuals who have permitted the use of copyright material by the following authors.

W. H. AUDEN: Seven selections from *Shorter Collected Poems* by W. H. Auden; reprinted by permission of Faber and Faber Ltd.

MARGARET AVISON: 'Hiatus' from *Winter Sun* by Margaret Avison; reprinted by permission of University of Toronto Press.

EARLE BIRNEY: 'David', 'Status quo', and 'Time-bomb' from *The Strait of Anian* by Earle Birney, Ryerson Press, Toronto; reprinted by permission of the author. 'For George Lamming' from *Near False Creek Mouth* by Earle Birney; reprinted by permission of the author and McClelland and Stewart Limited.

LEONARD COHEN: 'Les Vieux' and 'Prayer for Sunset' from *Let Us Compare Mythologies* by Leonard Cohen, Contact Press, Toronto; reprinted by permission of the author. 'The Bus' from *Flowers for Hitler* by Leonard Cohen; reprinted by permission of the author and McClelland and Stewart Limited.

ALEX COMFORT: 'Notes for My Son' from *The Song of Lazarus* by Alex Comfort, copyright 1945 by Alex Comfort; reprinted by permission of The Viking Press, Inc.

HART CRANE: Three selections from *The Collected Poems of Hart Crane*; reprinted by permission of Liveright, Publishers, N.Y. Copyright (C) R, 1961 by Liveright Publishing Corp.

E. E. CUMMINGS: 'the sky was' and 'Buffalo Bill's defunct' (copyright 1923, 1951 by E. E. Cummings); 'Poem, or Beauty Hurts Mr. Vinal' (copyright 1926 by Horace Liveright, copyright 1954 by E. E. Cummings); 'r-p-o-p-h-e-s-s-a-g-r' (copyright 1935 by E. E. Cummings, renewed © 1963 by Marion Morehouse Cummings). All from *Poems 1923-1954* by E. E. Cummings; reprinted by permission of Harcourt, Brace & World, Inc.

ROY DANIELLS: Two selections from *The Chequered Shade* by Roy Daniells; reprinted by permission of McClelland and Stewart Limited.

LOUIS DUDEK: 'Tree in a Street' and 'In Spring' from *East of the City* by Louis Dudek; reprinted by permission of The Ryerson Press, Toronto. 'Midnight Train' and 'News' from *The Transparent Sea* by Louis Dudek, Contact Press, Toronto; reprinted by permission of the author.

T. S. ELIOT: Seven selections from *Collected Poems 1909-1962* by T. S. Eliot; reprinted by permission of Faber and Faber Ltd.

R. G. EVERSON: Two selections from *Blind Man's Holiday* by R. G. Everson, The Ryerson Press, Toronto; reprinted by permission of the author.

LAWRENCE FERLINGHETTI: 'Constantly risking absurdity ...' from *A Coney Island of the Mind* by Lawrence Ferlinghetti; copyright 1955 by Lawrence Ferlinghetti, copyright © 1958 by Lawrence Ferlinghetti; reprinted by permission of New Directions Publishing Corp., New York.

ROBERT FROST: Four selections from *Complete Poems of Robert Frost*, copyright 1916, 1930, 1934, 1939 by Holt, Rinehart and Winston, Inc. Copyright 1942, 1944, © 1958, 1962 by Robert Frost. Reprinted by permission of Holt, Rinehart and Winston, Inc., New York.

SAINT-DENYS GARNEAU: Three selections from *Poésies complètes* by Saint-Denys Garneau; reprinted by permission of Les Editions Fides. English translations: 'Bird Cage' and 'Accompaniment' from *Translations of S.-D. Garneau and Anne Hébert* by F. R. Scott, Klanak Press, Vancouver; reprinted by permission of the author. 'Portrait' by Louis Dudek; reprinted by permission of the author.

ALLEN GINSBERG: 'A Supermarket in California' and lines from 'Howl' from *Howl and Other Poems* by Allen Ginsberg. Copyright © 1956 by Allen Ginsberg. Reprinted by permission of City Light Books.

JOHN GLASSCO: 'Quebec Farmhouse' from *A Point of Sky* by John Glassco; reprinted by permission of Oxford University Press, Canadian Branch.

ALAIN GRANDBOIS: Three selections from *Poèmes* by Alain Grandbois, Editions de l'Hexagone; reprinted by permission of the author. English translations: 'It is to all of you ...' from *Selected Poems of Alain Grandbois* by Peter Miller, Contact Press, Toronto, and 'What remains ...' and 'Forgotten Childhood' by Peter Miller. All reprinted by permission of the author.

All from *Collected Poems* by Marianne Moore; reprinted by permission of The Macmillan Company, New York.

ÉMILE NELLIGAN: 'Le Vaisseau d'Or' from *Poésies complètes* by Emile Nelligan; reprinted by permission of Les Editions Fides. English translation from *Selected Poems of Emile Nelligan*, edited by P. F. Widdows; reprinted by permission of The Ryerson Press, Toronto.

ALDEN NOWLAN: Two selections from *The Things Which Are* by Alden Nowlan, Contact Press, Toronto; reprinted by permission of the author.

P. K. PAGE: 'The Bands and the Beautiful Children' from *As Ten As Twenty* by P. K. Page, The Ryerson Press, Toronto; 'The Permanent Tourists' from *The Metal and the Flower* by P. K. Page, McClelland and Stewart Limited; both reprinted by permission of Mrs. W. A. Irwin.

JEAN-GUY PILON: 'Noces' from *La Mouette et le Large* by Jean-Guy Pilon, Editions de l'Hexagone; reprinted by permission of the author. 'L'Exigence du pays! . . . ' from *Pour saluer une ville* by Jean-Guy Pilon; reprinted by permission of Editions Seghers. English translations by Louis Dudek; reprinted by permission of the author.

EZRA POUND: 'What thou lovest well remains . . . ' from *The Cantos* by Ezra Pound, Faber and Faber Ltd.; all other poems from *Personae* by Ezra Pound, Faber and Faber Ltd. Reprinted by permission of Arthur V. Moore, literary agent for Ezra Pound.

E. J. PRATT: Three selections and lines from 'From Stone to Steel' from *Collected Poems* by E. J. Pratt; reprinted by permission of The Macmillan Company of Canada Limited.

ALFRED PURDY: Two selections from *Poems for All the Annettes* by Alfred Purdy, Contact Press, Toronto; reprinted by permission of the author.

JOHN CROWE RANSOM: Two selections from *Selected Poems*, Revised Edition, by John Crowe Ransom, copyright 1927 by Alfred A. Knopf, Inc.; renewed 1955 by John Crowe Ransom; reprinted by permission of Alfred A. Knopf, Inc.

JAMES REANEY: Two selections from *The Red Heart* by James Reaney, McClelland and Stewart Limited; reprinted by permission of Sybil Hutchinson, literary agent for James Reaney.

EDWIN ARLINGTON ROBINSON: 'Richard Cory' from *The Children of the Night* by Edwin Arlington Robinson (1897), and lines from 'Miniver Cheevy' from *The Town Down the River* by Edwin Arlington Robinson. Both reprinted by permission of Charles Scribner's Sons.

Editor's Note

In the preparation of this anthology I am grateful to several teachers and experts with books who have examined the selections and critical notes and have offered useful comments and suggestions. Among these I would like to thank especially Cecil J. Porter, Head of the English Department, Cobourg District Collegiate Institute East; M. Gnarowski, English Department, Lakehead College of Arts, Science and Technology, Port Arthur, Ontario; Miss Verna Collins, Marymount High School, Montreal; Mrs. Andrea Rutland, Redpath Library, McGill University; and Miss Aileen Collins, Holy Names High School, Montreal. For valuable assistance I owe thanks to the editorial staff of the School Book Department, Macmillan Company of Canada Limited, Toronto. I am also grateful for typing assistance and helpful criticism to my sister, Lillian Dudek.

Louis Dudek, M.A., PH.D. (Columbia)
Associate Professor of English Literature
McGill University

Contents

Poetry of Our Time

Twentieth-Century Poetry

The poetry of this century is radically different in many ways from that of the last century. This is only to be expected, since all things change. And poetry today — like painting, music, sculpture, and architecture — is different from that of the past.

The change has been so rapid and so great that many people find it hard to adapt themselves to the new kind of poetry. Many still refuse to accept the modern style in poetry, just as they refuse to accept the new styles in painting, sculpture, and music. This resistance will probably pass, but it is still strong and it is understandable. The result is that, in school texts and popular anthologies, contemporary poetry has often been represented by its more conventional examples, selections that too much resemble the poetry of the last century. In this way the characteristic elements of modernism are blurred and lost.

In this book we take the risk of looking at twentieth-century poetry as it really is. *Poetry of Our Time* is an introduction to modern poetry designed to present, vividly, its most characteristic features.

But there is one feature of modern poetry that we hope you will find absent; and this is its so-called 'obscurity'. The accusation, 'It's too difficult', has often been made by opponents of the new literature as part of their case against reading it. There has been a good deal of difficult poetry written in this century, but the same is true of any century. The difficult poem is for 'advanced' readers. In itself, 'obscurity' cannot be a real characteristic of the poetry of any age, since it is not any positive quality of poetry. Obscurity is a difficulty experienced by the reader in understanding the poetry.

Modern literature arose by reaction to the preceding period, perhaps more so than any other similar movement in the past. Elizabethan poetry came about without any such special quarrel with the past, although the humanists of that time did look back with some contempt at the whole period of the Middle

Ages. The neo-classical age, a century later, stressed classical learning, the adherence to ancient literary rules, and reason and common sense, as opposed to enthusiasm and uncontrolled imagination. The poetry of this age did think of itself as a great improvement over the 'barbarism' of the Elizabethans, but the neo-classical age was not a revolt. Romantic poetry, as written at the turn of the nineteenth century, was indeed a revolt against the neo-classical style; its spirit of rebellion does resemble that of the twentieth century. But our own literature is even more radically at odds with the past. And strangely enough, it is at odds with the late product of romanticism itself — the poetry of the Victorian Age.

Victorian poetry had fallen into the rut, so to speak, of the quatrain, a stanza of four lines, usually rhyming alternately. Its content had become a mere echo of the romantic expression of elevated emotion, parroting moral ideals and beliefs, often expressed in purely abstract terms against a background of idyllic 'nature'. Real nature had gone to the beauty parlour and come out as Victorian poetry. Against this poetry of decadent romanticism — a taste still today widespread and popular — the new poetry of the twentieth century has raised its battle cry. 'It's absolutely the *last* obsequies of the Victorian period,' boasted Ezra Pound, describing one of his modernistic poems of 1913. 'What soft cherubic creatures / These gentlewomen are!' wrote Emily Dickinson in one of her rare satirical poems. 'How beastly the bourgeois is,' echoed D. H. Lawrence later, more harshly. These are the voices of the modern revolt.

Here a word of caution may be in order. We don't believe everything we read. In an age of swift and radical changes, in manners and patterns of living, ideas will run rampant in the effort of men to find new order, or to break away from the rigid restraints of the past. Shelley, Byron, and Blake lived in such a time: Shelley was an atheist in his Cambridge days, a radical republican throughout his life; Blake was a moral rebel of the first water; Byron shocked his age with *Manfred* and

Don Juan. In our time, poets have appeared as violent critics of society in a time of change (Ezra Pound); as moralists preaching strange new doctrine (D. H. Lawrence); as prophets of despair (Robinson Jeffers); as cynics and laughing satirists on occasion (E. E. Cummings). None of them need be followed implicitly; all of them may have something to teach us.

Nor is the moral order of the past so much discredited. Poets are surely not destroyers; if anything, they are the architects of order, and they are sensitive recorders of distress and disorder. The past may need to be adapted to new conditions, or partially revised. Many modern poets have been deeply concerned about the loss of religious faith in our century, about the gross materialism of our commercial civilization, about the chaos apparent in our moral life. They have depicted this age in its throes of change with great vividness and with great honesty. As for what is to be done, that is for each individual to consider in his own life. The purpose of a diversity of views is that we should be moved to think and to decide for ourselves. Poetry does not persuade; it makes us feel and perceive.

We know that life in the twentieth century is radically different from life in the past. It is this difference that makes for the difference in our poetry; exciting experiments with forms, violent discords, passionate cries of distress or joy are all 'in the spirit of the age'. Huge populations have grown, cities have expanded immensely, industrial life has hit a new pace in each decade as new inventions appeared on the scene — the telephone, the radio, the airplane, moving pictures, television. Skyscrapers have sprung on the horizon. Terrifying political fanaticisms have swept the world. Masses of people compressed to anonymity by new methods of transit and communication listen bewildered to torrents of news, salesmanship, and entertainment, while jet planes, missiles, and atomic annihilation threaten. Leisure, affluence, and comforts such as the world has never known even in the courts of princes have come within the reach of millions, yet large areas of the world remain greatly impoverished. Such is the new world that poetry has tried to take into its province.

The break with the poetry of late romanticism came gradually. Two poets of the latter half of the nineteenth century, writing in seclusion, unknown to their own time, may be considered forerunners of the modern style: Emily Dickinson and Gerard Manley Hopkins. Three others, writing just before the turn of the century and after, stand on the brink of transition: A. E. Housman, Thomas Hardy, and Edwin Arlington Robinson. They are poets who wrote still chiefly in the quatrain form, still in the manner of Victorian meditative verse centred in nature, but who suggest a great discontent, a promise of change, by their pessimism, their bitter austerity, and the economy of their style.

Emily Dickinson suggests the coming mode by the eccentricity and compactness of her writing. Tension in her poetry hampers any free flow of romantic sentiment; lyricism has become analytic and self-critical. It is almost ready to pass to a modern kind of intellectuality.

Hopkins is similarly trapped in a secret conflict. His highly original metre, which he called 'sprung rhythm' – an effect like running on crutches – his bursts of enthusiasm and lapses of deep melancholy, seem to suggest a desperate need for the traditional faith which he embraced, as though the arguments of the world around him were being levelled against any easier belief. Hopkins became a Roman Catholic, a Jesuit, in the wake of the Oxford Movement, which was itself a movement of recoil from sceptical scientism and the disrupting forces already apparent in Victorian England. The movement sought to revitalize the Church of England, to restore a greater degree of ritual, and to place Anglicanism as a *via media* between Roman Catholicism and Evangelicalism.

Hardy, on the other hand, was a partisan of materialistic science. He felt that science had uprooted religion and that the arguments of science were unanswerable. His frankness on

4

sexual matters in his last novels and in his poetry makes him again a forerunner of the moderns. He joins with Housman and Robinson as a dark pessimist of the transition. We must recall that the romantic period was one of inspired affirmation, as in Shelley's 'Hymn to Intellectual Beauty' or Wordsworth's 'Tintern Abbey'. The last romantics appearing in a dejected mood announce the end of one movement in literature and the beginning of a new one.

The actual break with sentimental-romantic conventions came around the turn of the century, first in the popular realistic verse of Rudyard Kipling:

> Ah! What avails the classic bent
> And what the cultured word,
> Against the undoctored incident
> That actually occurred?
>
> And what is Art whereto we press
> Through paint and prose and rhyme —
> When Nature in her nakedness
> Defeats us every time?
>
> (from 'The Benefactors')

Kipling and Masefield rebelled against the past like bad boys on a short rebellious binge, only to return later to good behaviour and excessive conservatism. In the wonderful poem 'Mandalay', Kipling's hero wants to go 'Where there aren't no Ten Commandments an' a man can raise a thirst' — which sounds a bit like Huckleberry Finn grown up. And, in the poem 'M'Andrew's Hymn' (1893), the engineer of the *Mary Gloster* answers the sentimentalist:

> 'Mister M'Andrew, don't you think steam spoils romance
>   at sea?'
> Damned ijjit! I'd been doon that morn to see what ailed
>   the throws,
> Manholin', on my back — the cranks three inches off my nose.

5

Romance! Those first-class passengers they like it very well,
Printed and bound in little books; but why don't poets tell?
I'm sick of all their quirks an' turns — the loves an' doves
    they dream —
Lord, send a man like Robbie Burns to sing the Song o' Steam!

In the same vein, Masefield wrote his powerful realistic narrative *The Everlasting Mercy* (1911), the poem that won him fame. It tells the story of a tough bruiser, a boxer and heavy drinker, who sins, suffers, and 'gets religion' in the end. Both the violence of the action and the religious conversion in the poem are sensational versions of an idea that occurs in later, more sophisticated poetry.

Realism, clearly, is an ingredient of the modern view of life. In earlier poetry, realism had been excluded in favour of ideal perfection, the romantic ideal of beauty; only in the novels, not in the poems, of the last century did realism become a useful program and a source of powerful writing. In this century, the poem seems to have caught up with the novel. But realism is obviously not an easy and natural way for poetry; the problem of poetry is to transform dross and despair and to raise them — or at least to contrast them — to something that the heart desires, the ideal that is equally true and necessary. The effort to do this, even the bitter failure, but still the effort, runs through the entire history of poetry in this century.

The American side of first-stage realism in modern poetry appeared with Carl Sandburg, Vachel Lindsay, and Edgar Lee Masters, during the period of the First World War. Kipling and Masefield had whacked away in the old traditional metres; they were extremely conservative in form, while they explored new subject matter. Sandburg and Masters employed the new 'free verse' (*vers libre*), recently imported into England from France, and this became the characteristic verse form of the new movement.

Traditional metre, especially as it had been developed in the romantic period, tended to set up a large, sweeping wave of rhythm, like an ocean swell, in which the particular words and their meanings were carried along —

> This is the forest primeval. The murmuring pines and the
>   hemlocks,
> Bearded with moss, and with garments green, indistinct in the
>   twilight.
>
> (from 'Evangeline' by
Henry Wadsworth Longfellow)

while free verse built up its rhythmic effects out of the meaning and feeling of each particular group of words:

> Nobody knows now where Chick Lorimer went.
> Nobody knows why she packed her trunk . . . a few old things
> And is gone.
>   Gone with her little chin
>   Thrust ahead of her
>   And her soft hair blowing careless
>   From under a wide hat . . .
>
> (from 'Gone' by Carl Sandburg)

Carl Sandburg applied this kind of rhythm to his description of the landscape of industrial Chicago and the American Midwest. In his poetry, realistic toughness is tempered by the humanitarian and democratic ideal: a feeling for 'the common man', or 'the people', inspires all his poetry. This element of democracy had moved Walt Whitman, in the preceding century, to bring poetry down to common things — 'the Muse amid the kitchenware' — and Sandburg continued in Whitman's steps. As Sandburg applied the idea of 'the people', however, it became very much a sentimental good thing, since it shut his eyes to what makes actual people either bright or dull, extraordinary or insignificant. Poetry exists, surely, to make us see the scale of differences among people, not to level them down to a general equality. The praise of any one class — even the people — as if it had all the virtues, is absurd. If 'the people' is humanity — as it sometimes seems to be in Sandburg — an admiration for mankind has no point. Yet in a practical way, the generous acceptance of ordinary life and ordinary people is a valuable ingredient of democracy. And Sandburg has written some of the most charming and wistful poems of contemporary life: a humanitarian gentleness softens his occasional social anger and the hardness of his realistic subject matter to give us singing poetry of a very personal, unique kind.

Vachel Lindsay and Edgar Lee Masters provide variations of the democratic idea in poetry. Lindsay was something of a folk poet, an emotional visionary child, who took poetry to the people in the form of revivalist recitations (the jazz sessions and poetry readings of recent 'beat' poets resemble nothing so much as Lindsay in this):

> In a nation of one hundred fine, mob-hearted, lynching, relenting, repenting millions,
> There are plenty of sweeping, swinging, stinging, gorgeous things to shout about,
> And knock your old blue devils out.
>
> I brag and chant of Bryan, Bryan, Bryan,
> Candidate for president who sketched a silver Zion,
> The one American Poet who could sing outdoors,
> He brought in tides of wonder, of unprecedented splendor,
> Wild roses from the plains, that made hearts tender,
> All the funny circus silks
> Of politics unfurled,
> Bartlett pears of romance that were honey at the cores,
> And torchlights down the street, to the end of the world . . .

> (from 'Bryan, Bryan, Bryan, Bryan'
> by Vachel Lindsay)

Masters wrote a powerful and popular book *Spoon River Anthology*, in which the ordinary inhabitants of an American small town speak from their graves about life, suffering, injustice, sex, sudden death, and the search for the meaning of it all. It is still a great book to pick up and read from beginning to end.

So on both sides of the Atlantic the twentieth century in

poetry moved towards realism, at some points urban realism, and disenchantment. It abandoned the set metres of the quatrain and experimented with free-verse forms. But not all the major figures in poetry, we should note, have gone along with these currents of the age. Two, at least, have resisted the demands of modernism and have written great poetry by developing in the line of the old romantic tradition. These are W. B. Yeats writing in the British tradition and Robert Frost in the American.

Yeats (born 1865) began writing in the 1880s, so it is not surprising that his early poetry is bathed in aestheticism, dreams, and ethereal music. Withdrawal from life carried Yeats farther than any other poet towards an imaginary realm — to the study of mystical doctrines, theosophy, magic, and eastern religions. Then, as he matured, he turned more to actuality, but his poetry became as a result hard, small, and dry:

> Though leaves are many, the root is one;
> Through all the lying days of my youth
> I swayed my leaves and flowers in the sun;
> Now I may wither into the truth.
>
> (from 'The Coming of Wisdom With Time')

Out of this barren stage of truth-seeking, Yeats might have been expected to develop in a modernistic vein. But he did not. The astonishing growth of his poetry after 1910 was a further explosion of his mystical supernatural yearning into prophetic statement and vision.

'We were the last romantics . . .' Yeats said in a poem; and to the end he remained faithful to a high, uncompromising idealism. The subject of much of his poetry is love, his great life-long love for Maud Gonne; but love for Yeats is also a vehicle for a variety of statements, upon life, politics, history, beliefs, and the fading ideals of love itself. In the early poems love is the occasion for mourning 'that no new wonder may betide' — that the world had declined from its former nobility; and in the later poems love is a great memory that contrasts

9

with the troubles of the present and the future. Yeats was a bitter critic of our age. But he never presented clearly or specifically what it was he objected to in middle-class life, or what virtues he admired in the peasantry and aristocracy. His attitudes remain personal and temperamental; yet his poetry is a burst of authentic romanticism carried into the heart of the twentieth century.

Robert Frost, the American conservative voice in poetry, represents for many people exactly what a poet should be. Traditional verse metres and familiar nature setting are the perfect recipe to suit tastes formed in the romantic tradition and resistant to modern changes. But Frost is a realist of nature. And his metres go with a natural speaking voice which in spirit is close to free verse. (His metre and rhyme become more obtrusive in the later poetry, so that in criticism one could say: 'Mr. Frost, you stopped writing free verse.' A bit of a joke, since he had always been strongheaded against the free-verse form.) The theme of his poetry is an austere, realistic conception of nature and a stoical acceptance of its conditions, in no way a sentimental view of nature's comforts or beauty. 'The Death of the Hired Man' is a famous poem that well illustrates this: a homeless man comes to die on the farm where he had worked for many years — he has no other place to go; a young hard-working couple argue and discuss whether they should take him back, a useless burden on the farm. He dies before the conversation is finished. There is ironic compassion in the poem, kindness tempering the cruelty of our natural condition.

The austerity of Frost's attitude in the face of nature separates him from the sentimental line of minor poets; but the theme of nature also makes him perhaps too universal to be entirely relevant to the special problems of today. The problems of modern life and culture are urban — they are the problems of the industrialized city extending its influence throughout the countryside and even absorbing the country into the city. Robert Frost has set his back against the city, and has written of it only in the most general terms, to deplore the urbanized life: so that his poetry does not effectively reach the central issues of today. His comment that the truth of nature is what we should try to return to does indeed carry much wisdom, but it does not come down to cases in life as most of us live it. And the countryside is not something we can go to for comfort — except on a holiday.

The final break with romantic nature-worship, and with the verbal excesses that were a part of romanticism in decadence, came with the Imagist movement in poetry, beginning in 1912. This movement, fathered in London by Ezra Pound with the help of ideas from T. E. Hulme, Ford Madox Ford, and others, limited the poem in scope to the 'image' — defined as 'an intellectual and emotional complex in an instant of time'. The result was a series of short poems written by H. D. (Hilda Doolittle), Richard Aldington, Pound, Williams — even Lawrence and T. S. Eliot were drawn in — to depict some single visual or sensory experience with great precision and clarity. Then, as the image began to speak, that is, as the images of contemporary life began to yield their new meanings, modern poetry grew out of Imagism. This movement may be considered as the thin point of the hour-glass, where all romantic effusions are checked, and only the fine sand of contemporary images is allowed to pass.

T. S. Eliot is a notable writer in whom the clarity of contemporary images, speaking their own new language and meaning, appears with remarkable effect. He does not explain, he lets the images speak:

> Let us go then, you and I,
> When the evening is spread out against the sky
> Like a patient etherized upon a table;
> Let us go, through certain half-deserted streets,
> The muttering retreats
> Of restless nights in one-night cheap hotels . . .

> (from 'The Love Song of J. Alfred Prufrock')

More vividly than any other poet, he saw the realities of

modern life, and he viewed these realities in negative terms. Crowded cities, cheap restaurants and hotels, illicit loves, commercial chicanery, an atmosphere of cheap newspapers, crass entertainments, and pubs pervaded the sad world of Eliot's early poetry. By the feeling and connection of the images (as the critics eventually perceived) Eliot was really saying that this desert of emptiness — the Waste Land — was the result of a total absence of religious faith, specifically the decline in religious belief in the modern world.

It is true that in the sphere of ideas, where science has often been thrown into conflict with religion, and sceptical directions of thought have been widely explored, religious belief in our time has been undermined. The process of sceptical analysis and reduction has really been going on for two centuries, since the Age of Reason, which placed great emphasis on rational inquiry as opposed to unquestioning belief. Modern forces such as urbanization and applied science have accelerated this process of scepticism and some of its results may have reached public popularity in a destructively negative form. T. S. Eliot's thesis is not groundless. In his poetry it is passionately and personally realized. Moreover, it has rightly been said that his message is true for all time, not only for this particular age, since life is always a desert — in the Christian sense — when it is seen in terms of merely ephemeral pleasures and pursuits. But on the whole, the single-minded religious approach of T. S. Eliot to the complex problems of modern life does not seem to be objective enough. The analysis and solution seem to be determined by Eliot's own personal anxieties.

Ezra Pound, the great impresario of modern poetry, has also demanded nobility and higher meaning for life, but not in terms of religion; he has looked for the higher meaning in the form of art. Art, for this poet, is well-nigh the greatest good. And he has laboured unremittingly in its cause.

Like Eliot, Pound has looked at modern life with very critical eyes. He has analysed the deterioration of standards and values, as he sees it, both artistically and historically, and in terms of economic causes. His major work, the *Cantos*, is an epic of world history (it includes China, Europe, and America in its scope) making a drastic condemnation of present-day civilization, and aiming to show, by means of samples or 'ideograms', how things got that way. It is a difficult poem, especially since the samples are unfamiliar to most readers; but it is nevertheless a deeply-felt moral criticism of life, made from the standpoint of art. (There is, incidentally, no specific anti-Semitism in the *Cantos* — a charge against Pound that has been raised — although there is a good deal of irritation against many creeds, nations, and individuals.)

Pound is a great artistic craftsman, in fact a kind of literary forger who can reproduce at will the poetry and beauty of any past age: but his position is so uncompromising and critical that few readers dare to meet him on his own terms. His admirers are still a minority, but his influence in poetry is nevertheless very great. Perhaps no one so well as he epitomizes the predicament of modern poetry, the poet pitted against his age, and to all intents defeated by the immense pressures of actuality. And yet in the long run — who knows — the decision may be reversed in his favour.

Four poets who are true modernists, following in the footsteps of Eliot and Pound, or working out new methods of their own, have gained much attention in recent years. William Carlos Williams, E. E. Cummings, Marianne Moore, and Wallace Stevens, each in his own way, are extreme individualists, experimentalists in verse (experiments are interesting to watch), models of concreteness and of the modern sensibility.

Williams is an 'easy' poet of great charm. His fresh personality and spontaneous effects of line-arrangement on the page make him as authentic and American as Carl Sandburg, and more purely so, revealing everything by example. The real centre of interest in his poetry is his lively, candid, unpretentious self.

E. E. Cummings is our most exhibitionistic experimentalist, and yet behind it all he is almost as simple and direct as Williams. Think of playing with alphabet blocks in an adult way and you will understand Cummings. It's all great fun. Instead of giving us complete words and phrases, he breaks them up into their parts and asks us to put them together again. As we do it, we learn something about the world around us, about love, about the joy of living, about the seasons, of birth and death, and of ourselves.

Williams and Cummings praise the real world in which we live. They capture the instant of experience — 'the language of old ecstasies' (Williams) — and give it permanent form. Unlike Eliot and Pound, they are willing to accept the twentieth-century universe, at least in its moments of rare delight, and refrain from too much thought. 'Let's live suddenly without thinking,' says Cummings, thus giving a temporary answer to many doubts and misgivings.

Marianne Moore is a meticulous writer who counts her syllables and weighs every word. Her work, once you learn to read it, slowly, is a lesson in exact thinking and careful phrasing. It is also vivid, convincing, and wisely didactic. She loves animals and uses them to convey her moral reflections and perceptions. She likes to quote exotic phrases from the oddest places to build up her poems, but these phrases make perfect sense in the new context; you not need to look them up. Hers is a genuine world of personal discrimination.

> Openly, yes,
> with the naturalness
>   of the hippopotamus or the alligator
>   when it climbs out on the bank to experience the
> sun, I do these
> things which I do, which please
>   no one but myself . . .

> (from 'Melancthon')

Wallace Stevens attempts a larger philosophic ordering of experience. Difficult, sometimes too abstract, he is the philosopher among modern poets; and in a time of confusion such as ours philosophy is certainly in demand. There is no absolute truth, says Stevens, but only the truth expressed in poetry. All stories, myths, religions, are high poetry, in this view; they elevate and explain existence. Philosophers like Plato have argued that there exists an invisible absolute order behind the changing world we know, a world of 'ideas' which forms the unities of science, mathematics, ethics, and religion. Wallace Stevens agrees that these ideas of order exist, but he holds that they are man-made. 'Poetry is the supreme fiction, madame,' is his poetic philosophy in a nutshell. It is both harrowingly sceptical and constructively positive and beautiful, since we are enjoined to build our supreme fictions and to beautify life. If there were more Wallace Stevenses there would be less Waste Land; but that is of course assuming that poetry could become more effective and practical than it ever really is. Only for the individual reader is it ever a sovereign medicine and cure.

Society, however, needs doctoring in our time. We have seen that the major poets, Eliot, Yeats, and Pound, were obsessed with the problems of society, or with general culture. In 1929 the stock market in New York crashed; and a few years later bread-lines and relief lists began to stretch out alarmingly as more and more men and women could not find work. One devastating world war had decimated Europe; another loomed on the horizon. Fascism had exploded like a cancer in Italy in the 1920s; in 1933 Hitler came into power. These cataclysms, especially the economic collapse, forced thinking people to the conclusion that our economic system was at an end and another was soon to begin. Fascism was said to be the last stand of capitalism in its efforts to survive. Various forms of leftist, socialist, and Marxist theory became widely popular. In poetry, the view was soon common that Eliot's 'Waste Land' was but the picture of capitalist culture in its dying stages, and that socialism or communism would be the inevitable cure for these ills. The poetic version of this idea occurs in W. H. Auden's

'Spain' and other poems, in Stephen Spender's best early poems, and in the lighter verse of Louis MacNeice. None of these poets, however, were merely propagandists, and their political convictions — later renounced — were blended with other, more profoundly human concerns.

Socialism in Auden is in fact subordinate to a deep religious concern. Auden, however, is a rationalist by temperament; his mind is analytic, incredibly efficacious, witty, and satirical. The emotional nature, therefore, that seeks some religious resolution is forever restless in him, and cannot fully claim what it knows. He is one of the most gifted and versatile minds in our time, also one of the most intelligent and informed. Yet he lacks that core of quiet seriousness which makes even lesser poets succeed, and his best poetry is often only the best of verse by a virtuoso versifier, hardly poetry at all.

Stephen Spender's earlier, socially-inspired poetry is deeply moving, even if the ideology it contains is by now transparent. The idea of the working man's state as a 'golden hive' in which individuals become anonymous and efficiency for the common good governs (see the poem 'The Funeral') is a utopian mirage that melted away as soon as the Iron Curtain lifted somewhat and the West became aware of the real nature of Stalin's commissarism. The political vision of the future in Spender's early poetry and the poignant compassion for the poor and suffering which accompanies this are expressions of a romantic idealism akin to that of Shelley and Blake in another age. Since the 1930s, the struggle with failure and disillusionment and the search for new grounds of feeling have prevented Spender's poetry from rising to its former power.

Stephen Spender, however, introduces a new theme into our survey of modern poetry. He is obviously a romantic in character and expression, yet he is a poet turned to social realities and facts. (Some of his best poems are about machinery and modern industrial power.) With Spender we return to the theme of romanticism, reborn on new grounds.

The word 'romantic' has many uses; perhaps here we should define it for the present purpose. Let us say that romanticism is a frame of mind in which one's idealism — the highest striving for what should be — fills one's conception of reality, or even displaces it. In other words, the ideal becomes the primary motive. Historically, romanticism developed after rational scepticism, in France, had demolished religious belief among the intellectual class. The idealism contained in religion was released upon poetry and life — nature, and love, are made divine in the process. Since that time, whenever a similar process of idealizing reality occurs, it seems fair to call it a return to romanticism.

To those readers who are loyal to the great romantic poets (and it's all to their credit) it will be welcome news that modern poetry in its turning to realism was never a rejection of the true romantic principle. It is in many ways a return to the original sources of romanticism. The moderns repudiated the faint imitators of the romantic movement — the Alice Meynells and de la Mares — only to return to imaginative poetry with a more realistic fervour. Modernism in poetry might in fact be defined as romanticism brought down to earth. It often repeats the romantic poet's feeling of homelessness in the real world; and it overflows at the other extreme in rhetoric and high idealistic striving. The tendency is for the ideal to repel the real. But the modern effort to combine them can also result in great richness and dramatic contrast. And some of the truest successes of modernism happen when the real and ideal meet in harmony and fusion, as in the poetry of Williams, Cummings, Hart Crane, D. H. Lawrence, or Stephen Spender.

During the 1920s in America, Hart Crane wrote his powerful poem *The Bridge*, an epic of the industrial age and a vision of its goals. The actual subject is Brooklyn Bridge, but the bridge is symbolic of industrial America and its properties are highly spiritual. The opening poem apostrophizes the bridge in the manner of a god:

And Thee, across the harbor, silver-paced
As though the sun took step of thee, yet left
Some motion ever unspent in thy stride, —
Implicitly thy freedom staying thee! ...

O sleepless as the river under thee,
Vaulting the sea, the prairies' dreaming sod,
Unto us lowliest sometime sweep, descend
And of the curveship lend a myth to God.

Despite its astonishing beauty, the poem fails in its ultimate aim. It is highly charged with visionary idealism — seeing the realities of the modern world, the subway, Columbus Circle, the Twentieth Century Limited, and the bridge itself in terms of huge promise and wonder — but its definition of the ultimate goal, to which all this is to serve as a bridge, seems inflated and unconvincing. The heaven of this world is impossible to imagine in romantic terms; it always seems too forced, too far from the actual, to be literally true.

There is, nevertheless, a line of modern romantics, or neo-romantics, whose work proposes this kind of vision of an earthly paradise. D. H. Lawrence is a prophet of resurrection through love, sexuality, and nature. A highly moral and chaste writer, he envisioned every natural process, especially the sexual, in the highest terms. He believed that salvation for modern man is only possible through some such return to natural life; and the natural world seemed to him filled with native powers and spiritual connections that lead inevitably to mysticism. (For this side of Lawrence, see his book *Apocalypse*.)

Robinson Jeffers also belongs in this group of prophetic voices in our time. Like Lawrence — and like so many of the poets we have noted — he saw the modern world as standing very much in need of salvation. But he could see no salvation in store for us. His apocalyptic vision is one of black despair. Man is an incestuous, self-destructive force, an infection on the face of the globe, an error of the gods, destined to vanish. Nature alone is clean and pristine in its purity. This verdict on modern life is chastening, and often its specific detail is piercingly true. Jeffers writes a beautiful, long-flowing line, as natural as the world of nature he admires. The heroic element of nobility stands forth in the tone of prophetic condemnation, and in the structure of his poems; it is the positive vision of great good that contrasts with his fearful message.

Dylan Thomas is of course the English (strictly, Welsh) counterpart of this romantic return in poetry. Since he follows the writers we have so far mentioned, he is possibly the culmination of the romantic return. In Thomas's powerful rhetorical poetry, the artifacts of modern life disappear entirely, to be replaced by a surrealist world of inner vision. The recurrent subjects are death and birth; and the glory of a visionary childhood is the ecstatic point of repose. But Dylan Thomas is a product of the twentieth century through the awesome reality of his inner vision. There is nothing sentimental about it. We move in blood and marrow, coffins walk, seed-bulbs burst in growth, lovers bleed in love, and die. The vision of first and last things converges here in a great cataclysm of imagery and language. It is an experience in poetry that has been very moving to modern readers. We know there will be nothing like it again, since all poets are inimitable and unique. But Dylan Thomas has many imitators.

In Dylan Thomas, perhaps, we see the failure of poetry in its effort to redeem reality, the sad withdrawal of the modern muse into the inner world of subjectivity. Minor poets, in the meantime, have moved into the academies. After the first generation of poets which included Eliot and Pound had done their work, the critical analysis of modern poetry seemed to become primary. Young poets have pitched on the methods of these earlier poets and developed the same methods further, but in imitative fashion. As the Victorian Age was a continuation and diminution of the romantic movement, so it seems that twentieth-century poetry at this time is a continuation of the great period of modernism in the early part of this century.

Two new developments, however, are worth considering before we close this brief survey. One is the poetry of protest that has appeared in England during and after the Second World War, the other is the poetry of the so-called 'beat' generation in America. Both are extreme iconoclastic movements of revolt. In both England and the United States, poetry seems split into two parties. On the one hand we have the poetry of the so-called 'establishment', which means that it is approved by reputable critics and quality journals. On the other hand, there is the poetry of angry protest, with its own following among the young writers and 'little magazines'. The 'establishment' kind of poetry is often excellent, as in the case of Richard Wilbur or Robert Lowell in America, or John Betjeman in England. But the angry protesters are probably more significant mirrors of this age.

During the last war, a surprising number of the young English poets were conscientious objectors, pacifists who refused to participate in war under any condition. They spent their time in prison or on assignment to peaceful chores. In addition to this, a good number of the poets have been anarchists by conviction, espousing the doctrine that the state as such is an evil, a cause of war, and that the limitation and eventual abolition of the state is desirable. The elderly English poet and art critic, Herbert Read, has been a leader in this movement. Alex Comfort is a younger representative.

In America, the passionate iconoclasm of the so-called 'beat' generation is only too familiar. The protest of these young people, against the moneyed materialism of American life, against threats of war and the war economy, against the ignorance of a mass society led by advertising and shallow entertainment, runs parallel to the English post-war generation. Nor is it something new in our poetry. The 'howl' of the beats (the title of Allen Ginsberg's wild and tragic long poem) is a violent *cri du coeur* containing the same essential verdict on modern life as that of Robinson Jeffers, of D. H. Lawrence, of

T. S. Eliot and Ezra Pound, and of the great Irishman W. B. Yeats.

So we have seen that, in the twentieth century, poetry has made the effort to master reality. Because poetry speaks for ultimate perfection, it has tended to repudiate reality, or at least to judge it severely. Only rarely has it been able to transmute fragments of the world into itself. We treasure poetry greatly when it does this, not because we agree with the poetry, or because we approve of it, but because it is something permanent that contains human value. In fact, eventually we are very likely to come to agree with and to approve of the things we love. But perfection is very rare. And the twentieth century has still a long way to go.

LOUIS DUDEK

WALT WHITMAN (1819-1892)

Walt Whitman, the great American poet of democracy, is often considered the father of the modern style — for his liberation of the form of poetry (his use of the long unmetrical line), and for his treatment of realistic subject matter. Actually, he represents original romanticism in America, expressing (like Wordsworth) a highly idealistic or spiritual conception of reality. But in Whitman romantic idealism was turned especially toward reality, both by the conditions of life in America and by the idea of democracy, which aims to redeem the common life from contempt and asserts the dignity of every individual.

Whitman was appreciated by a small group of admirers during his lifetime (Emerson among them), but he had no success with publishers and critics, and the great public ignored him. At the end of his life he was reduced to peddling his books from a basket in the streets of Philadelphia. His fame after his death has placed him in the forefront of American poets, and many an anthology of twentieth-century poetry begins with a sampling from this prophet of our age.

'The little one sleeps in its cradle'

(From *Song of Myself*)

The little one sleeps in its cradle,
I lift the gauze and look a long time, and silently brush away
    flies with my hand.

The youngster and the red-faced girl turn aside up the bushy
    hill,
I peeringly view them from the top.
The suicide sprawls on the bloody floor of the bedroom,
I witness the corpse with its dabbled hair, I note where the
    pistol has fallen.

The blab of the pave, tires of carts, sluff of boot-soles, talk of
    the promenaders,

The heavy omnibus, the driver with his interrogating thumb,
    the clank of the shod horses on the granite floor,
The snow-sleighs, clinking, shouted jokes, pelts of snow-balls,
The hurrahs for popular favorites, the fury of rous'd mobs,
The flap of the curtain'd litter, a sick man inside borne to the
    hospital,
The meeting of enemies, the sudden oath, the blows and fall,
The excited crowd, the policeman with his star quickly work-
    ing his passage to the centre of the crowd,
The impassive stones that receive and return so many echoes,
What groans of over-fed or half-starv'd who fall sunstruck or
    in fits,
What exclamations of women taken suddenly who hurry home
    and give birth to babes,
What living and buried speech is always vibrating here, what
    howls restrain'd by decorum,
Arrests of criminals, slights, adulterous offers made, accept-
    ances, rejections with convex lips,
I mind them or the show or resonance of them — I come and
    I depart.

GERARD MANLEY HOPKINS (1844-1889)

Hopkins is yet another nineteenth-century prophet of things to come. An Anglican, he became converted to the Roman Catholic faith in the aftermath of that religious revival in England known as the Oxford Movement, a renewal of deep traditional Christianity that was partly a reaction to modern scientific thought and to rational scepticism.

Hopkins joined the Jesuit Order and was eventually ordained a priest (Cardinal Newman officiated at his ordination); as a teaching Jesuit, for many years he taught Greek at University College in Dublin.

As a token of devotion he destroyed his early poetry on entering the Church, and during his lifetime none of his later poetry was published. (Actually, he offered some of his most important poems for publication, with the permission of his superiors, but the originality of these poems prevented their acceptance.) It was nearly thirty years after his death that his one-time friend and confidant Robert Bridges brought out the *Poems of Gerard Hopkins* (1918). In the midst of modern experiment and poetic change, Hopkins was quickly recognized as a poet of great originality and tense intellectual energy. His influence on modern poets has been widespread, ranging from Edith Sitwell and Hart Crane to W. H. Auden and Dylan Thomas.

Spring

Nothing is so beautiful as spring —
    When weeds, in wheels, shoot long and lovely and lush;
    Thrush's eggs look little low heavens, and thrush
Through the echoing timber does so rinse and wring
The ear, it strikes like lightnings to hear him sing;
    The glassy peartree leaves and blooms, they brush
    The descending blue; that blue is all in a rush
With richness; the racing lambs too have fair their fling.

What is all this juice and all this joy?
    A strain of the earth's sweet being in the beginning

In Eden garden. — Have, get, before it cloy,
   Before it cloud, Christ, lord, and sour with sinning,
Innocent mind and Mayday in girl and boy,
   Most, O maid's child, thy choice and worthy the
      winning.

Spring and Fall:

to a young child

> Margaret, are you grieving
> Over Goldengrove unleaving?
> Leaves, like the things of man, you
> With your fresh thoughts care for, can you?
> Ah! as the heart grows older
> It will come to such sights colder
> By and by, nor spare a sigh
> Though worlds of wanwood leafmeal lie;
> And yet you will weep and know why.
> Now no matter, child, the name:
> Sorrow's springs are the same.
> Nor mouth had, no nor mind, expressed
> What heart heard of, ghost guessed:
> It is the blight man was born for.
> It is Margaret you mourn for.

'No worst, there is none'

No worst, there is none. Pitched past pitch of grief,
More pangs will, schooled at forepangs, wilder wring.
Comforter, where, where is your comforting?
Mary, mother of us, where is your relief?

My cries heave, herds-long; huddle in a main, a chief
Woe, world-sorrow; on an age-old anvil wince and sing —
Then lull, then leave off. Fury had shrieked 'No ling-
ering! Let me be fell: force I must be brief'.

O the mind, mind has mountains; cliffs of fall
Frightful, sheer, no-man-fathomed. Hold them cheap
May who ne'er hung there. Nor does long our small
Durance deal with that steep or deep. Here! creep,
Wretch, under a comfort serves in a whirlwind: all
Life death does end and each day dies with sleep.

EMILY DICKINSON (1830-1886)

Like Hopkins, Emily Dickinson published virtually nothing during her lifetime. She lived in seclusion in her father's house in Amherst, Massachusetts, shutting herself up from her twenty-sixth year so that few townspeople ever saw her. Yet she had warm friendships and wrote prolific letters to her friends. Speculation about an ill-starred love for the Reverend Charles Wadsworth — a married man — whom she met during a visit to Philadelphia, has suggested an explanation for her retreat from life. Actually, her poems reveal several emotional attachments in early life, and her imagination dwelt on these. But her nature was shy and withdrawn, and no single cause will explain her originality of character.

After her death hundreds of poems were discovered among her private papers, some of them masterpieces, all of them meticulously worked over, and often unfinished, with numerous alternative readings in the manuscript. Her poetry was first published in 1890 but after a short period of interest the poems fell into neglect, until in 1924 a new collected edition, together with a life of Emily Dickinson, combined to establish her as one of the greatest women poets of all time.

She is a nature poet of the romantic century, but steeped in earlier English poetry, especially of the seventeenth century, a fact which brings her close to some of the moderns. Atomic, passionate, yet at the same time intellectual, she demands close reading; but labour is well repaid by the nuggets of meaning packed in her strange, original words.

'A narrow fellow in the grass'

A narrow fellow in the grass
Occasionally rides;
You may have met him, — did you not?
His notice sudden is.

The grass divides as with a comb,
A spotted shaft is seen;
And then it closes at your feet
And opens further on.

27

He likes a boggy acre,
A floor too cool for corn.
Yet when a child, and barefoot,
I more than once, at morn,

Have passed, I thought, a whip-lash
Unbraiding in the sun, —
When, stooping to secure it,
It wrinkled, and was gone.

Several of nature's people
I know, and they know me;
I feel for them a transport
Of cordiality;

But never met this fellow,
Attended or alone,
Without a tighter breathing,
And zero at the bone.

'I died for beauty'

I died for beauty, but was scarce
Adjusted in the tomb,
When one who died for truth was lain
In an adjoining room.

He questioned softly why I failed?
'For beauty,' I replied.
'And I for truth, — the two are one;
We brethren are,' he said.

And so, as kinsmen met a night,
We talked between the rooms,
Until the moss had reached our lips,
And covered up our names.

'Some keep the Sabbath going to church'

Some keep the Sabbath going to church;
I keep it staying at home,
With a bobolink for a chorister,
And an orchard for a dome.

Some keep the Sabbath in surplice;
I just wear my wings,
And instead of tolling the bell for church,
Our little sexton sings.

God preaches, — a noted clergyman, —
And the sermon is never long;
So instead of getting to heaven at last,
I'm going all along!

'I taste a liquor never brewed'

I taste a liquor never brewed,
From tankards scooped in pearl;
Not all the vats upon the Rhine
Yield such an alcohol!

Inebriate of air am I,
And debauchee of dew,
Reeling, through endless summer days,
From inns of molten blue.

When landlords turn the drunken bee
Out of the foxglove's door,
When butterflies renounce their drams,
I shall but drink the more!

Till seraphs swing their snowy hats,
And saints to windows run,
To see the little tippler
Leaning against the sun!

A. E. HOUSMAN (1859-1936)

First published in 1896, Housman's *A Shropshire Lad* was virtually ignored until the outbreak of the Second World War, when his pessimism and hedonism suddenly found an echo in the hearts of thousands. His poems have remained modern classics ever since. (The pattern of long neglect and of rediscovery seems to apply to several poets in this period of transition.) Housman's strain of cynical pessimism springs from a disillusionment with the romantic ideals of the past, and a deep hurt from something in the present. Stoically, he prefers death to life, in many a poem, yet he affirms the sweetness of life in the face of death. Courage and endurance are the virtues he inculcates against a bitter fate.

A professed atheist, yet a dutiful, practising Anglican, Housman was a noted classical scholar and teacher. His purity of thought and style is presumably derived from classical sources; but the classics have inspired Milton and Spenser, religious poets, as well as Housman. The materialism which led Hardy to pessimistic conclusions no doubt lurks behind the pessimism of this perfect lyricist whose feelings are cloaked in tales of pastoral simplicity, set in a world of orchard trees and roses.

To an Athlete Dying Young

The time you won your town the race
We chaired you through the market-place;
Man and boy stood cheering by,
And home we brought you shoulder-high.

To-day, the road all runners come,
Shoulder-high we bring you home,
And set you at your threshold down,
Townsman of a stiller town.

Smart lad, to slip betimes away
From fields where glory does not stay
And early though the laurel grows
It withers quicker than the rose.

Eyes the shady night has shut
Cannot see the record cut,
And silence sounds no worse than cheers
After earth has stopped the ears:

Now you will not swell the rout
Of lads that wore their honours out,
Runners whom renown outran
And the name died before the man.

So set, before its echoes fade,
The fleet foot on the sill of shade,
And hold to the low lintel up
The still-defended challenge-cup.

And round that early-laurelled head
Will flock to gaze the strengthless dead,
And find unwithered on its curls
The garland briefer than a girl's.

'Into my heart an air that kills'

Into my heart an air that kills
        From yon far country blows:
What are those blue remembered hills,
        What spires, what farms are those?

That is the land of lost content,
        I see it shining plain,
The happy highways where I went
        And cannot come again.

THOMAS HARDY (1840-1928)

Thomas Hardy was already a famous novelist when he turned exclusively to poetry in later life. In his last two novels, *Tess of the D'Urbervilles* (1891) and *Jude the Obscure* (1896), he had challenged the Victorian reading public by writing with frankness about sex and with sceptical pessimism about religious belief. Strongly impressed by scientific materialism and determinism, he often presents nature as austere and cruel, sex as a tyrannical instinct, and man's life as doomed to misery and death. The reception of his last novels was so unfriendly that he abandoned novel-writing altogether and turned to his first love, poetry. In his stoic truthfulness, in the best poems, he is a transitional poet from the nineteenth century to the twentieth, and poets as different as Stephen Spender and Ezra Pound have admired his integrity and craft. *The Dynasts*, an epic poem on the Napoleonic Wars, is his most ambitious work; and *The Return of the Native* is perhaps his greatest novel.

The Darkling Thrush

I leant upon a coppice gate
  When Frost was spectre-gray,
And Winter's dregs made desolate
  The weakening eye of day.
The tangled bine-stems scored the sky
  Like strings of broken lyres,
And all mankind that haunted nigh
  Had sought their household fires.

The land's sharp features seemed to be
  The Century's corpse outleant,
His crypt the cloudy canopy,
  The wind his death-lament.
The ancient pulse of germ and birth
  Was shrunken hard and dry,
And every spirit upon earth
  Seemed fervourless as I.

At once a voice arose among
   The bleak twigs overhead
In a full-hearted evensong
   Of joy illimited;
An aged thrush, frail, gaunt, and small,
   In blast-beruffled plume,
Had chosen thus to fling his soul
   Upon the growing gloom.

So little cause for carolings
   Of such ecstatic sound
Was written on terrestrial things
   Afar or nigh around,
That I could think there trembled through
   His happy good-night air
Some blessed Hope, whereof he knew
   And I was unaware.

Where the Picnic Was

Where we made the fire
In the summer time
Of branch and briar
On the hill to the sea,
I slowly climb
Through winter mire,
And scan and trace
The forsaken place
Quite readily.

Now a cold wind blows,
And the grass is gray,
But the spot still shows
As a burnt circle — aye,

And stick-ends, charred,
Still strew the sward
Whereon I stand,
Last relic of the band
Who came that day!

Yes, I am here
Just as last year,
And the sea breathes brine
From its strange straight line
Up hither, the same
As when we four came.
— But two have wandered far
From this grassy rise
Into urban roar
Where no picnics are,
And one — has shut her eyes
For evermore.

EDWIN ARLINGTON ROBINSON (1869-1935)

Edwin Arlington Robinson's first book was published in 1896 and an enlarged collection appeared in the following year, under the title *The Children of the Night*. He achieved little recognition, however — despite the admiration of the President of the United States, Theodore Roosevelt — though he published two further volumes at the beginning of the century. He was already forty-seven when the book that brought him fame, *The Man Against the Sky*, appeared in 1916. A long series of titles followed, enlarging his reputation, including the best-seller *Tristram* in 1927 and a *Collected Poems* in 1921, both of which won the Pulitzer Prize.

Robinson was a lonely man, given to drinking excessively at times; he never married; his philosophy was one of extreme darkness unrelieved by any natural optimism. (He pictures life, in one poem, as 'a stairway to the sea / Where down the blind are driven'; and in another he wonders whether in the face of 'pangs and terrors' one might not 'curse God and die'.) Many of his characters suffer a tragic fate or bear a burden of inescapable failure. The theme of the romantic born too late in a world of sordid vanity seems to haunt him:

> Miniver cursed the commonplace
> > And eyed a khaki suit with loathing;
> He missed the medieval grace
> > Of iron clothing.

> (from 'Miniver Cheevy')

A master of traditional metres worn to a smoothness almost without relief, yet compact with bitter meaning, Robinson is a poet standing just before the break-up of traditional style and the emergence of new poetic energies in poetry.

Richard Cory

Whenever Richard Cory went down town,
We people on the pavement looked at him:
He was a gentleman from sole to crown,
Clean favored, and imperially slim.

And he was always quietly arrayed,
And he was always human when he talked;
But still he fluttered pulses when he said,
'Good-morning,' and he glittered when he walked.

And he was rich — yes, richer than a king —
And admirably schooled in every grace:
In fine, we thought that he was everything
To make us wish that we were in his place.

So on we worked, and waited for the light,
And went without the meat, and cursed the bread;
And Richard Cory, one calm summer night,
Went home and put a bullet through his head.

RUDYARD KIPLING (1865-1936)

Rudyard Kipling was a great writer of novels and stories, for both adults and children, as well as a powerful poet. In contrast to the recluse poets preceding, he was a popular bard who travelled throughout many parts of the world and expressed a variety of life with vigour and dramatic skill. His prose books are well known: the Jungle Books (1894-5), *Captains Courageous* (1897), *Kim* (1901). His poetry is available in an inclusive edition, and also in a selection, *A Choice of Kipling's Verse*, prepared by T. S. Eliot in 1941.

Kipling was born in Bombay, India, of English parents — his father was the curator of a museum — but he was sent at an early age to an English public school, where he was homesick and unhappy. On his return to India as a young man he worked on a newspaper and soon began to write light verse for the paper; this was collected in his first book, *Departmental Ditties* (1886). He had already made a reputation as a short-story writer before the appearance of *Barrack-Room Ballads* established him as a poet in 1892.

These vigorous poems are in a sense a take-off on the romantic ballad of sentimental love and idealism, even as the title is a realistic parallel to Wordsworth's and Coleridge's *Lyrical Ballads* (1798). Kipling wrote about rough soldiers, greasy engineers, ship-owners who had come up the hard way, bridge-builders and empire-builders, in a poetry that appealed to multitudes of readers. His songs were set to music and played on bandstands and in music halls, and entered into the common culture of the age.

He travelled, lived in America for some years, and settled finally in Sussex, England. After his death his reputation declined somewhat, but he remains a household word, sentimentalized out of recognition sometimes, as in the song-hit 'Robins and Roses' a few years ago: 'And then life will be / A poem by Kipling while troubles go rippling by!'

L'Envoi to *The Seven Seas*

When Earth's last picture is painted and the tubes are twisted
    and dried,
When the oldest colours have faded, and the youngest critic
    has died,

We shall rest, and, faith, we shall need it — lie down for an
    aeon or two,
Till the Master of All Good Workmen shall put us to work
    anew!

And those that were good shall be happy: they shall sit in a
    golden chair;
They shall splash at a ten-league canvas with brushes of
    comets' hair.
They shall find real saints to draw from — Magdalene, Peter,
    and Paul;
They shall work for an age at a sitting and never be tired at
    all!

And only The Master shall praise us, and only The Master
    shall blame;
And no one shall work for money, and no one shall work for
    fame,
But each for the joy of the working, and each, in his separate
    star,
Shall draw the Thing as he sees It for the God of Things as
    They are!

Gunga Din

You may talk o' gin and beer
When you're quartered safe out 'ere,
An' you're sent to penny-fights an' Aldershot it;
But when it comes to slaughter
You will do your work on water,
An' you'll lick the bloomin' boots of 'im that's got it.
Now in Injia's sunny clime,
Where I used to spend my time
A-servin' of 'Er Majesty the Queen,

Of all them blackfaced crew
The finest man I knew
Was our regimental bhisti, Gunga Din.
　　　　He was 'Din! Din! Din!
　'You limpin' lump o' brick-dust, Gunga Din!
　　　　'Hi! slippery *hitherao*!
　　　　'Water, get it! *Panee lao*!
　'You squidgy-nosed old idol, Gunga Din.'

The uniform 'e wore
Was nothin' much before,
An' rather less than 'arf o' that be'ind,
For a piece o' twisty rag
An' a goatskin water-bag
Was all the field-equipment 'e could find.
When the sweatin' troop-train lay
In a sidin' through the day,
Where the 'eat would make your bloomin' eyebrows
　crawl,
We shouted 'Harry By!'
Till our throats were bricky-dry,
Then we wopped 'im 'cause 'e couldn't serve us all.
　　　　It was 'Din! Din! Din!
　'You 'eathen, where the mischief 'ave you been?
　　　　'You put some *juldee* in it
　　　　'Or I'll *marrow* you this minute
　'If you don't fill up my helmet, Gunga Din!'

'E would dot an' carry one
Till the longest day was done;
An' 'e didn't seem to know the use o' fear.
If we charged or broke or cut,
You could bet your bloomin' nut,
'E'd be waitin' fifty paces right flank rear.
With 'is mussick on 'is back,
'E would skip with our attack,

An' watch us till the bugles made 'Retire,'
An' for all 'is dirty 'ide
'E was white, clear white, inside
When 'e went to tend the wounded under fire!
      It was 'Din! Din! Din!'
  With the bullets kickin' dust-spots on the green.
     When the cartridges ran out,
     You could hear the front-files shout,
  'Hi! ammunition-mules an' Gunga Din!'

I shan't forgit the night
When I dropped be'ind the fight
With a bullet where my belt-plate should 'a' been.
I was chokin' mad with thirst,
An' the man that spied me first
Was our good old grinnin', gruntin' Gunga Din.
'E lifted up my 'ead,
An' he plugged me where I bled,
An' 'e guv me 'arf-a-pint o' water-green:
It was crawlin' and it stunk,
But of all the drinks I've drunk,
I'm gratefullest to one from Gunga Din.
      It was 'Din! Din! Din!
   ' 'Ere's a beggar with a bullet through 'is spleen;
     ' 'E's chawin' up the ground,
     'An' 'e's kickin' all around:
  'For Gawd's sake git the water, Gunga Din!'

'E carried me away
To where a dooli lay,
An' a bullet come an' drilled the beggar clean.
'E put me safe inside,
An' just before 'e died,
'I 'ope you liked your drink,' sez Gunga Din.
So I'll meet 'im later on
At the place where 'e is gone —

Where it's always double drill and no canteen;
'E 'll be squattin' on the coals
Givin' drink to poor damned souls,
An' I'll get a swig in hell from Gunga Din!
      Yes, Din! Din! Din!
   You Lazarushian-leather Gunga Din!
      Though I've belted you and flayed you,
      By the livin' Gawd that made you,
You're a better man than I am, **Gunga Din**.

JOHN MASEFIELD (1878-   )

John Masefield went off to sea as a boy, and like Kipling he saw much of the world outside the genteel drawing-room before he turned to poetry. For a time he was a bartender in a saloon in New York and then he worked in a carpet factory in Yonkers. He tells us in his autobiography that reading a poem by a Canadian, Duncan Campbell Scott, in a New York weekly, first inspired him to write poetry. This was Scott's poem 'The Piper of Arl', a romantic ballad after the manner of Coleridge. When Masefield discovered his own subject, it was a salty mixture of realism and sentimentality, like Kipling's popular ballads and songs, full of the life of sailors, working men, the poor, and the oppressed.

Salt Water Ballads appeared in 1902, and Ballads in 1903. But it was the long narrative poem The Everlasting Mercy (1911) that made him famous; and several narrative poems of this type followed: Dauber (1912), The Widow of the Bye Street (1912), The Daffodil Fields (1913). (Note that the long narrative poem is characteristic of the transition to modernism, but it vanishes with the chief modern poets, Eliot, Pound, Cummings, etc.) Masefield became softer and more sentimental in his later poems, as though relapsing into a milder nature. He was appointed Poet Laureate in 1930.

The Fight

(From *The Everlasting Mercy*)

The stakes were drove, the ropes were hitched,
Into the ring my hat I pitched.
My corner faced the Squire's park
Just where the fir trees make it dark;
The place where I begun poor Nell
Upon the woman's road to hell.
I thought of 't, sitting in my corner
After the time-keep struck his warner
(Two brandy flasks, for fear of noise,
Clinked out the time to us two boys).

And while my seconds chafed and gloved me
I thought of Nell's eyes when she loved me,
And wondered how my tot would end,
First Nell cast off and now my friend;
And in the moonlight dim and wan
I knew quite well my luck was gone;
And looking round I felt a spite
At all who'd come to see me fight;
The five and forty human faces
Inflamed by drink and going to races,
Faces of men who'd never been
Merry or true or live or clean . . .

· · ·

From the beginning of the bout
My luck was gone, my hand was out.
Right from the start Bill called the play,
But I was quick and kept away
Till the fourth round, when work got mixed,
And then I knew Bill had me fixed.
My hand was out, why, Heaven knows;
Bill punched me when and where he chose.
Through two more rounds we quartered wide,
And all the time my hands seemed tied;
Bill punched me when and where he pleased.
The cheering from my backers eased,
But every punch I heard a yell
Of 'That's the style, Bill, give him hell.'
No one for me, but Jimmy's light
'Straight left! Straight left!' and 'Watch his right.'

I don't know how a boxer goes
When all his body hums from blows;
I know I seemed to rock and spin,
I don't know how I saved my chin;
I know I thought my only friend

43

Was that clinked flask at each round's end
When my two seconds, Ed and Jimmy,
Had sixty seconds help to gimme.
But in the ninth, with pain and knocks
I stopped: I couldn't fight nor box.
Bill missed his swing, the light was tricky,
But I went down, and stayed down, dicky.
'Get up,' cried Jim.   I said, 'I will.'
Then all the gang yelled, 'Out him, Bill.
Out him.' Bill rushed . . . and Clink, Clink, Clink.
Time! and Jim's knee, and rum to drink.
And round the ring there ran a titter:
'Saved by the call, the bloody quitter.'

They drove (a dodge that never fails)
A pin beneath my finger nails.
They poured what seemed a running beck
Of cold spring water down my neck;
Jim with a lancet quick as flies
Lowered the swellings round my eyes.
They sluiced my legs and fanned my face
Through all that blessed minute's grace;
They gave my calves a thorough kneading,
They salved my cuts and stopped the bleeding.
A gulp of liquor dulled the pain,
And then the two flasks clinked again.
Time!
      There was Bill as grim as death,
He rushed, I clinched, to get more breath,
And breath I got, though Billy bats
Some stinging short-arms in my slats.
And when we broke, as I foresaw,
He swung his right in for the jaw.
I stopped it on my shoulder bone,
And at the shock I heard Bill groan —

A little groan or moan or grunt
As though I'd hit his wind a bunt.
At that, I clinched, and while we clinched,
His old time right arm dig was flinched,
And when we broke he hit me light
As though he didn't trust his right,
He flapped me somehow with his wrist
As though he couldn't use his fist,
And when he hit he winced with pain.
I thought, 'Your sprained thumb's crocked again.'
So I got strength and Bill gave ground,
And that round was an easy round.

During the wait my Jimmy said,
'What's making Billy fight so dead?
He's all to pieces. Is he blown?'
'His thumb's out.'
'No? Then it's your own.
It's all your own, but don't be rash —
He's got the goods if you've got cash,
And what one hand can do he'll do,
Be careful this next round or two.'

Time. There was Bill, and I felt sick
That luck should play so mean a trick
And give me leave to knock him out
After he'd plainly won the bout.
But by the way the man came at me
He made it plain he meant to bat me;
If you'd a seen the way he come
You wouldn't think he'd crocked a thumb.
With all his skill and all his might
He clipped me dizzy left and right;
The Lord knows what the effort cost,
But he was mad to think he'd lost,

And knowing nothing else could save him
He didn't care what pain it gave him.
He called the music and the dance
For five rounds more and gave no chance.

Try to imagine if you can
The kind of manhood in the man,
And if you'd like to feel his pain
You sprain your thumb and hit the sprain.
And hit it hard, with all your power
On something hard for half-an-hour,
While someone thumps you black and blue,
And then you'll know what Billy knew.
Bill took that pain without a sound
Till halfway through the eighteenth round,
And then I sent him down and out,
And Silas said, 'Kane wins the bout.'

When Bill came to, you understand,
I ripped the mitten from my hand
And went across to ask Bill shake.
My limbs were all one pain and ache,
I was so weary and so sore
I don't think I'd a stood much more.
Bill in his corner bathed his thumb,
Buttoned his shirt and glowered glum.
'I'll never shake your hand,' he said.
'I'd rather see my children dead.
I've been about and had some fun with you,
But you're a liar and I've done with you.
You've knocked me out, you didn't beat me;
Look out the next time that you meet me,
There'll be no friend to watch the clock for you
And no convenient thumb to crock for you,
And I'll take care, with much delight,

You'll get what you'd a got to-night;
That puts my meaning clear, I guess,
Now go to hell; I want to dress.'

I dressed. My backers one and all
Said, 'Well done you,' or 'Good old Saul.'
'Saul is a wonder and a fly 'un,
What'll you have, Saul, at the Lion?'
With merry oaths they helped me down
The stony wood path to the town.

WILLIAM BUTLER YEATS (1865-1939)

'We were the last romantics,' Yeats wrote in a poem, although we may doubt whether romantics of this type will ever cease to exist. He is a poet of idealism, imaginative vision, irresistible music. In the opinion of most critics he ranks higher than any other poet of our time.

He was born at Sandymount near Dublin in 1865. His mother, a beautiful woman, taught him to love the western hills and lakes of Ireland, especially the district of Sligo, where he spent his vacations. He studied in schools in Dublin (he was a 'poor speller' and said that he could never learn to 'scan poetry') and he spent some time in an art school, but never went to a university. Early in life he tried to become a painter like his father, but gave that up. For many years he lived in London as a writer, meeting with literary friends and studying — years when he often lacked the money for bus fares, walked a lot, and haunted the homes of friends for a square meal to stave off hunger.

His father loved to read aloud, a habit that gave Yeats a love for Shakespeare and the romantic poets. He became interested in Irish folklore and collected two books of the folk tales of Ireland. At the same time, the philosophy of mysticism and the eastern religions fascinated him, as a substitute for the religion which he had lost under the influence of his father's scientific outlook. 'I was deeply religious,' he later wrote; but he said he had made himself a private religion out of 'a fardel of stories', the folklore of Ireland.

He fell passionately in love in the 1890s with a famous Irish beauty, an actress and political enthusiast, Maud Gonne. She refused to marry him, however, fearing that marriage might 'hurt his poetry' and this ideal of a great romantic love continued in his poetry throughout his life. It is the subject of many of his poems, and provides a vehicle for much that he has to say about life, death, old age, civilization, art, and politics. For Maud Gonne he wrote *The Countess Cathleen* and other plays; in fact, his contribution to the Irish theatre at the end of the century is no less than his work as a poet.

He published *The Wanderings of Oisin* in 1889, a long 'medieval romance' in the manner of William Morris. This was followed by *Poems* (1895), *The Wind among the Reeds* (1899), and *In the Seven Woods* (1904). As he grew to maturity his poetry in the late-Victorian vein was followed after 1910 by a growing interest in clarity and directness in language and imagery. This culminated in a firm, declarative kind of poetry in *Responsibilities* (1914) and *The Wild Swans of Coole* (1917).

Yeats was now a famous poet in his middle age. His final development in the period of old age is an astonishing illustration of powerful imagination and thought in its full maturity. He was married at fifty-two to Georgie Hyde-Lees (Ezra Pound serving as best man), and with the help of his wife developed a new philosophic conception of man and history. (He actually claimed that the ideas were communicated to him by 'spirits'.) This philosophy appeared in the book, *A Vision*, in 1925.

Yeats at the very end turned back to simple lyrics, sometimes shockingly sensual, always profoundly moving and complex in their structure. He died at Roquebrune on the French Riviera on January 28, 1939, at the age of seventy-three.

He Thinks of Those Who Have
Spoken Evil of His Beloved

Half close your eyelids, loosen your hair,
And dream about the great and their pride;
They have spoken against you everywhere,
But weigh this song with the great and their pride;
I made it out of a mouthful of air,
Their children's children shall say they have lied.

He Wishes for the Cloths of Heaven

Had I the heavens' embroidered cloths,
Enwrought with golden and silver light,
The blue and the dim and the dark cloths
Of night and light and the half-light,
I would spread the cloths under your feet:
But I, being poor, have only my dreams;
I have spread my dreams under your feet;
Tread softly because you tread on my dreams.

The Coming of Wisdom with Time

Though leaves are many, the root is one;
Through all the lying days of my youth
I swayed my leaves and flowers in the sun;
Now I may wither into the truth.

Adam's Curse

We sat together at one summer's end,
That beautiful mild woman, your close friend,
And you and I, and talked of poetry.
I said, 'A line will take us hours maybe;
Yet if it does not seem a moment's thought,
Our stitching and unstitching has been naught.

Better go down upon your marrow-bones
And scrub a kitchen pavement, or break stones
Like an old pauper, in all kinds of weather;
For to articulate sweet sounds together
Is to work harder than all these, and yet
Be thought an idler by the noisy set
Of bankers, schoolmasters, and clergymen
The martyrs call the world.'

                 And thereupon
That beautiful mild woman for whose sake
There's many a one shall find out all heartache
On finding that her voice is sweet and low
Replied, 'To be born woman is to know —
Although they do not talk of it at school —
That we must labour to be beautiful.'

I said, 'It's certain there is no fine thing
Since Adam's fall but needs much labouring.

There have been lovers who thought love should be
So much compounded of high courtesy
That they would sigh and quote with learned looks
Precedents out of beautiful old books;
Yet now it seems an idle trade enough.'

We sat grown quiet at the name of love;
We saw the last embers of daylight die,
And in the trembling blue-green of the sky
A moon, worn as if it had been a shell
Washed by time's waters as they rose and fell
About the stars and broke in days and years.

I had a thought for no one's but your ears:
That you were beautiful, and that I strove
To love you in the old high way of love;
That it had all seemed happy, and yet we'd grown
As weary-hearted as that hollow moon.

The Second Coming

Turning and turning in the widening gyre
The falcon cannot hear the falconer;
Things fall apart; the centre cannot hold;
Mere anarchy is loosed upon the world,
The blood-dimmed tide is loosed, and everywhere
The ceremony of innocence is drowned;
The best lack all conviction, while the worst
Are full of passionate intensity.

Surely some revelation is at hand;
Surely the Second Coming is at hand.
The Second Coming! Hardly are those words out
When a vast image out of *Spiritus Mundi*

Troubles my sight: somewhere in sands of the desert
A shape with lion body and the head of a man,
A gaze blank and pitiless as the sun,
Is moving its slow thighs, while all about it
Reel shadows of the indignant desert birds.
The darkness drops again; but now I know
That twenty centuries of stony sleep
Were vexed to nightmare by a rocking cradle,
And what rough beast, its hour come round at last,
Slouches towards Bethlehem to be born?

On Being Asked for a War Poem

I think it better that in times like these
A poet's mouth be silent, for in truth
We have no gift to set a statesman right;
He has had enough of meddling who can please
A young girl in the indolence of her youth,
Or an old man upon a winter's night.

CARL SANDBURG (1878-   )

America's troubadour, Carl Sandburg is perhaps analogous to Kipling and Masefield in his mixture of toughness and mystical gentleness. Born of Swedish parents in Galesburg, Illinois, he worked as a young man at various odd jobs that gave him the flavour of common life. He was everything from milkman and dishwasher to harvest hand and journalist in the burgeoning Midwest of the turn of the century. In 1914 he achieved recognition with the publication of the prize-winning poem 'Chicago' in *Poetry: a Magazine of Verse*. Two years later, the book *Chicago Poems* established him as the most vigorous and challenging voice of the free-verse movement.

Notable books followed — *Cornhuskers* in 1918, *Smoke and Steel* in 1920, *Good Morning, America* in 1928. Sandburg was rapidly becoming the spokesman for the popular ideal of democracy, just as Kipling had spoken for British imperialism. This is both his source of appeal and his weakness. As a poet of America he toured the States with his guitar, collected folk songs in *The American Songbag* (1927) — a true forerunner to the folk-song revival of our time — and compiled a six-volume biography of Abraham Lincoln. (*The War Years* section of this biography was awarded the Pulitzer Prize in 1939.) *The People, Yes* (1936), a vast poem composed of gags, speechways, and paeans to democracy, is perhaps his most revealing work of collection and creation, a tribute to the common man carried out as an actual collaboration between the poet and the people.

Chicago

Hog Butcher for the World,
Tool Maker, Stacker of Wheat,
Player with Railroads and the Nation's Freight Handler;
Stormy, husky, brawling,
City of the Big Shoulders:

They tell me you are wicked and I believe them, for I have seen
    your painted women under the gas lamps luring the farm
    boys.

And they tell me you are crooked and I answer: Yes, it is
true I have seen the gunman kill and go free to kill again.

And they tell me you are brutal and my reply is: On the faces
of women and children I have seen the marks of wanton
hunger.

And having answered so I turn once more to those who sneer
at this my city, and I give them back the sneer and say to
them:

Come and show me another city with lifted head singing so
proud to be alive and coarse and strong and cunning.

Flinging magnetic curses amid the toil of piling job on job,
here is a tall bold slugger set vivid against the little soft
cities;

Fierce as a dog with tongue lapping for action, cunning as a
savage pitted against the wilderness.

   Bareheaded,
   Shoveling,
   Wrecking,
   Planning,
   Building, breaking, rebuilding,

Under the smoke, dust all over his mouth, laughing with white
teeth,

Under the terrible burden of destiny laughing as a young man
laughs,

Laughing even as an ignorant fighter laughs who has never
lost a battle,

Bragging and laughing that under his wrist is the pulse, and
under his ribs the heart of the people,

   Laughing!

Laughing the stormy, husky, brawling, laughter of Youth,
half-naked, sweating, proud to be Hog Butcher, Tool
Maker, Stacker of Wheat, Player with Railroads and
Freight Handler to the Nation.

Cool Tombs

When Abraham Lincoln was shoveled into the tombs, he
forgot the copperheads and the assassin ... in the dust, in
the cool tombs.

And Ulysses Grant lost all thought of con men and Wall
Street, cash and collateral turned ashes ... in the dust, in
the cool tombs.

Pocahontas' body, lovely as a poplar, sweet as a red haw in
November or a pawpaw in May, did she wonder? does she
remember? ... in the dust, in the cool tombs?

Take any streetful of people buying clothes and groceries,
cheering a hero or throwing confetti and blowing tin horns
... tell me if the lovers are losers ... tell me if any get more
than the lovers ... in the dust ... in the cool tombs.

Gone

Everybody loved Chick Lorimer in our town.
          Far off
       Everybody loved her.
So we all love a wild girl keeping a hold
       On a dream she wants.
Nobody knows now where Chick Lorimer went.
Nobody knows why she packed her trunk ... a few old
   things
And is gone,
          Gone with her little chin
          Thrust ahead of her
          And her soft hair blowing careless
          From under a wide hat,
Dancer, singer, a laughing passionate lover.

Were there ten men or a hundred hunting Chick?
Were there five men or fifty with aching hearts?
    Everybody loved Chick Lorimer.
        Nobody knows where she's gone.

Working Girls

The working girls in the morning are going to work — long
    lines of them afoot amid the downtown stores and factories,
    thousands with little brick-shaped lunches wrapped in
    newspapers under their arms.
Each morning as I move through this river of young-woman
    life I feel a wonder about where it is all going, so many with
    a peach bloom of young years on them and laughter of red
    lips and memories in their eyes of dances the night before
    and plays and walks.
Green and gray streams run side by side in a river and so here
    are always the others, those who have been over the way,
    the women who know each one the end of life's gamble for
    her, the meaning and the clue, the how and the why of the
    dances and the arms that passed around their waists and the
    fingers that played in their hair.
Faces go by written over: 'I know it all, I know where the
    bloom and the laughter go and I have memories,' and the
    feet of these move slower and they have wisdom where the
    others have beauty.
So the green and the gray move in the early morning on the
    downtown streets.

Happiness

I asked professors who teach the meaning of life to tell me
    what is happiness.

And I went to famous executives who boss the work of
   thousands of men.
They all shook their heads and gave me a smile as though I
   was trying to fool with them.
And then one Sunday afternoon I wandered out along the
   Desplaines river
And I saw a crowd of Hungarians under the trees with their
   women and children and a keg of beer and an accordion.

The Shovel Man

         On the street
Slung on his shoulder is a handle half way across,
Tied in a big knot on the scoop of cast iron
Are the overalls faded from sun and rain in the ditches;
Spatter of dry clay sticking yellow on his left sleeve
         And a flimsy shirt open at the throat,
         I know him for a shovel man,
         A dago working for a dollar six bits a day
And a dark-eyed woman in the old country dreams of him
         for one of the world's ready men with a pair of fresh
         lips and a kiss better than all the wild grapes that ever
         grew in Tuscany.

' "Do tell!" . . . "I want to know!" '

(From *The People, Yes*)

         'Do tell!'
         'I want to know!'
         'You don't say so!'
         'For the land's sake!'
         'Gosh all fish-hooks!'

'Tell me some more.
I don't believe a word you say
but I love to listen
to your sweet harmonica
to your chin-music.
Your fish stories hang together
when they're just a pack of lies:
you ought to have a leather medal:
you ought to have a statue
carved of butter: you deserve
a large bouquet of turnips.'

. . .

The people, yes, the customers,
In short-order lunch rooms they read signs:
 If the ice-box gets on fire ring the towel.
 Don't tip the waiters — it upsets them.
 Eat here — why go somewhere else to be cheated?
 Your face is good but it won't go in the cash register.
'There ain't no strong coffee, there's only weak people,'
 said one heavy on the java.

The people is a child at school writing howlers,
writing answers half wrong and half right:
 The government of England is a limited mockery.
 Gravitation is that which if there were none we
 would all fly away.
 There were no Christians among the early Gauls;
 they were mostly lawyers.

. . .

When Chicago has a debate whether there is a hell someone
 always says, 'Down in hell they debate whether there is a
 Chicago.'
'Too bad you have to work in this kind of a soup parlor,'
 the customer sympathized, the waiter refusing the
 sympathy: 'I work here but I don't eat here.'

A short-order lunch room in Waterloo hangs up a sign for
visiting Hawkeyes: 'We eat our own hash — think it over.'
A college boarding house in Ann Arbor instructs the
scissorbill: 'God hates a glutton — learn to say No.'
The slim little wiry Texas Ranger answering a riot call heard
from the town committee that they certainly expected at
least a company of troopers, which brought his query,
'There's only one riot — isn't there?'
'Are you happy?' the evangelist asked the new half-convert.
'Well, parson, I'm not damn happy, just *happy*, that's all.'

· · ·

Wedlock is a padlock.
Take a good look at the mother before
getting tied up with the daughter.
Let a mother be ever so bad she wishes
her daughter to be good.
The man hardly ever marries the woman
he jokes about: she often marries the
man she laughs at.
Keep your eyes open before marriage,
half-shut afterward.

In heaven an angel is nobody in particular.
Even if your stomach be strong, eat as few cockroaches as
possible.
The curse of the Spanish gypsy: May you be a mail carrier
and have sore feet.
Well lathered is half shaved.
A wife is not a guitar you hang on the wall after playing it.
The liar forgets.
A redheaded man in the orchestra is a sure sign of trouble.
The shabby genteel would better be in rags.
As sure as God made little apples he was busy as a cranberry
merchant.

It will last about as long as a snowball in hell.
I wouldn't take a million dollars for this baby and I wouldn't
   give ten cents for another.

Blue eyes say love me or I die.
Black eyes say love me or I kill you.
The sun rises and sets in her eyes.
   Wishes won't wash dishes.
May all your children be acrobats.
   Leave something to wish for.
   Lips however rosy must be fed.
   Some kill with a feather.
   By night all cats are gray.
Life goes before we know what it is.
   One fool is enough in a house.
Even God gets tired of too much hallelujah.
Take it easy and live long are brothers.
   The baby's smile pays the bill.

EDGAR LEE MASTERS (1869-1950)

The author of one extraordinarily successful book, *Spoon River Anthology*, Edgar Lee Masters, like Carl Sandburg, is an example of rugged midwestern individualism. His father was a barrister of standing, his mother a descendant of old New England stock. But the poet was brought up in small towns in Illinois, and largely educated himself by reading widely. He attended schools in Petersburg and at Lewistown, near the Spoon River, which is about 200 miles from Chicago. A term at Knox college whetted his appetite for education, but he had to give place to a younger sister and left college.

By apprenticeship in his father's law office he eventually became an attorney and moved to Chicago. He worked for a while as a bill collector, but soon set up in law practice. His mind, however, was set on poetry, and he had published conventional poems for many years in Chicago newspapers. Three books he published attracted no attention. For some years, also, he had been planning to write a novel using his experience of small-town life. In the spring of 1914, when he was already forty-four, his mother visited him in Chicago and for some days they talked of the lives of people they had known in the Spoon River country. Out of this stuff of memory came the first poems of *Spoon River Anthology*, realistic, bitter, passionate sketches of small-town life.

The first batch of poems appeared in *Reedy's Mirror*, a St. Louis periodical, on May 29, 1914, under the pseudonym of Webster Ford. The poems continued weekly for the next six months until more than 250 poems had been written. Masters collapsed from nervous exhaustion after completing the book; but he was already a national figure, and *Spoon River* has gone through numerous editions since then.

Subsequently, Masters wrote much and ranged widely, in poems, plays, novels, biography, history, and autobiography. He was a prolific writer, turning out one, sometimes two, books a year. But neither the public nor critics have ever given him his due after the success of *Spoon River*. A study of his complete work is still to come. He died at Melrose Park, Pennsylvania, in his eightieth year.

Seth Compton

When I died, the circulating library
Which I built up for Spoon River,
And managed for the good of inquiring minds,
Was sold at auction on the public square,
As if to destroy the last vestige
Of my memory and influence.
For those of you who could not see the virtue
Of knowing Volney's 'Ruins' as well as Butler's 'Analogy'
And 'Faust' as well as 'Evangeline',
Were really the power in the village,
And often you asked me,
'What is the use of knowing the evil in the world?'
I am out of your way now, Spoon River,
Choose your own good and call it good.
For I could never make you see
That no one knows what is good
Who knows not what is evil;
And no one knows what is true
Who knows not what is false.

Minerva Jones

I am Minerva, the village poetess,
Hooted at, jeered at by the Yahoos of the street
For my heavy body, cock-eye, and rolling walk,
And all the more when 'Butch' Weldy
Captured me after a brutal hunt.
He left me to my fate with Doctor Meyers;
And I sank into death, growing numb from the feet up,
Like one stepping deeper and deeper into a stream of ice.
Will some one go to the village newspaper,

And gather into a book the verses I wrote? —
I thirsted so for love!
I hungered so for life!

Doctor Meyers

No other man, unless it was Doc Hill,
Did more for people in this town than I.
And all the weak, the halt, the improvident
And those who could not pay flocked to me.
I was good-hearted, easy Doctor Meyers.
I was healthy, happy, in comfortable fortune,
Blessed with a congenial mate, my children raised,
All wedded, doing well in the world.
And then one night, Minerva, the poetess,
Came to me in her trouble, crying.
I tried to help her out — she died —
They indicted me, the newspapers disgraced me,
My wife perished of a broken heart.
And pneumonia finished me.

Daisy Fraser

Did you ever hear of Editor Whedon
Giving to the public treasury any of the money he received
For supporting candidates for office?
Or for writing up the canning factory
To get people to invest?
Or for suppressing the facts about the bank,
When it was rotten and ready to break?
Did you ever hear of the Circuit Judge
Helping anyone except the 'Q' railroad,
Or the bankers? Or did Rev. Peet or Rev. Sibley

Give any part of their salary, earned by keeping still,
Or speaking out as the leaders wished them to do,
To the building of the water works?
But I — Daisy Fraser who always passed
Along the streets through rows of nods and smiles,
And coughs and words such as 'there she goes',
Never was taken before Justice Arnett
Without contributing ten dollars and costs
To the school fund of Spoon River!

Judge Somers

How does it happen, tell me,
That I who was most erudite of lawyers,
Who knew Blackstone and Coke
Almost by heart, who made the greatest speech
The court-house ever heard, and wrote
A brief that won the praise of Justice Breese —
How does it happen, tell me,
That I lie here unmarked, forgotten,
While Chase Henry, the town drunkard,
Has a marble block, topped by an urn,
Wherein Nature, in a mood ironical,
Has sown a flowering weed?

Emily Sparks

Where is my boy, my boy —
In what far part of the world?
The boy I loved best of all in the school? —
I, the teacher, the old maid, the virgin heart,
Who made them all my children.

Did I know my boy aright,
Thinking of him as spirit aflame,
Active, ever aspiring?
Oh, boy, boy, for whom I prayed and prayed
In many a watchful hour at night,
Do you remember the letter I wrote you
Of the beautiful love of Christ?
And whether you ever took it or not,
My boy, wherever you are,
Work for your soul's sake,
That all the clay of you, all of the dross of you,
May yield to the fire of you,
Till the fire is nothing but light! . . .
Nothing but light!

Reuben Pantier

Well, Emily Sparks, your prayers were not wasted,
Your love was not all in vain.
I owe whatever I was in life
To your hope that would not give me up,
To your love that saw me still as good.
Dear Emily Sparks, let me tell you the story.
I pass the effect of my father and mother;
The milliner's daughter made me trouble
And out I went in the world,
Where I passed through every peril known
Of wine and women and joy of life.
One night, in a room in the Rue de Rivoli,
I was drinking wine with a black-eyed cocotte,
And the tears swam into my eyes.
She thought they were amorous tears and smiled
For thought of her conquest over me.

But my soul was three thousand miles away,
In the days when you taught me in Spoon River.
And just because you no more could love me,
Nor pray for me, nor write me letters,
The eternal silence of you spoke instead.
And the black-eyed cocotte took the tears for hers,
As well as the deceiving kisses I gave her.
Somehow, from that hour, I had a new vision —
Dear Emily Sparks!

Fiddler Jones

The earth keeps some vibration going
There in your heart, and that is you.
And if the people find you can fiddle,
Why, fiddle you must, for all your life.
What do you see, a harvest of clover?
Or a meadow to walk through to the river?
The wind's in the corn; you rub your hands
For beeves hereafter ready for market;
Or else you hear the rustle of skirts
Like the girls when dancing at Little Grove.
To Cooney Potter a pillar of dust
Or whirling leaves meant ruinous drouth;
They looked to me like Red-Head Sammy
Stepping it off, to 'Toor-a-Loor'.
How could I till my forty acres
Not to speak of getting more,
With a medley of horns, bassoons and piccolos
Stirred in my brain by crows and robins
And the creak of a wind-mill — only these?
And I never started to plow in my life
That some one did not stop in the road

And take me away to a dance or picnic.
I ended up with forty acres;
I ended up with a broken fiddle —
And a broken laugh, and a thousand memories,
And not a single regret.

ROBERT FROST (1874-1963)

The best-loved and most popular poet of America, Robert Frost did not become well known until his middle life, after he had suffered many disappointments. He was already forty when *North of Boston* (1914), the book that brought him fame, was published. Before that he had sent poetry for years to magazines and newspapers, only to collect rejection slips in return. Once established, however, his reputation has been lasting and deep-rooted. He is the poet of New England, but his poetry has a profound significance that goes far beyond the regional setting.

He was in fact born in San Francisco in 1874, and did not see New England until the age of nine. His father had been a strong sympathizer with the South over the Civil War, and had therefore moved out of New England and settled in the far west. He had named his first-born, the poet-to-be, Robert Lee, after the Confederate general Robert E. Lee. After the father's death, the young widow travelled with her two children, Robert and his sister, across the continent to bury their father in Massachusetts; and they afterwards lived there. Robert attended Lawrence High School. At graduation he was class poet and co-valedictorian with the girl whom he later married.

He had early discovered his vocation as a poet, and he drifted with apparent aimlessness from one job to another for many years, writing and perfecting his craft. He studied for a semester at Dartmouth College; worked as a bobbin boy in a woollen mill, then as a newspaper reporter. His first published poem, 'My Butterfly', appeared in the *New York Independent* in November 1894; and he printed six of his poems in an edition of two copies — one for his fiancée and one for himself — under the title *Twilight*.

After two more years of study at Harvard, he settled on a small farm at Derry, New Hampshire, where he raised poultry and became known as 'the egg man'. He also taught school for a while; he was now married, and a growing family (three daughters and a son) added to his responsibilities. But he was writing his best work: by 1905 most of the poems in *North of Boston* had already been written. Suddenly in 1912 he risked everything, sold his farm, and sailed with his family for England to try his fortune with poetry.

In England, he quickly found good friends in Edward Thomas, F. S. Flint, T. E. Hulme, Lascelles Abercrombie, and Ezra Pound. His first book, *A Boy's Will*, appeared in 1913 in England, and *North of Boston* the following year. In America, *North of Boston* soon became a best-seller and Frost returned to find himself a national figure. As the years passed he gave readings and lectures in a score of universities and taught as writer-in-residence at Amherst, the University of Michigan, Harvard, and Dartmouth. He won the Pulitzer Prize four times, receiving honours from many great universities, including Oxford and Cambridge. He even had a mountain named after him in the State of Vermont; and on his seventy-fifth birthday he received formal felicitations from the United States Senate. His death on January 29, 1963, was a day of sadness for thousands who had delighted and thrilled to his lectures, readings, and published poems.

The Pasture

I'm going out to clean the pasture spring;
I'll only stop to rake the leaves away
(And wait to watch the water clear, I may):
I sha'n't be gone long. — You come too.

I'm going out to fetch the little calf
That's standing by the mother. It's so young,
It totters when she licks it with her tongue.
I sha'n't be gone long. — You come too.

Mowing

There was never a sound beside the wood but one,
And that was my long scythe whispering to the ground.
What was it it whispered? I knew not well myself;
Perhaps it was something about the heat of the sun,
Something, perhaps, about the lack of sound —
And that was why it whispered and did not speak.
It was no dream of the gift of idle hours,
Or easy gold at the hand of fay or elf:
Anything more than the truth would have seemed too weak

To the earnest love that laid the swale in rows,
Not without feeble-pointed spikes of flowers
(Pale orchises), and scared a bright green snake.
The fact is the sweetest dream that labor knows.
My long scythe whispered and left the hay to make.

'Out, Out – '

The buzz-saw snarled and rattled in the yard
And made dust and dropped stove-length sticks of wood,
Sweet-scented stuff when the breeze drew across it.
And from there those that lifted eyes could count
Five mountain ranges one behind the other
Under the sunset far into Vermont.
And the saw snarled and rattled, snarled and rattled,
As it ran light, or had to bear a load.
And nothing happened: day was all but done.
Call it a day, I wish they might have said
To please the boy by giving him the half hour
That a boy counts so much when saved from work.
His sister stood beside them in her apron
To tell them 'Supper.' At the word, the saw,
As if to prove saws knew what supper meant,
Leaped out at the boy's hand, or seemed to leap –
He must have given the hand. However it was,
Neither refused the meeting. But the hand!
The boy's first outcry was a rueful laugh,
As he swung toward them holding up the hand
Half in appeal, but half as if to keep
The life from spilling. Then the boy saw all –
Since he was old enough to know, big boy
Doing a man's work, though a child at heart –
He saw all spoiled. 'Don't let him cut my hand off –

The doctor, when he comes. Don't let him, sister!'
So. But the hand was gone already.
The doctor put him in the dark of ether.
He lay and puffed his lips out with his breath.
And then — the watcher at his pulse took fright.
No one believed. They listened at his heart.
Little — less — nothing! — and that ended it.
No more to build on there. And they, since they
Were not the one dead, turned to their affairs.

A Considerable Speck

(Microscopic)

A speck that would have been beneath my sight
On any but a paper sheet so white
Set off across what I had written there.
And I had idly poised my pen in air
To stop it with a period of ink
When something strange about it made me think.
This was no dust speck by my breathing blown,
But unmistakably a living mite
With inclinations it could call its own.
It paused as with suspicion of my pen,
And then came racing wildly on again
To where my manuscript was not yet dry;
Then paused again and either drank or smelt —
With loathing, for again it turned to fly.
Plainly with an intelligence I dealt.
It seemed too tiny to have room for feet,
Yet must have had a set of them complete
To express how much it didn't want to die.
It ran with terror and with cunning crept.

It faltered: I could see it hesitate;
Then in the middle of the open sheet
Cower down in desperation to accept
Whatever I accorded it of fate.
I have none of the tenderer-than-thou
Collectivistic regimenting love
With which the modern world is being swept.
But this poor microscopic item now!
Since it was nothing I knew evil of
I let it lie there till I hope it slept.
I have a mind myself and recognize
Mind when I meet with it in any guise.
No one can know how glad I am to find
On any sheet the least display of mind.

EZRA POUND (1885-   )

The most controversial, dynamic, and stimulating figure in modern literature, Pound is the experimentalist, initiator of movements, and showman of modern letters. He has directed and inspired scores of 'little magazines' — small-circulation literary periodicals — and he has influenced and helped a dozen important writers ranging from Robert Frost and T. S. Eliot to Hemingway. And he has written the most astonishing and complex poetry of our time.

Born in Hailey, Idaho, in 1885 (on his mother's side he is distantly related to the poet Longfellow), Pound grew up as a boy in Pennsylvania and entered the university at the precocious age of fifteen. He received degrees from Hamilton College and Pennsylvania University, then began teaching at Wabash College, Indiana. He was dismissed from his post, however, following a minor scandal. (He had given shelter to a homeless chorus girl stranded in the streets, giving her his bed while he himself slept on the couch; but this quixotic action was misunderstood by the authorities, with tragic results for Pound.) Clearly he was of the 'bohemian type'.

Leaving America, Pound sailed for Spain and Italy with $80 in his pocket. In Venice he published his first book, *A Lume Spento* (1908). He then settled in London, England, where for twelve years he dominated the literary scene, directing the poetry movement called Imagism, creating another movement called Vorticism, editing and contributing to such periodicals as *The Little Review*, *Blast*, *Poetry* (Chicago), and *The Egoist*. His books, *Personae* (1909), *Exultations* (1909), *Cathay* (1915), and others, won him a notable reputation. He was married to Dorothy Shakespear in 1914.

In 1920 Pound left London, and after four years' stay in Paris settled in Rapallo on the Italian Riviera. There he continued to write his epic poem *The Cantos* which he had begun in 1917. Living in Italy, he became a partisan of Mussolini's Fascism, which he saw in the light of his Renaissance theories of the heroic leader and the economic doctrine of social control on behalf of art and culture. Guided by these ideas, he accepted an offer to broadcast without pay to American troops during the Second World War. This ill-considered action earned him the charge of treason from his own country, to which he was always deeply devoted, and when the war ended he was brought to America for trial. He was conveniently declared of unsound mind, however, before the trial could take place, and was committed to St. Elizabeths Hospital, Washington, D.C.

Pound spent twelve years in the asylum, writing, translating, and receiving distinguished visitors (the Bolingen Award which he received at this time for his Pisan Cantos created a great sensation). Released in 1958, he returned to Italy, where he now lives in retirement, an ageing man, having suffered several severe paralytic strokes.

The River-Merchant's Wife: A Letter

(After Rihaku)

While my hair was still cut straight across my forehead
I played about the front gate, pulling flowers.
You came by on bamboo stilts, playing horse,
You walked about my seat, playing with blue plums.
And we went on living in the village of Chokan:
Two small people, without dislike or suspicion.

At fourteen I married My Lord you.
I never laughed, being bashful.
Lowering my head, I looked at the wall.
Called to, a thousand times, I never looked back.

At fifteen I stopped scowling,
I desired my dust to be mingled with yours
Forever and forever and forever.
Why should I climb the look out?

At sixteen you departed,
You went into far Ku-to-yen, by the river of swirling eddies,
And you have been gone five months.
The monkeys make sorrowful noise overhead.

You dragged your feet when you went out.
By the gate now, the moss is grown, the different mosses,
Too deep to clear them away!
The leaves fall early this autumn, in wind.

The paired butterflies are already yellow with August
Over the grass in the West garden;
They hurt me. I grow older.
If you are coming down through the narrows of the river
   Kiang,
Please let me know beforehand,
And I will come out to meet you
                  As far as Cho-fu-Sa.

N.Y.

My City, my beloved, my white! Ah, slender,
Listen! Listen to me, and I will breathe into thee a soul.
Delicately upon the reed, attend me!

Now do I know that I am mad,
For here are a million people surly with traffic;
This is no maid.
Neither could I play upon any reed if I had one.

My City, my beloved,
Thou art a maid with no breasts,
Thou art slender as a silver reed.
Listen to me, attend me!
And I will breathe into thee a soul,
And thou shalt live for ever.

The Study in Aesthetics

The very small children in patched clothing,
Being smitten with an unusual wisdom,
Stopped in their play as she passed them
And cried up from their cobbles:

*Guarda! Ahi, guarda! ch' è be'a!**

But three years after this
I heard the young Dante, whose last name I do not know —
For there are, in Sirmione, twenty-eight young Dantes and
   thirty-four Catulli;
And there had been a great catch of sardines,
And his elders
Were packing them in the great wooden boxes
For the market in Brescia, and he
Leapt about, snatching at the bright fish
And getting in both of their ways;
And in vain they commanded him to *sta fermo*!
And when they would not let him arrange
The fish in the boxes
He stroked those which were already arranged,
Murmuring for his own satisfaction
This identical phrase:

   Ch' è be'a

And at this I was mildly abashed.

Meditatio

When I carefully consider the curious habits of dogs
I am compelled to conclude
That man is the superior animal.

When I consider the curious habits of man
I confess, my friend, I am puzzled.

**bella*

76

Salutation I

O generation of the thoroughly smug
   and thoroughly uncomfortable,

I have seen fishermen picnicking in the sun,

I have seen them with untidy families,

I have seen their smiles full of teeth
     and heard ungainly laughter.

And I am happier than you are,

And they were happier than I am;

And the fish swim in the lake
     and do not even own clothing.

The Rest

O helpless few in my country,
O remnant enslaved!

Artists broken against her,
A-stray, lost in the villages,
Mistrusted, spoken-against,

Lovers of beauty, starved,
Thwarted with systems,
Helpless against the control;

You who can not wear yourselves out
By persisting to successes,
You who can only speak,
Who can not steel yourselves into reiteration;

You of the finer sense,
Broken against false knowledge,
You who can know at first hand,
Hated, shut in, mistrusted:

Take thought:
I have weathered the storm,
I have beaten out my exile.

Commission

Go, my songs, to the lonely and the unsatisfied,
Go also to the nerve-wracked, go to the enslaved-by-
    convention,
Bear to them my contempt for their oppressors.
Go as a great wave of cool water,
Bear my contempt of oppressors.

Speak against unconscious oppression,
Speak against the tyranny of the unimaginative,
Speak against bonds.
Go to the bourgeoise who is dying of her ennuis,
Go to the women in suburbs.
Go to the hideously wedded,
Go to them whose failure is concealed,
Go to the unluckily mated,
Go to the bought wife,
Go to the woman entailed.

Go to those who have delicate lust,
Go to those whose delicate desires are thwarted,
Go like a blight upon the dulness of the world;
Go with your edge against this,
Strengthen the subtle cords,
Bring confidence upon the algae and the tentacles of the soul.

Go in a friendly manner,
Go with an open speech.
Be eager to find new evils and new good,
Be against all forms of oppression.
Go to those who are thickened with middle age,
To those who have lost their interest.

Go to the adolescent who are smothered in family —
Oh how hideous it is
To see three generations of one house gathered together!
It is like an old tree with shoots,
And with some branches rotted and falling.

Go out and defy opinion,
Go against this vegetable bondage of the blood.
Be against all sorts of mortmain.

'These fought in any case'

(From *Hugh Selwyn Mauberley*)

These fought in any case,
   and some believing,
      pro domo, in any case . . .

Some quick to arm,
some for adventure,
some from fear of weakness,
some from fear of censure,
some for love of slaughter, in imagination,
learning later . . .
some in fear, learning love of slaughter;

Died some, pro patria,
   non 'dulce' non 'et decor' . . .
walked eye-deep in hell

believing in old men's lies, then unbelieving
came home, home to a lie,
home to many deceits,
home to old lies and new infamy;
usury age-old and age-thick
and liars in public places.

Daring as never before, wastage as never before.
Young blood and high blood,
fair cheeks, and fine bodies;

fortitude as never before

frankness as never before,
disillusions as never told in the old days,
hysterias, trench confessions,
laughter out of dead bellies.

'There died a myriad'

(From *Hugh Selwyn Mauberley*)

There died a myriad,
And of the best, among them,
For an old bitch gone in the teeth,
For a botched civilization.

Charm, smiling at the good mouth,
Quick eyes gone under earth's lid,

For two gross of broken statues,
For a few thousand battered books.

'What thou lovest well remains . . .'

(From *Canto LXXXI*)

What thou lovest well remains,
                    the rest is dross
What thou lov'st well shall not be reft from thee
What thou lov'st well is thy true heritage
Whose world, or mine or theirs
                    or is it of none?
First came the seen, then thus the palpable
  Elysium, though it were in the halls of hell,
What thou lovest well is thy true heritage

The ant's a centaur in his dragon world.
Pull down thy vanity, it is not man
Made courage, or made order, or made grace,
  Pull down thy vanity, I say pull down.
Learn of the green world what can be thy place
In scaled invention or true artistry,
Pull down thy vanity,
                    Paquin pull down!
The green casque has outdone your elegance.

'Master thyself, then others shall thee beare'
        Pull down thy vanity
Thou art a beaten dog beneath the hail,
A swollen magpie in a fitful sun,
Half black half white
Nor knowst'ou wing from tail
Pull down thy vanity
                How mean thy hates
Fostered in falsity,
                Pull down thy vanity,
Rathe to destroy, niggard in charity,

Pull down thy vanity,
                    I say pull down.

But to have done instead of not doing
                    this is not vanity
To have, with decency, knocked
That a Blunt should open
                    To have gathered from the air a live tradition
or from a fine old eye the unconquered flame
This is not vanity.
                  Here error is all in the not done,
all in the diffidence that faltered.

T. S. ELIOT (1888-1965)

The mentor of modern poetry, a classicist, traditionalist, and convinced religious voice in the twentieth century, T. S. Eliot is undoubtedly a central character in the complex drama of modern literature. He seems to have gone counter to all the unexamined assumptions of the majority: easy liberalism, scepticism, worldliness, pleasure-seeking, slovenliness in art and life, and unduly optimistic belief in progress. Against these he directed a rigorous critical mind, disciplined in a Christian pre-romantic tradition, seeking hope and spiritual illumination in the present.

Born in 1888 in St. Louis, Missouri, where his father was in business, Eliot belonged to a family of choice New England stock that carried culture, Emerson's philosophy, faith, and poetry into the heart of the American frontier. His grandfather was a distinguished Unitarian minister, one of the founders of Washington University in St. Louis. (Later, when Eliot attended Harvard, a distant relative, Charles William Eliot, was president of that university.) His mother wrote a dramatic poem on Savonarola. After studying at Smith and Milton academies, Eliot went to Harvard where he showed special interest in philosophy, and he published his first poems in the *Harvard Advocate*. (He took his B.A. in 1909, and a master's degree in 1910.) At Harvard, also, he composed the poem 'The Love Song of J. Alfred Prufrock', the source of his early reputation. (It was first published in *Poetry* (Chicago), in 1915.)

For a time he continued graduate studies in French literature at the Sorbonne, and in philosophy in Germany, and at Oxford; but soon after he taught school near London, then worked in a bank. After meeting Ezra Pound in the fall of 1914 he turned to a purely literary career and with the publication of 'Prufrock' in 1915 entered into the mainstream of the modernist movement. His style was novel and full of surprises, derived from the French poets Baudelaire, Laforgue, Corbière, and Rimbaud. 'The kind of poetry that I needed,' he later explained, '... did not exist in English at all; it was only to be found in French.'

Eliot's career from this point is the history of his literary life and of the domination he has exerted over modern letters. His first appearance in the role of critic was an anonymous essay on Pound in 1917. Provocative and influential critical essays appeared in *The Sacred Wood* in 1920. His first book of poetry, *Prufrock and Other Observations*, appeared in 1917, and the sensational poem *The Waste Land* in 1922. In that year he began his own periodical, *The Criterion*, at present sponsored by the firm of which he later became a director, Faber and Faber. In 1928, in a critical preface, he defined his position as 'classical in literature, royalist in politics, anglo-catholic in religion' — a three-pronged bone that stuck in the throats of most of his critics. *The Waste Land* and 'The Hollow Men' (1925) had seemed to proclaim the end of all religious faith in our time; but now the poet of scepticism seemed to revert to a firm belief in the tenets of the Anglican faith. The logic of Eliot's development, however, was much more consistent than anyone realized: he had always been concerned with the absence of religion.

Eliot's 1928 announcement of his convictions was followed by *Ash Wednesday* in 1930; and in the next years by religious plays, *The Rock* in 1934, and *Murder in the Cathedral* in 1935. Eliot later wrote several successful plays in which the religious thought and conviction was masked by social satire, comedy, and contemporary subjects: *The Cocktail Party* (1949) and *The Confidential Clerk* (1953). His later poetry is represented in *Four Quartets,* philosophic, personal, religious meditations written in the period from 1934 to 1943. His poetic productivity was not large, but his work is demanding, intense, and highly unified in content. The critical writings are more considerable, but they too are unified by the poet's programmatic and priest-like role in an age of scepticism and disorder. Eliot more than any other writer has given this century its image of itself as one of disintegration, fragmented neurosis, and imminent chaos — with an insistence on the order we need to cure us of this distress.

Preludes

I

The winter evening settles down
With smell of steaks in passageways.
Six o'clock.
The burnt-out ends of smoky days.
And now a gusty shower wraps
The grimy scraps
Of withered leaves about your feet
And newspapers from vacant lots;

And showers beat
On broken blinds and chimney-pots,
And at the corner of the street
A lonely cab-horse steams and stamps.
And then the lighting of the lamps.

II

The morning comes to consciousness
Of faint stale smells of beer
From the sawdust-trampled street
With all its muddy feet that press
To early coffee-stands.
With the other masquerades
That time resumes,
One thinks of all the hands
That are raising dingy shades
In a thousand furnished rooms.

III

You tossed a blanket from the bed,
You lay upon your back, and waited;
You dozed, and watched the night revealing
The thousand sordid images
Of which your soul was constituted;
They flickered against the ceiling.
And when all the world came back
And the light crept up between the shutters
And you heard the sparrows in the gutters,
You had such a vision of the street
As the street hardly understands;
Sitting along the bed's edge, where
You curled the papers from your hair,
Or clasped the yellow soles of feet
In the palms of both soiled hands.

IV

His soul stretched tight across the skies
That fade behind a city block,
Or trampled by insistent feet
At four and five and six o'clock;
And short square fingers stuffing pipes,
And evening newspapers, and eyes
Assured of certain certainties,
The conscience of a blackened street
Impatient to assume the world.

I am moved by fancies that are curled
Around these images, and cling:
The notion of some infinitely gentle
Infinitely suffering thing.

Wipe your hand across your mouth, and laugh;
The worlds revolve like ancient women
Gathering fuel in vacant lots.

Morning at the Window

They are rattling breakfast plates in basement kitchens,
And along the trampled edges of the street
I am aware of the damp souls of housemaids
Sprouting despondently at area gates.

The brown waves of fog toss up to me
Twisted faces from the bottom of the street,
And tear from a passer-by with muddy skirts
An aimless smile that hovers in the air
And vanishes along the level of the roofs.

Portrait of a Lady

Among the smoke and fog of a December afternoon
You have the scene arrange itself — as it will seem to do —
With 'I have saved this afternoon for you';
And four wax candles in the darkened room,
Four rings of light upon the ceiling overhead,
An atmosphere of Juliet's tomb
Prepared for all the things to be said, or left unsaid.
We have been, let us say, to hear the latest Pole
Transmit the Preludes, through his hair and fingertips.
'So intimate, this Chopin, that I think his soul
Should be resurrected only among friends
Some two or three, who will not touch the bloom
That is rubbed and questioned in the concert room.'
— And so the conversation slips
Among velleities and carefully caught regrets
Through attenuated tones of violins
Mingled with remote cornets
And begins.

'You do not know how much they mean to me, my friends,
And how, how rare and strange it is, to find
In a life composed so much, so much of odds and ends,
[For indeed I do not love it . . . you knew? you are not blind!
How keen you are!]
To find a friend who has these qualities,
Who has, and gives
Those qualities upon which friendship lives.
How much it means that I say this to you —
Without these friendships — life, what *cauchemar*!'

Among the windings of the violins
And the ariettes

87

Of cracked cornets
Inside my brain a dull tom-tom begins
Absurdly hammering a prelude of its own,
Capricious monotone
That is at least one definite 'false note'.
— Let us take the air, in a tobacco trance,
Admire the monuments,
Discuss the late events,
Correct our watches by the public clocks.
Then sit for half an hour and drink our bocks.

II

Now that lilacs are in bloom
She has a bowl of lilacs in her room
And twists one in her fingers while she talks.
'Ah, my friend, you do not know, you do not know
What life is, you who hold it in your hands';
(Slowly twisting the lilac stalks)
'You let it flow from you, you let it flow,
And youth is cruel, and has no remorse
And smiles at situations which it cannot see.'
I smile, of course,
And go on drinking tea.
'Yet with these April sunsets, that somehow recall
My buried life, and Paris in the Spring,
I feel immeasurably at peace, and find the world
To be wonderful and youthful, after all.'

The voice returns like the insistent out-of-tune
Of a broken violin on an August afternoon:
'I am always sure that you understand
My feelings, always sure that you feel,
Sure that across the gulf you reach your hand.

You are invulnerable, you have no Achilles' heel.
You will go on, and when you have prevailed

You can say: at this point many a one has failed.
But what have I, but what have I, my friend,
To give you, what can you receive from me?
Only the friendship and the sympathy
Of one about to reach her journey's end.

I shall sit here, serving tea to friends . . .

I take my hat: how can I make a cowardly amends
For what she has said to me?
You will see me any morning in the park
Reading the comics and the sporting page.
Particularly I remark
An English countess goes upon the stage.
A Greek was murdered at a Polish dance,
Another bank defaulter has confessed.
I keep my countenance,
I remain self-possessed
Except when a street piano, mechanical and tired
Reiterates some worn-out common song
With the smell of hyacinths across the garden
Recalling things that other people have desired.
Are these ideas right or wrong?

III

The October night comes down: returning as before
Except for a slight sensation of being ill at ease
I mount the stairs and turn the handle of the door
And feel as if I had mounted on my hands and knees.
'And so you are going abroad; and when do you return?
But that's a useless question.
You hardly know when you are coming back,
You will find so much to learn.
My smile falls heavily among the bric-à-brac.

'Perhaps you can write to me.'
My self-possession flares up for a second;

This is as I had reckoned.
'I have been wondering frequently of late
(But our beginnings never know our ends!)
Why we have not developed into friends.'
I feel like one who smiles, and turning shall remark
Suddenly, his expression in a glass.
My self-possession gutters; we are really in the dark.

'For everybody said so, all our friends,
They all were sure our feelings would relate
So closely! I myself can hardly understand.
We must leave it now to fate.
You will write, at any rate.
Perhaps it is not too late.
I shall sit here, serving tea to friends.'

And I must borrow every changing shape
To find expression . . . dance, dance
Like a dancing bear,
Cry like a parrot, chatter like an ape.
Let us take the air, in a tobacco trance —

Well! and what if she should die some afternoon,
Afternoon grey and smoky, evening yellow and rose;
Should die and leave me sitting pen in hand
With the smoke coming down above the housetops;
Doubtful, for a while
Not knowing what to feel or if I understand
Or whether wise or foolish, tardy or too soon . . .
Would she not have the advantage, after all?
This music is successful with a 'dying fall'
Now that we talk of dying —
And should I have the right to smile?

A Game of Chess

(From *The Waste Land*)

The Chair she sat in, like a burnished throne,
Glowed on the marble, where the glass
Held up by standards wrought with fruited vines
From which a golden Cupidon peeped out
(Another hid his eyes behind his wing)
Doubled the flames of sevenbranched candelabra
Reflecting light upon the table as
The glitter of her jewels rose to meet it,
From satin cases poured in rich profusion;
In vials of ivory and coloured glass
Unstoppered, lurked her strange synthetic perfumes,
Unguent, powdered, or liquid — troubled, confused
And drowned the sense in odours; stirred by the air
That freshened from the window, these ascended
In fattening the prolonged candle-flames,
Flung their smoke into the laquearia,
Stirring the pattern on the coffered ceiling.
Huge sea-wood fed with copper
Burned green and orange, framed by the coloured stone,
In which sad light a carvèd dolphin swam.
Above the antique mantel was displayed
As though a window gave upon the sylvan scene
The change of Philomel, by the barbarous king
So rudely forced; yet there the nightingale
Filled all the desert with inviolable voice
And still she cried, and still the world pursues,
'Jug Jug' to dirty ears.
And other withered stumps of time
Were told upon the walls; staring forms
Leaned out, leaning, hushing the room enclosed.
Footsteps shuffled on the stair.

Under the firelight, under the brush, her hair
Spread out in fiery points
Glowed into words, then would be savagely still.

'My nerves are bad to-night. Yes, bad. Stay with me.
'Speak to me. Why do you never speak. Speak.
    'What are you thinking of? What thinking? What?
'I never know what you are thinking. Think.'

I think we are in rats' alley
Where the dead men lost their bones.

'What is that noise?'
                        The wind under the door.
'What is that noise now? What is the wind doing?'
                        Nothing again nothing.
                                            'Do
'You know nothing? Do you see nothing? Do you remember
'Nothing?'

    I remember
Those are pearls that were his eyes.
'Are you alive, or not? Is there nothing in your head?'
                                            But

O O O O that Shakespeherian Rag —
It's so elegant
So intelligent
'What shall I do now? What shall I do?'
'I shall rush out as I am, and walk the street
'With my hair down, so. What shall we do tomorrow?
'What shall we ever do?'
                        The hot water at ten.
And if it rains, a closed car at four.
And we shall play a game of chess,
Pressing lidless eyes and waiting for a knock upon the door.

When Lil's husband got demobbed, I said —
I didn't mince my words, I said to her myself,
HURRY UP PLEASE ITS TIME
Now Albert's coming back, make yourself a bit smart.
He'll want to know what you done with that money he
    gave you
To get yourself some teeth. He did, I was there.
You have them all out, Lil, and get a nice set,
He said, I swear, I can't bear to look at you.
And no more can't I, I said, and think of poor Albert,
He's been in the army four years, he wants a good time,
And if you don't give it him, there's others will, I said.
Oh is there, she said. Something o' that, I said.
Then I'll know who to thank, she said, and give me a
    straight look.
HURRY UP PLEASE ITS TIME
If you don't like it you can get on with it, I said.
Others can pick and choose if you can't.
But if Albert makes off, it won't be for lack of telling.
You ought to be ashamed, I said, to look so antique.
(And her only thirty-one.)
I can't help it, she said, pulling a long face,
It's them pills I took, to bring it off, she said.
(She's had five already, and nearly died of young George.)
The chemist said it would be all right, but I've never been
    the same.
You *are* a proper fool, I said.
Well, if Albert won't leave you alone, there it is, I said,
What you get married for if you don't want children?
HURRY UP PLEASE ITS TIME
Well, that Sunday Albert was home, they had a hot gammon,
And they asked me in to dinner, to get the beauty of it hot —
HURRY UP PLEASE ITS TIME
HURRY UP PLEASE ITS TIME
Goonight Bill. Goonight Lou. Goonight May. Goonight.

Ta ta. Goonight. Goonight.
Good night, ladies, good night, sweet ladies, good night, good
  night.

Death by Water

(From *The Waste Land*)

Phlebas the Phoenician, a fortnight dead,
Forgot the cry of gulls, and the deep sea swell
And the profit and loss.
                          A current under sea
Picked his bones in whispers. As he rose and fell
He passed the stages of his age and youth
Entering the whirlpool.
                          Gentile or Jew
O you who turn the wheel and look to windward,
Consider Phlebas, who was once handsome and tall as you.

Journey of the Magi

'A cold coming we had of it,
Just the worst time of the year
For a journey, and such a long journey:
The ways deep and the weather sharp,
The very dead of winter.'
And the camels galled, sore-footed, refractory,
Lying down in the melting snow.
There were times we regretted
The summer palaces on slopes, the terraces,
And the silken girls bringing sherbet.
Then the camel men cursing and grumbling

94

And running away, and wanting their liquor and women,
And the night-fires going out, and the lack of shelters,
And the cities hostile and the towns unfriendly
And the villages dirty and charging high prices:
A hard time we had of it.
At the end we preferred to travel all night,
Sleeping in snatches,
With the voices singing in our ears, saying
That this was all folly.

Then at dawn we came down to a temperate valley,
Wet, below the snow line, smelling of vegetation;
With a running stream and a water-mill beating the darkness,
And three trees on the low sky,
And an old white horse galloped away in the meadow.
Then we came to a tavern with vine-leaves over the lintel,
Six hands at an open door dicing for pieces of silver,
And feet kicking the empty wine-skins.
But there was no information, and so we continued
And arrived at evening, not a moment too soon
Finding the place; it was (you may say) satisfactory.

All this was a long time ago, I remember,
And I would do it again, but set down
This set down
This: were we led all that way for
Birth or Death? There was a Birth, certainly,
We had evidence and no doubt. I had seen birth and death,
But had thought they were different; this Birth was
Hard and bitter agony for us, like Death, our death.
We returned to our places, these Kingdoms,
But no longer at ease here, in the old dispensation,
With an alien people clutching their gods.
I should be glad of another death.

Choruses from 'The Rock'

The Word of the LORD came unto me, saying:
O miserable cities of designing men,
O wretched generation of enlightened men,
Betrayed in the mazes of your ingenuities,
Sold by the proceeds of your proper inventions:
I have given you hands which you turn from worship,
I have given you speech, for endless palaver,
I have given you my Law, and you set up commissions,
I have given you lips, to express friendly sentiments,
I have given you hearts, for reciprocal distrust.
I have given you power of choice, and you only alternate
Between futile speculation and unconsidered action.
Many are engaged in writing books and printing them,
Many desire to see their names in print,
Many read nothing but the race reports.
Much is your reading, but not the Word of GOD,
Much is your building, but not the House of GOD.
Will you build me a house of plaster, with corrugated roofing,
To be filled with a litter of Sunday newspapers?

1st Male Voice:
A Cry from the East:
What shall be done to the shore of smoky ships?
Will you leave my people forgetful and forgotten
To idleness, labour, and delirious stupor?
There shall be left the broken chimney,
The peeled hull, a pile of rusty iron,
In a street of scattered brick where the goat climbs,
Where My Word is unspoken.

2nd Male Voice:
A Cry from the North, from the West and from the South
Whence thousands travel daily to the timekept City;

Where My Word is unspoken,
In the land of lobelias and tennis flannels
The rabbit shall burrow and the thorn revisit,
The nettle shall flourish on the gravel court,
And the wind shall say: 'Here were decent godless people:
Their only monument the asphalt road
And a thousand lost golf balls.

Chorus:

We build in vain unless the LORD build with us.
Can you keep the City that the LORD keeps not with you?
A thousand policemen directing the traffic
Cannot tell you why you come or where you go.
A colony of cavies or a horde of active marmots
Build better than they that build without the LORD.
Shall we lift up our feet among perpetual ruins?
I have loved the beauty of Thy House, the peace of Thy
    sanctuary,
I have swept the floors and garnished the altars.
Where there is no temple there shall be no homes,
Though you have shelters and institutions,
Precarious lodgings while the rent is paid,
Subsiding basements where the rat breeds
Or sanitary dwellings with numbered doors
Or a house a little better than your neighbour's;
When the Stranger says: 'What is the meaning of this city?
Do you huddle close together because you love each other?'
What will you answer? 'We all dwell together
To make money from each other'? or 'This is a community'?
And the Stranger will depart and return to the desert.
O my soul, be prepared for the coming of the Stranger,
Be prepared for him who knows how to ask questions.

O weariness of men who turn from GOD
To the grandeur of your mind and the glory of your action,

To arts and inventions and daring enterprises,
To schemes of human greatness thoroughly discredited,
Binding the earth and the water to your service,
Exploiting the seas and developing the mountains,
Dividing the stars into common and preferred,
Engaged in devising the perfect refrigerator,
Engaged in working out a rational morality,
Engaged in printing as many books as possible,
Plotting of happiness and flinging empty bottles,
Turning from your vacancy to fevered enthusiasm
For nation or race or what you call humanity;
Though you forget the way to the Temple,
There is one who remembers the way to your door:
Life you may evade, but Death you shall not.
You shall not deny the Stranger.

D. H. LAWRENCE (1885-1930)

D. H. Lawrence was born in a small mining town near Nottingham; his mother was a schoolteacher, his father a coal-miner. A scholarship helped him through high school, after which he taught for a time, but he soon abandoned teaching for novel-writing. His health was poor and he was to die in middle life, but the flame of creative energy burned fiercely in him. On first reading his work, Ford Madox Ford, the editor of the *English Review*, immediately recognized him as 'a genius', a tribute to the spontaneous vitality of his writing.

Lawrence's flowing prose is like a natural force welling up from primal sources: he would not revise a novel, but would rewrite it from the beginning, as he did three times with *Lady Chatterley's Lover*, his last novel. He described poems as fragments of 'chaos' rather than as rationally structured forms. Beginning with *The White Peacock* (1911), he showed a passionate concern for sexual truthfulness, and saw the need for a true love relationship as the core of our social problems. He attacked the class system, industrialism, and the mechanical organization of modern life as inimical to man's natural instincts and his capacity for love. The relations between men and women, their cruel incompatibilities and conflicts, and the desire for love perfectly realized, he depicted in such novels as *Sons and Lovers* (1913), *The Rainbow* (1915), *Women in Love* (1921), and *Lady Chatterley's Lover* (1928).

Although he was primarily a novelist, Lawrence also wrote and published poetry throughout his life, beginning with *Love Poems and Others* in 1913. His *Collected Poems* in two volumes was brought out in 1929, just before his death, and *Last Poems* posthumously in 1933. In search of lost innocence, he travelled to New Mexico, Italy, Sicily, and Sardinia, and he died of tuberculosis at Vence, France, in 1930.

Snake

A snake came to my water-trough
On a hot, hot day, and I in pyjamas for the heat,
To drink there.

In the deep, strange-scented shade of the great dark carob tree
I came down the steps with my pitcher
And must wait, must stand and wait, for there he was at the
    trough before me.

He reached down from a fissure in the earth-wall in the gloom
And trailed his yellow-brown slackness soft-bellied down,
    over the edge of the stone trough
And rested his throat upon the stone bottom,
And where the water had dripped from the tap, in a small
    clearness,
He sipped with his straight mouth,
Softly drank through his straight gums, into his slack long
    body,
Silently.

Someone was before me at my water-trough,
And I, like a second comer, waiting.

He lifted his head from his drinking, as cattle do,
And looked at me vaguely, as drinking cattle do,
And flickered his two-forked tongue from his lips, and mused
    a moment,
And stooped and drank a little more,
Being earth-brown, earth-golden from the burning bowels
    of the earth
On the day of Sicilian July, with Etna smoking.

The voice of my education said to me
He must be killed,
For in Sicily the black, black snakes are innocent, the gold are
    venomous.

And voices in me said, If you were a man
You would take a stick and break him now, and finish
    him off.

But must I confess how I liked him,
How glad I was he had come like a guest in quiet, to drink at
    my water-trough
And depart peaceful, pacified, and thankless,
Into the burning bowels of this earth?

Was it cowardice, that I dared not kill him?
Was it perversity, that I longed to talk to him?
Was it humility, to feel so honoured?
I felt so honoured.

And yet those voices:
If you were not afraid, you would kill him!

And truly I was afraid, I was most afraid,
But even so, honoured still more
That he should seek my hospitality
From out the dark door of the secret earth.

He drank enough
And lifted his head, dreamily, as one who has drunken,
And flickered his tongue like a forked night on the air, so
    black,
Seeming to lick his lips,
And looked around like a god, unseeing, into the air,
And slowly turned his head,
And slowly, very slowly, as if thrice adream,
Proceeded to draw his slow length curving round
And climb again the broken bank of my wall-face.

And as he put his head into that dreadful hole,
And as he slowly drew up, snake-easing his shoulders, and
    entered farther,
A sort of horror, a sort of protest against his withdrawing into
    that horrid black hole,

Deliberately going into the blackness, and slowly drawing
  himself after,
Overcame me now his back was turned.

I looked around, I put down my pitcher,
I picked up a clumsy log
And threw it at the water-trough with a clatter.

I think I did not hit him,
But suddenly that part of him that was left behind convulsed
  in undignified haste,
Writhed like lightning, and was gone
Into the black hole, the earth-lipped fissure in the wall-front,
At which, in the intense still noon, I stared with fascination.

And immediately I regretted it.
I thought how paltry, how vulgar, what a mean act!
I despised myself and the voices of my accursed human
  education.

And I thought of the albatross,
And I wished he would come back, my snake.

For he seemed to me again like a king,
Like a king in exile, uncrowned in the underworld,
Now due to be crowned again.

And so, I missed my chance with one of the lords
Of life.
And I have something to expiate;
A pettiness.

Green

The dawn was apple-green,
  The sky was green wine held up in the sun,
The moon was a golden petal between.

She opened her eyes, and green
    They shone, clear like flowers undone
For the first time, now for the first time seen.

A Young Wife

The pain of loving you
Is almost more than I can bear.

I walk in fear of you.
The darkness starts up where
You stand, and the night comes through
Your eyes when you look at me.

Ah, never before did I see
The shadows that live in the sun!

Now every tall glad tree
Turns round its back to the sun
And looks down on the ground, to see
The shadow it used to shun.

At the foot of each glowing thing
A night lies looking up.

Oh, and I want to sing
And dance, but I can't lift up
My eyes from the shadows: dark
They lie split round the cup.

What is it? — Hark
The faint fine seethe in the air!

Like the seething sound in a shell!
It is death still seething where
The wild-flower shakes its bell
And the skylark twinkles blue —

The pain of loving you
Is almost more than I can bear.

After the Opera

Down the stone stairs
Girls with their large eyes wide with tragedy
Lift looks of shocked and momentous emotion up at me.
And I smile.

Ladies
Stepping like birds, with their bright and pointed feet
Peer anxiously forth, as if for a boat to carry them out of the
    wreckage;
And among the wreck of the theatre crowd
I stand and smile.
They take tragedy so becomingly;
Which pleases me.

But when I meet the weary eyes
The reddened, aching eyes of the bar-man with thin arms,
I am glad to go back to where I came from.

WILLIAM CARLOS WILLIAMS (1883-1963)

William Carlos Williams was a doctor by profession, and throughout his life practised medicine in his native city of Rutherford, New Jersey. Yet poetry was his real vocation. He tells in his autobiography how he would be working on a poem when a patient appeared at the door: bang! the typewriter was pushed aside and the doctor appeared. As soon as the patient had gone, up came the typewriter again and the poem would be resumed.

He was the author of numerous books of poetry, beginning with *Poems* (1909), published at his own expense. His last book, written just before his death, was *Pictures from Brueghel* (1962). In addition, he wrote several novels, many short stories, an imaginative work on history (*In the American Grain*), and a long poem, *Paterson*.

The poetry of William Carlos Williams may strike the reader as very easy and unpretentious. Ordinary life is often his subject and a naturalness of language conveys simple images and ideas. However, there is also a characteristic complexity — even opacity — which belongs to this poet. And the rhythmic flow of the words is carefully fashioned into original forms. Cleanness, both of perception and of artistic design, is the main feature of his poetry. To elevate the fleeting moment, even the most commonplace, and to give it permanence, is his object.

For many years a peripheral figure among modern poets, William Carlos Williams emerged as the chief influence among the young American writers after the Second World War. The relaxed style of the so-called 'beat poetry' — a term covering many different strains — owes much to his example.

Love Song

>Sweep the house clean,
>hang fresh curtains
>in the windows
>put on a new dress
>and come with me!
>The elm is scattering

its little loaves
of sweet smells
from a white sky!

Who shall hear of us
in the time to come?
Let him say there was
a burst of fragrance
from black branches.

The Act

There were the roses, in the rain.
Don't cut them, I pleaded.
            They won't last, she said
But they're so beautiful
            where they are.
Agh, we were all beautiful once, she
            said,
and cut them and gave them to me
            in my hand.

Complaint

They call me and I go.
It is a frozen road
past midnight, a dust
of snow caught
in the rigid wheeltracks.
The door opens.
I smile, enter and
shake off the cold.

Here is a great woman
on her side in the bed.
She is sick,
perhaps vomiting,
perhaps laboring
to give birth to
a tenth child. Joy! Joy!
Night is a room
darkened for lovers,
through the jalousies the sun
has sent one gold needle!
I pick the hair from her eyes
and watch her misery
with compassion.

The Red Wheelbarrow

so much depends
upon

a red wheel
barrow

glazed with rain
water

beside the white
chickens.

Young Woman at a Window

She sits with
tears on

her cheek
her cheek on

her hand
the child

in her lap
his nose

pressed
to the glass

Poem

As the cat
climbed over
the top of

the jamcloset
first the right
forefoot

carefully
then the hind
stepped down

into the pit of
the empty
flowerpot

To a Poor Old Woman

munching a plum on
the street a paper bag
of them in her hand

They taste good to her
They taste good
to her. They taste
good to her

You can see it by
the way she gives herself
to the one half
sucked out in her hand

Comforted
a solace of ripe plums
seeming to fill the air
They taste good to her

Contemporania

The corner of a great rain
Steamy with the country
Has fallen upon my garden.

I go back and forth now
And the little leaves follow me
Talking of the great rain,
Of branches broken,
And the farmer's curses!

But I go back and forth
In this corner of a garden
And the green shoots follow me
Praising the great rain.

We are not curst together,
The leaves and I,
Framing devices, flower devices

And other ways of peopling
The barren country.
Truly it was a very great rain
That makes the little leaves follow me.

Education a Failure

The minor stupidities
of my world
dominate that world —
as when

with two bridges across
the river and one
closed for repairs
the other also

will be closed by
the authorities
for painting! But then
there is heaven

and the ideal state
closed also
before the aspiring soul.
I had rather

watch a cat threading
a hedge with
another sitting by
while the bird

screams overhead
athrash
in the cover of the
low branches.

WALLACE STEVENS (1879-1955)

More reticent even than T. S. Eliot — and perhaps on the same principle, that the 'life' is not essential to the poetry — Wallace Stevens has provided little biographical information for the use of his readers. We hardly know whether he had a father and mother, whether he had ever been a boy, or any other details of his home or family life. Yet he is an exquisite poet, of an aesthetic purity that does not need such homely facts to illumine the poetic reality. Indeed, the abstract question of 'reality' and 'imagination', and their interrelation, is the central theme of his poetry.

A few essential facts we do have: he was born in Reading, Pennsylvania, in 1879. For three years he studied at Harvard University, then at the New York Law School, where he took his degree in 1903. He was admitted to the bar in New York City the following year. In 1916 he joined the Hartford Accident and Indemnity Company, and he advanced to the rank of vice-president with that firm in 1934. He offers a striking example of a successful businessman and an outstanding poet in the same flesh, a combination that most people would consider improbable, if not impossible.

His first book, *Harmonium*, appeared in 1923 when he was already forty-four. The imagery of his poetry is exotic, sensuous, and imaginative. Often it is derived from holiday experiences in the Caribbean and at other seaside resorts, filled with an atmosphere of swank hotels and nature's opulence. Rarely does it touch the rude world of business, money, and mortgages, or the market-place and the city streets.

Yet Stevens has won the admiration of his readers as an original and varied artist in words and an inventor of mental pictures. He plays many changes on a central philosophical paradox. The world, for him, is reduced to cold, unadorned reality if it is not coloured with imagination. Poetry is then 'the supreme fiction' that gives value and beauty to life. But the truth of poetry, for Wallace Stevens, is not an absolute ideal order; it, too, is a changing, unstable invention of our minds, which the imagination enriches and renews.

The Man with the Blue Guitar appeared in 1937, *Parts of a World* in 1942, *Transport to Summer* in 1947, and *The Auroras of Autumn* in 1950. His *Collected Poems* were published in 1954, the year before his death. He died following an operation in his seventy-fifth year.

The Emperor of Ice-Cream

Call the roller of big cigars,
The muscular one, and bid him whip
In kitchen cups concupiscent curds.
Let the wenches dawdle in such dress
As they are used to wear, and let the boys
Bring flowers in last month's newspapers.
Let be be finale of seem.
The only emperor is the emperor of ice-cream.

Take from the dresser of deal,
Lacking the three glass knobs, that sheet
On which she embroidered fantails once
And spread it so as to cover her face.
If her horny feet protrude, they come
To show how cold she is, and dumb.
Let the lamp affix its beam.
The only emperor is the emperor of ice-cream.

The Worms at Heaven's Gate

Out of the tomb, we bring Badroulbadour,
Within our bellies, we her chariot.
Here is an eye. And here are, one by one,
The lashes of that eye and its white lid.
Here is the cheek on which that lid declined,
And, finger after finger, here, the hand,
The genius of that cheek. Here are the lips,
The bundle of the body and the feet.

 .   .   .   .

Out of the tomb we bring Badroulbadour.

Gubbinal

That strange flower, the sun,
Is just what you say.
Have it your way.

The world is ugly.
And the people are sad.

That tuft of jungle feathers,
That animal eye,
Is just what you say.

That savage of fire,
That seed,
Have it your way.

The world is ugly,
And the people are sad.

Another Weeping Woman

Pour the unhappiness out
From your too bitter heart,
Which grieving will not sweeten.

Poison grows in this dark.
It is in the water of tears
Its black blooms rise.

The magnificent cause of being,
The imagination, the one reality
In this imagined world

Leaves you
With him for whom no phantasy moves,
And you are pierced by a death.

To the Roaring Wind

What syllable are you seeking,
Vocalissimus,
In the distances of sleep?
Speak it.

Tattoo

The light is like a spider.
It crawls over the water.
It crawls over the edges of the snow.
It crawls under your eyelids
And spreads its webs there —
Its two webs.

The webs of your eyes
Are fastened
To the flesh and bones of you
As to rafters or grass.

There are filaments of your eyes
On the surface of the water
And in the edges of the snow.

The Snow Man

One must have a mind of winter
To regard the frost and the boughs
Of the pine-trees crusted with snow;

And have been cold a long time
To behold the junipers shagged with ice,
The spruces rough in the distant glitter

Of the January sun; and not to think
Of any misery in the sound of the wind,
In the sound of a few leaves,

Which is the sound of the land
Full of the same wind
That is blowing in the same bare place

For the listener, who listens in the snow,
And, nothing himself, beholds
Nothing that is not there and the nothing that is.

Frogs Eat Butterflies. Snakes Eat
Frogs. Hogs Eat Snakes.
Men Eat Hogs

It is true that the rivers went nosing like swine,
Tugging at banks, until they seemed
Bland belly-sounds in somnolent troughs,

That the air was heavy with the breath of these swine,
The breath of turgid summer, and
Heavy with thunder's rattapallax,

That the man who erected this cabin, planted
This field, and tended it awhile,
Knew not the quirks of imagery,

That the hours of his indolent, arid days,
Grotesque with this nosing in banks,
This somnolence and rattapallax,

Seemed to suckle themselves on his arid being,
As the swine-like rivers suckled themselves
While they went seaward to the sea-mouths.

Bantams in Pine-Woods

Chieftain Iffucan of Azcan in caftan
Of tan with henna hackles, halt!

Damned universal cock, as if the sun
Was blackamoor to bear your blazing tail.

Fat! Fat! Fat! Fat! I am the personal.
Your world is you. I am my world.

You ten-foot poet among inchlings. Fat!
Begone! An inchling bristles in these pines,

Bristles, and points their Appalachian tangs,
And fears not portly Azcan nor his hoos.

MARIANNE MOORE (1887-   )

'I am against the stock phrase,' writes Marianne Moore, 'and an easier use of words in verse than would be tolerated in prose.' Every phrase of her poetry is a finely polished piece of expression, so that the total effect is often to bewilder the reader with its originality and exquisite detail. Obviously she must be read slowly and each point must be relished separately.

Marianne Moore was born in St. Louis, Missouri, in 1887, one year before T. S. Eliot, who was also born in that city. (Much later, in 1935, T. S. Eliot was to write an introduction for her *Selected Poems*.) She received her B.A. degree from Bryn Mawr in 1909. For some years she taught stenography at Carlisle, Pennsylvania, then worked as a librarian in a branch of the New York Public Library in New York. Some of her unique experimental poetry was published in 1921 by her friends in a book entitled *Poems*, and she received a notable award from one of the leading little magazines of the time, *The Dial*. A year later she became editor of *The Dial* and continued until the magazine's demise in 1929.

She was a strict and effective editor, in the vanguard of modern letters, an occasional critic in the pages of the magazine, and a key figure in the poetry movement of the 1920s. Her second book, *Observations*, appeared in 1924. Other volumes followed, culminating in a *Collected Poems* in 1951 which won three major awards – the Pulitzer Prize, the Bollingen, and the National Book Award. Her poems in large-circulation magazines like *The New Yorker* and *Cosmopolitan* have brought her name to a larger public. There is a *Marianne Moore Reader* (1961) which brings together some of her prose writings and correspondence as well as poetry.

Poetry

I, too, dislike it: there are things that are important beyond
          all this fiddle.
  Reading it, however, with a perfect contempt for it, one
          discovers in
  it after all, a place for the genuine.

Hands that can grasp, eyes
that can dilate, hair that can rise
if it must, these things are important not because a

high-sounding interpretation can be put upon them but
because they are
useful. When they become so derivative as to become
unintelligible,
the same thing may be said for all of us, that we
do not admire what
we cannot understand: the bat
holding on upside down or in quest of something to

eat, elephants pushing, a wild horse taking a roll, a tireless
wolf under
a tree, the immovable critic twitching his skin like a horse
that feels a flea, the base-
ball fan, the statistician —
nor is it valid
to discriminate against 'business documents and

school-books'; all these phenomena are important. One
must make a distinction
however: when dragged into prominence by half poets,
the result is not poetry,
nor till the poets among us can be
'literalists of
the imagination' — above
insolence and triviality and can present

for inspection, 'imaginary gardens with real toads in them',
shall we have
it. In the meantime, if you demand on the one hand,
the raw material of poetry in
all its rawness and
that which is on the other hand
genuine, you are interested in poetry.

The Fish

wade
through black jade.
  Of the crow-blue mussel-shells, one keeps
  adjusting the ash-heaps;
    opening and shutting itself like

an
injured fan.
  The barnacles which encrust the side
  of the wave, cannot hide
    there for the submerged shafts of the

sun
split like spun
  glass, move themselves with spotlight swiftness
  into the crevices —
    in and out, illuminating

the
turquoise sea
  of bodies. The water drives a wedge
  of iron through the iron edge
    of the cliff; whereupon the stars,

pink
rice-grains, ink-
  bespattered jelly-fish, crabs like green
  lilies, and submarine
    toadstools, slide each on the other.

All
external
  marks of abuse are present on this
  defiant edifice —
    all the physical features of

ac-
cident — lack
   of cornice, dynamite grooves, burns, and
   hatchet strokes, these things stand
      out on it; the chasm-side is

dead.
Repeated
   evidence has proved that it can live
   on what can not revive
      its youth. The sea grows old in it.

Bird-Witted

With innocent wide penguin eyes, three
   large fledgling mocking-birds below
the pussy-willow tree,
   stand in a row,
wings touching, feebly solemn,
till they see
      their no longer larger
      mother bringing
something which will partially
feed one of them.

Toward the high-keyed intermittent squeak
   of broken carriage-springs, made by
the three similar, meek-
   coated bird's-eye
freckled forms she comes; and when
from the beak
      of one, the still living
      beetle has dropped
out, she picks it up and puts
it in again.

Standing in the shade till they have dressed
   their thickly-filamented, pale
pussy-willow-surfaced
   coats, they spread tail
and wings, showing one by one,
the modest
         white stripe lengthwise on the
         tail and crosswise
underneath the wing, and the
accordion

is closed again. What delightful note
   with rapid unexpected flute-
sounds leaping from the throat
   of the astute
grown bird, comes back to one from
the remote
         unenergetic sun-
         lit air before
the brood was here? How harsh
the bird's voice has become.

A piebald cat observing them,
   is slowly creeping toward the trim
trio on the tree-stem.
   Unused to him
the three make room — uneasy
new problem.
         A dangling foot that missed
         its grasp, is raised
and finds the twig on which it
planned to perch. The

parent darting down, nerved by what chills
   the blood, and by hope rewarded —

of toil — since nothing fills
    squeaking unfed
mouths, wages deadly combat,
and half kills
        with bayonet beak and
        cruel wings, the
intellectual cautious-
ly creeping cat.

E. E. CUMMINGS (1894-1962)

The experimentalist of modern poetry, E. E. Cummings is usually quite easy to read and to understand once the method of his poetry is accepted. He is a man of *letters*: the alphabet for him contains the units of which poems are made; letters, not words or phrases. It's really child's play, like building-blocks. The themes, also, are fundamental: love (and sex), springtime, death, children, happiness, ignorance, and inhumanity. His purpose is to make a perfect poem; he is an artist *par excellence* and a craftsman. But all he asks us to do is to enjoy.

His father was a Unitarian minister, a notable preacher, at one time a lecturer in English at Harvard. (He was killed in a railroad accident in 1926.) When Cummings graduated from Harvard in English and Classics the First World War was raging in Europe and he enlisted in the Ambulance Corps. In France, however, he ran into trouble; he was imprisoned and kept in a cell for three months as a result of ill-considered statements, and of some prankish letters he had written which were read by the censor. This experience later provided material for his novel, *The Enormous Room*.

After the war Cummings shuttled between Paris and Greenwich Village, New York, painting and writing poetry. His first book of poems, *Tulips and Chimneys*, appeared in 1923. It was followed by a new title every few years, until the publication of the impressive *Collected Poems* in 1954. He visited Soviet Russia in 1931 and wrote the highly-critical book on Russia, *Eimi*. Several experimental plays also came from his pen.

For long considered extremely *avant-garde*, Cummings came to be recognized before his death in 1962 as one of the chief poets of modern America, serious and consistent, even traditional, in the universal quality of his poetic effects.

'the sky was'

the
    sky
        was
can   dy   lu
minous

              edible
spry
        pinks shy
lemons
greens   coo   l choc
olate
s.

    un   der,
    a   lo
co
mo
    tive   s pout
                      ing
                       vi
                        o
                        lets

'r-p-o-p-h-e-s-s-a-g-r'

                          r-p-o-p-h-e-s-s-a-g-r
                  who
      a)s w(e loo)k
      upnowgath
                 PPEGORHRASS
                              eringint(o-
      aThe):l
            eA
              !p:
      S   a
                      (r
      rIvInG   .gRrEaPsPhOs)
                                      to
      rea(be)rran(com)gi(e)ngly
      ,grasshopper;

'Buffalo Bill's defunct'

Buffalo Bill's
defunct
      who used to
      ride a watersmooth-silver
                   stallion
and break onetwothreefourfive pigeonsjustlikethat
                             Jesus

he was a handsome man
                   and what i want to know is
how do you like your blueeyed boy
Mister Death

Poem, or Beauty Hurts Mr. Vinal

take it from me kiddo
believe me
my country, 'tis of

you, land of the Cluett
Shirt Boston Garter and Spearmint
Girl With The Wrigley Eyes(of you
land of the Arrow Ide
and Earl &
Wilson
Collars)of you i
sing: land of Abraham Lincoln and Lydia E. Pinkham,
land above all of Just Add Hot Water And Serve —
from every B.V.D.

let freedom ring

amen. i do however protest, anent the un
-spontaneous and otherwise scented merde which

greets one(Everywhere Why)as divine poesy per
that and this radically defunct periodical.   i would

suggest that certain ideas gestures
rhymes, like Gillette Razor Blades
having been used and reused
to the mystical moment of dullness emphatically are
Not To Be Resharpened.   (Case in point

if we are to believe these gently O sweetly
melancholy trillers amid the thrillers
these crepuscular violinists among my and your
skyscrapers — Helen & Cleopatra were Just Too Lovely,
The Snail's On The Thorn enter Morn and God's
In His andsoforth

do you get me?)according
to such supposedly indigenous
throstles Art is O World O Life
a formula: example, Turn Your Shirttails Into
Drawers and If It Isn't An Eastman It Isn't A
Kodak therefore my friends let
us now sing each and all fortissimo A-
mer
i

ca, I
love,
You.   And there're a
hun-dred-mil-lion-oth-ers, like
all of you successfully if
delicately gelded (or spaded)
gentlemen(and ladies) — pretty

littleliverpill-
hearted-Nujolneeding-There's-A-Reason
americans(who tensetendoned and with

upward vacant eyes, painfully
perpetually crouched, quivering, upon the
sternly allotted sandpile
— how silently
emit a tiny violetflavoured nuisance: Odor?

ono.
comes out like a ribbon lies flat on the brush

EDITH SITWELL (1887-1964)

Edith Sitwell, who died in December 1964, was, like E. E. Cummings, one of the most extravagant experimentalists in modern poetry. She puzzled her readers by often abandoning rational meaning and relying on amusing effects of sound and the combination of incompatible objects and images:

> WHEN
> Sir
> Beelzebub called for his syllabub in the hotel in Hell
>   Where Proserpine first fell,
> Blue as the gendarmerie were the waves of the sea
>
>   (Rocking and shocking the bar-maid) . . .
>
> (from 'Sir Beelzebub')

Born of an aristocratic English family (her brothers Osbert and Sacheverell Sitwell are also writers of distinction), she had a nostalgic attachment to a romantic, exotic world that cut her off from actuality. Out of this she made her fantastic poems, the poems in the magazine *Wheels* which she edited, and those in her early books beginning with *The Mother and Other Poems* in 1915.

As the 1920s advanced, this poetry of pure sound and of surrealist effects began to combine with an acid, satirical vein directed at the modern world. It was the period of T. S. Eliot's *The Waste Land*; and Edith Sitwell paralleled Eliot's satire in her own long poem, *Gold Coast Customs* (1930). In that same year her first *Collected Poems* was published (to be enlarged in 1957); but her development was still only in mid career. With the outbreak of the Second World War and the terror of war bombing in London, harsh reality became dominant in her poetry, in the books *Street Song* (1942) and *The Song of the Cold* (1948). In addition to poetry, Edith Sitwell published a biography of Alexander Pope, works of literary criticism and history, and a critical anthology.

The Mauve Summer Rain

> The mauve summer rain
> Is falling again —
> It soaks through the eaves

And the ladies' sleeves —
It soaks through the leaves

That like silver fish fall
In the fountains, recall
Afternoons when I
Was a child small and shy
In the palace. . . . Fish lie

On the grass with lives darkling.
Our laughter falls sparkling
As the mauve raindrops bright
When they fall through the light
With the briefest delight.
The pavilions float
On the lake like a boat. . . .
Mauve rains from trees fall
Like wistaria flowers . . . all
My life is like this
And drifts into nothingness!

The strange ladies sigh
'The autumn is nigh'. . . .
The King bows and mutters. . . .
His eyelids seem shutters
Of a palace pavilion
Deserted a million

Echoing years ago.
Oh, but the rain falls slow.

Song of the Man from a Far Country

Rose and Alice,
Oh, the pretty lassies,

With their mouths like a calice
And their hair a golden palace —
Through my heart like a lovely wind they blow.

Though I am black and not comely,
Though I am black as the darkest trees,
I have swarms of gold that will fly like honey-bees,
By the rivers of the sun I will feed my words
Until they skip like those fleecèd lambs
The waterfalls, and the rivers (horned rams);
Then for all my darkness I shall be
The peacefulness of a lovely tree —
A tree wherein the golden birds
Are singing in the darkest branches, oh!

HART CRANE (1899-1932)

Hart Crane died by suicide, stepping off a steamer on which he was returning from Mexico, in his thirty-third year. An offspring of separated parents whose conflict tore him apart, he never completed high school, worked for short periods at various jobs, fell into abnormal and excessive ways — with love, and drink — suffering always from guilt and a sense of persecution. He had immense talent, however, a genius for words, which could put him among the first poets of the age.

He was in the midst of his struggle with neurosis and bohemian poverty when a wealthy philanthropist and art critic came to his help. Otto H. Kahn provided him with sufficient funds to enable him to write a long poem, *The Bridge*, interpreting modern America and the age of machinery in epic, visionary terms. Crane believed that machinery must be absorbed into poetry, that the poet must 'surrender' to the industrial environment and so express its form and pressure. To 'acclimatize' the machine in this sense Crane used a powerful rhetoric and an almost religious intensity of conception; in fact, his highly-charged idealism is none other than the romantic vision of a Blake, a Wordsworth, or a Whitman, concentrated like a cobalt bomb upon the materials of modern life.

The Collected Poems of Hart Crane appeared in 1933, the year after his death. During his lifetime he had published two books, *White Buildings* (1926) and *The Bridge* (1930).

'The nasal whine of power ...'

(From *The Bridge*)

The nasal whine of power whips a new universe ...
Where spouting pillars spoor the evening sky,
Under the looming stacks of the gigantic power house
Stars prick the eyes with sharp ammoniac proverbs,
New verities, new inklings in the velvet hummed
Of dynamos, where hearing's leash is strummed ...
Power's script, — wound, bobbin-bound, refined —

Is stropped to the slap of belts on booming spools, spurred
Into the bulging bouillon, harnessed jelly of the stars.
Towards what? The forked crash of split thunder parts
Our hearing momentwise; but fast in whirling armatures,
As bright as frogs' eyes, giggling in the girth
Of steely gizzards — axle-bound, confined
In coiled precision, bunched in mutual glee
The bearings glint, — O murmurless and shined
In oilrinsed circles of blind ecstasy!

Van Winkle

(From *The Bridge*)

Macadam, gun-grey as the tunny's belt,
Leaps from Far Rockaway to Golden Gate:
Listen! the miles a hurdy-gurdy grinds —
Down gold arpeggios mile on mile unwinds.

Times earlier, when you hurried off to school
— It is the same hour though a later day —
You walked with Pizarro in a copybook,
And Cortez rode up, reining tautly in —
Firmly as coffee grips the taste, — and away!

There was Priscilla's cheek close in the wind,
And Captain Smith, all beard and certainty,
And Rip Van Winkle bowing by the way, —
'Is this Sleepy Hollow, friend — ?' And he —

And Rip forgot the office hours,
                    and he forgot the pay;
        Van Winkle sweeps a tenement
                    . way down on Avenue A, —

The grind-organ says ... Remember, remember
The cinder pile at the end of the backyard
Where we stoned the family of young
Garter snakes under ... And the monoplanes
We launched — with paper wings and twisted
Rubber bands ... Recall — recall

                      the rapid tongues
That flittered from under the ash heap day
After day whenever your stick discovered
Some sunning inch of unsuspecting fibre —
It flashed back at your thrust, as clean as fire.

And Rip was slowly made aware
       that he, Van Winkle, was not here
    nor there. He woke and swore he'd seen Broadway
      a Catskill daisy chain in May —

So memory, that strikes a rhyme out of a box
Or splits a random smell of flowers through glass —
Is it the whip stripped from the lilac tree
One day in spring my father took to me,
Or is it the Sabbatical, unconscious smile
My mother almost brought me once from church
And once only, as I recall — ?

It flickered through the snow screen, blindly
It forsook her at the doorway, it was gone
Before I had left the window. It
Did not return with the kiss in the hall.

Macadam, gun-grey as the tunny's belt,
Leaps from Far Rockaway to Golden Gate. . . .
Keep hold of that nickel for car-change, Rip, —
Have you got your 'Times' — ?
And hurry along, Van Winkle — it's getting late!

Virginia

(From *The Bridge*)

O rain at seven,
Pay-check at eleven —
Keep smiling the boss away,
Mary (what are you going to do?)
Gone seven — gone eleven,
And I'm still waiting you —

O blue-eyed Mary with the claret scarf,
Saturday Mary, mine!

It's high carillon
From the popcorn bells!
Pigeons by the million —
And Spring in Prince Street
Where green figs gleam
By oyster shells!

O Mary, leaning from the high wheat tower,
Let down your golden hair!

High in the noon of May
On cornices of daffodils
The slender violets stray.
Crap-shooting gangs in Bleecker reign,
Peonies with pony manes —
Forget-me-nots at windowpanes:

Out of the way-up nickel-dime tower shine,
Cathedral Mary,
shine! —

JOHN CROWE RANSOM (1888-   )

A scholarly poet, John Crowe Ransom was a Rhodes Scholar from Tennessee, a classicist at Oxford, and later a professor at Kenyon College, Ohio. There he founded *The Kenyon Review*, one of the most important critical journals of modern letters. His first book of poetry appeared in 1919, *Poems about God*. In 1924 he published *Chills and Fevers*, a book that defined his characteristic style: irony, extreme precision in the use of words, a restrained romanticism of feeling.

Ransom is a representative voice of the American South in poetry, a convinced agrarian and conservative, turning back with feeling to a vanished time before the Civil War. In perspective, he stands closer to Edwin Arlington Robinson and Thomas Hardy than to the Greenwich Village modernism of an E. E. Cummings. He has also written excellent criticism and discussion of social and religious problems, in *God Without Thunder* (1930), *I'll Take My Stand* (1930), *The World's Body* (1938), and *The New Criticism* (1941).

Blue Girls

Twirling your blue skirts, travelling the sward
Under the towers of your seminary,
Go listen to your teachers old and contrary
Without believing a word.

Tie the white fillets then about your hair
And think no more of what will come to pass
Than bluebirds that go walking on the grass
And chattering on the air.

Practise your beauty, blue girls, before it fail;
And I will cry with my loud lips and publish
Beauty which all our power shall never establish,
It is so frail.

For I could tell you a story which is true;
I know a lady with a terrible tongue,
Blear eyes fallen from blue,
All her perfections tarnished — yet it is not long
Since she was lovelier than any of you.

Janet Waking

Beautifully Janet slept
Till it was deeply morning. She woke then
And thought about her dainty-feathered hen,
To see how it had kept.

One kiss she gave her mother,
Only a small one gave she to her daddy
Who would have kissed each curl of his shining baby;
No kiss at all for her brother.

'Old Chucky, old Chucky!' she cried,
Running across the world upon the grass
To Chucky's house, and listening. But alas,
Her Chucky had died.

It was a transmogrifying bee
Came droning down on Chucky's old bald head
And sat and put the poison. It scarcely bled,
But how exceedingly

And purply did the knot
Swell with the venom and communicate
Its rigor! Now the poor comb stood up straight
But Chucky did not.

So there was Janet
Kneeling on the wet grass, crying her brown hen
(Translated far beyond the daughters of men)
To rise and walk upon it.

And weeping fast as she had breath
Janet implored us, 'Wake her from her sleep!'
And would not be instructed in how deep
Was the forgetful kingdom of death.

ARCHIBALD MacLEISH (1892-   )

A prolific writer for radio, the theatre, and other public media, Archibald MacLeish was educated for the law but abandoned his practice in Boston for literature and journalism. For a time he lived in Paris, returning for his summers to the Berkshires in New England; then he settled in New York, where he was an editor of *Fortune*.

His career as a poet began with *Tower of Ivory* in 1917. Many books followed, the most notable being *Streets in the Moon* (1926), *The Hamlet of A. MacLeish* (1928), *New Found Land* (1930), *Conquistador* (1932), and *Public Speech* (1936). MacLeish is a conscious craftsman in verse, a technician who adopts and explores the modern techniques of other poets with great effect.

With *Panic* (1935) MacLeish entered the theatre. *The Fall of the City* (1937), a radio classic, was broadcast in 1937. *Air Raid* followed in 1938. At the same time, MacLeish collaborated with Ernest Hemingway and Lillian Hellman in writing a movie script, *The Spanish Earth*. In 1959, the successful play *J.B.*, a modern version of the Book of Job, won the Pulitzer Prize and achieved success on Broadway. His enlarged *Collected Poems: 1917-1952* brings together an extremely varied display of experimental and oratorical poetry.

Psyche with the Candle

Love which is the most difficult mystery
Asking from every young one answers
And most from those most eager and most beautiful —
Love is a bird in a fist:
To hold it hides it, to look at it lets it go.
It will twist loose if you lift so much as a finger.
It will stay if you cover it — stay but unknown and invisible.
Either you keep it forever with fist closed
Or let it fling
Singing in fervor of sun and in song vanish.
There is no answer other to this mystery.

ROBERT GRAVES (1895-   )

A vigorous prose writer, Robert Graves has also grown in stature as a poet since his first book was published in 1916. His father, Alfred Percival Graves, was himself an Irish poet. The boy attended Charterhouse, the famous and ancient boys' school in London, entered the army at the outbreak of the First World War, and saw action at the front. (He returned with a head wound that left a permanent scar.) His early poems place him beside Wilfred Owen and Siegfried Sassoon, as a realist rejecting the patriotic attitude to war – the same kind of realism that was to appear in Hemingway's *A Farewell to Arms*. Graves, however, had a knack for fantasy and humour, which appeared in his whimsical, childlike poems and ballads in the book *Fairies and Fusiliers* (1917).

Numerous prose works and books of poetry followed (despite his professional prose writing, Graves is constant in his dedication as a poet). *The White Goddess* and *The Greek Myths* show his maturing conviction of the importance of myth and symbol in the interpretation of literature – a natural outgrowth of nineteenth-century romanticism. He has lived for some years in the Spanish island of Majorca, which has become something of a literary colony as a result. In recent years he has been recognized as one of the most impressive of living English poets.

A Slice of Wedding Cake

Why have such scores of lovely, gifted girls
    Married impossible men?
Simple self-sacrifice may be ruled out,
    And missionary endeavour, nine times out of ten.

Repeat 'impossible men': not merely rustic,
    Foul-tempered or depraved
(Dramatic foils chosen to show the world
    How well women behave, and always have behaved).

Impossible men: idle, illiterate,
    Self-pitying, dirty, sly,

For whose appearance even in City parks
  Excuses must be made to casual passers-by.

Has God's supply of tolerable husbands
  Fallen, in fact, so low?
Or do I always over-value woman
  At the expense of man?

                    Do I?

                              It might be so.

LOUIS MacNEICE (1907-1963)

Too easily shelved as one of the 'poets of the Thirties', Louis MacNeice brings his own vital and positive personality into the treatment of modern subjects. Born in Ireland, he studied at Oxford in the late 1920s when Auden and Spender were students there. Later he collaborated with Auden on the book *Letters from Iceland* (1937). His own first book, *Blind Fireworks*, appeared in 1929, but he did not find his own voice until 1935, in the book *Poems*. His style is direct and explicit, crisp, charged with physical vitality and high spirits; contemporary life is his conscious subject, and he treats it with critical awareness and intelligence. In addition to poetry, MacNeice has written criticism — *Modern Poetry* (1938) and *The Poetry of W. B. Yeats* (1941) — as well as a play in verse, *Out of the Picture* (1937). His verse is available in a collected edition, *Poems: 1925-40*.

The Daily News

The news that blows around the streets
Or vibrates over the air
Whether it is rape, embezzlement or murder
Seems frivolous, if not farcical, without dignity.
Whereas the actual fact before it becomes news
Is often tragic even when commonplace.
The daily press gives neither laughter nor tears
But the stage of life gives both.
We wish to remind you that upon this stage
Slapstick may turn to swordplay,
The cottage flowers may give a sudden hiss
The trees curve down their hands in heavy gloves —
A malediction on the nape of the neck.
We will tell you a little fable:
There was a picnic party in the eighteenth century
Strayed out of canvas with their lutes and beakers

And called among the rocks to the lady Echo
But Echo missed her cue
And instead of returning the same coin they gave her,
Phrases of music and gallant phrases,
Echo like a gorgon glared from the sudden rocks
And cried in a stony voice the one word 'Death'.
These possibilities should always be remembered
But for the moment let us go back to our farce.

Morning Sun

Shuttles of trains going north, going south, drawing threads
    of blue
The shining of the lines of trams like swords,
Thousands of posters asserting a monopoly of the good, the
    beautiful, the true,
Crowds of people all in the vocative, you and you,
The haze of the morning shot with words.

Yellow sun comes white off the wet streets but bright
Chromium yellows in the gay sun's light,
Filleted sun streaks the purple mist,
Everything is kissed and reticulated with sun
Scooped-up and cupped in the open fronts of shops
And bouncing on the traffic that never stops.

And the street fountain blown across the square
Rainbow-trellises the air and sunlight blazons
The red butcher's and scrolls of fish on marble slabs,
Whistled bars of music crossing silver sprays
And horns of cars, touché, touché, rapiers' retort, a moving
    cage,
A turning page of shine and sound, the day's maze.

But when the sun goes out, the streets go cold, the hanging
  meat
And tiers of fish are colourless and merely dead,
And the hoots of cars neurotically repeat and the tiptoed feet
Of women hurry and falter whose faces are dead;
And I see in the air but not belonging there
The blown grey powder of the fountain grey as the ash
That forming on a cigarette covers the red.

Sunday Morning

Down the road some one is practising scales,
The notes like little fishes vanish with a wink of tails,
Man's heart expands to tinker with his car
For this is Sunday morning, Fate's great bazaar;
Regard these means as ends, concentrate on this Now,
And you may grow to music or drive beyond Hindhead
  anyhow,
Take corners on two wheels until you go so fast
That you can clutch a fringe or two of the windy past,
That you can abstract this day and make it to the week of
  time
A small eternity, a sonnet self-contained in rhyme.

But listen, up the road, something gulps, the church spire
Opens its eight bells out, skulls' mouths which will not tire
To tell how there is no music or movement that ensures
Escape from the weekday time. Which deadens and endures.

Snow

The room was suddenly rich and the great bay-window was
Spawning snow and pink roses against it

Soundlessly collateral and incompatible:
World is suddener than we fancy it.

World is crazier and more of it than we think,
Incorrigibly plural. I peel and portion
A tangerine and spit the pips and feel
The drunkenness of things being various.

And the fire flames with a bubbling sound for world
Is more spiteful and gay than one supposes —
On the tongue on the eyes on the ears in the palms of your
    hands —
There is more than glass between the snow and the huge roses.

W. H. AUDEN (1907-   )

The acknowledged leader of the group of leftist poets in England in the 1930s, W. H. Auden dominated a generation by his clever, intellectual, allusive poetry about a sick culture, a dying bourgeoisie, the need for a change of heart and a new social order. Michael Roberts, editor of the anthology *New Signatures* (1932), wrote that Auden's *Poems* (1930) and C. Day Lewis's *From Feathers to Iron* (1931) were 'the first books in which imagery taken from contemporary life consistently appeared as the natural and spontaneous expression of the poet's thought and feeling'.

Auden was born on February 21, 1907, in York, England. His father was soon after appointed medical officer and professor of Public Health at Birmingham University. Auden's interests from the beginning were scientific, indicating a rationalist bent of mind; but the atmosphere of the home was devoutly Anglo-Catholic, and four uncles in the family were clergymen. Auden, however, early became sceptical in religious matters. His friend Christopher Isherwood, who knew him at Gresham's School, describes him as 'precociously clever, untidy, lazy, and, with the masters, inclined to be insolent'.

At the age of nineteen, Auden discovered the poetry of T. S. Eliot; he himself was already writing verse. In Oxford, he co-edited two editions of *Oxford Poetry*, the latter jointly with his fellow poet C. Day Lewis. In 1928 appeared his first book of poetry, *Poems*, printed privately on a hand press by Stephen Spender. Two years later Faber and Faber in London brought out his first published book, with the same title.

During the 1930s, working as a schoolmaster at various schools in Scotland and England, Auden was abundantly producing poetry, anthologies, plays, criticism, and books of travel. His fame was well established from the beginning of the decade. In 1936, during the Hitler period, he married Erika Mann, daughter of Thomas Mann, although he had never met her, in order to provide her with a passport to freedom. In 1937 he went to Spain during the Spanish Civil War; the result was the poem 'Spain', perhaps the most explicit statement of Auden's leftist political commitment. The same year saw the publication of *Letters from Iceland*, containing his 'Letter to Lord Byron', the most clever and entertaining of his poems in the light-verse manner. He visited China in 1938, then the United States, and decided to return and settle in America. He became an American citizen immediately after the war, in 1946.

In the United States Auden has been teaching at various colleges and universities, he has collaborated with Benjamin Britten and others in operatic and choral compositions, and he has continued to publish widely. For some time, however, the emphasis of his poetry has been changing from a chiefly political commitment to one deeply concerned with the philosophical and religious problems involved with human isolation, responsibility, and historical evil. The turning point came in *The Double Man* (1941), where Auden explicitly returned to his faith as a Christian.

As a poet, Auden is an extremely clever versifier, an essayist in verse on all the subjects that interest intelligent minds; at other times, he is a lyric poet of unexampled smoothness and refinement. He has poeticized for our time the ideas of Freud, Marx, D. H. Lawrence, Kafka, Kierkegaard, and Pascal. But he has also written some poems not dependent on the ideas of a particular time that record in words a quality of feeling that gives them a permanent place in the annals of English literature.

'Say this city has ten million souls'

Say this city has ten million souls,
Some are living in mansions, some are living in holes:
Yet there's no place for us, my dear, yet there's no place for
   us.

Once we had a country and we thought it fair,
Look in the atlas and you'll find it there:
We cannot go there now, my dear, we cannot go there now.

In the village churchyard there grows an old yew,
Every spring it blossoms anew:
Old passports can't do that, my dear, old passports can't do
   that.

The consul banged the table and said:
'If you've got no passport you're officially dead';
But we are still alive, my dear, but we are still alive.

Went to a committee; they offered me a chair;
Asked me politely to return next year:
But where shall we go to-day, my dear, but where shall we
   go to-day?

Came to a public meeting; the speaker got up and said:
'If we let them in, they will steal our daily bread';
He was talking of you and me, my dear, he was talking of you
   and me.

Thought I heard the thunder rumbling in the sky;
It was Hitler over Europe, saying: 'They must die';
O we were in his mind, my dear, O we were in his mind.

Saw a poodle in a jacket fastened with a pin,
Saw a door opened and a cat let in:
But they weren't German Jews, my dear, but they weren't
   German Jews.

Went down the harbour and stood upon the quay,
Saw the fish swimming as if they were free:
Only ten feet away, my dear, only ten feet away.

Walked through a wood, saw the birds in the trees;
They had no politicians and sang at their ease:
They weren't the human race, my dear, they weren't the
   human race.

Dreamed I saw a building with a thousand floors,
A thousand windows and a thousand doors;
Not one of them was ours, my dear, not one of them was ours.

Stood on a great plain in the falling snow;
Ten thousand soldiers marched to and fro:
Looking for you and me, my dear, looking for you and me.

Schoolchildren

Here are all the captivities; the cells are as real:
But these are unlike the prisoners we know
Who are outraged or pining or wittily resigned
  Or just wish all away.

For they dissent so little, so nearly content
With the dumb play of the dog, the licking and rushing;
The bars of love are so strong, their conspiracies
  Weak like the vows of drunkards.

Indeed their strangeness is difficult to watch:
The condemned see only the fallacious angels of a vision;
So little effort lies behind their smiling,
  The beast of vocation is afraid.

But watch them, O, set against our size and timing
The almost neuter, the slightly awkward perfection;
For the sex is there, the broken bootlace is broken,
  The professor's dream is not true.

Yet the tyranny is so easy. The improper word
Scribbled upon the fountain, is that all the rebellion?
The storm of tears shed in the corner, are these
  The seeds of the new life?

The Unknown Citizen

(To JS/07/M/378
This Marble Monument
is Erected by the State)

He was found by the Bureau of Statistics to be
One against whom there was no official complaint,

And all the reports on his conduct agree
That, in the modern sense of an old-fashioned word, he was
    a saint,
For in everything he did he served the Greater Community.
Except for the War till the day he retired
He worked in a factory and never got fired,
But satisfied his employers, Fudge Motors Inc.
Yet he wasn't a scab or odd in his views,
For his Union reports that he paid his dues,
(Our report on his Union shows it was sound)
And our Social Psychology workers found
That he was popular with his mates and liked a drink.
The Press are convinced that he bought a paper every day
And that his reactions to advertisements were normal in
    every way.
Policies taken out in his name prove that he was fully insured,
And his Health-card shows he was once in hospital but left
    it cured.
Both Producers Research and High-Grade Living declare
He was fully sensible to the advantages of the Instalment Plan
And had everything necessary to the Modern Man,
A phonograph, a radio, a car and a frigidaire.
Our researchers into Public Opinion are content
That he held the proper opinions for the time of year;
When there was peace, he was for peace; when there was
    war, he went.
He was married and added five children to the population,
Which our Eugenist says was the right number for a parent
    of his generation,
And our teachers report that he never interfered with their
    education.
Was he free? Was he happy? The question is absurd:
Had anything been wrong, we should certainly have heard.

Who's Who

A shilling life will give you all the facts:
How Father beat him, how he ran away,
What were the struggles of his youth, what acts
Made him the greatest figure of his day:
Of how he fought, fished, hunted, worked all night,
Though giddy, climbed new mountains; named a sea:
Some of the last researchers even write
Love made him weep pints like you and me.

With all his honours on, he sighed for one
Who, say astonished critics, lived at home;
Did little jobs about the house with skill
And nothing else; could whistle; would sit still
Or potter round the garden; answered some
Of his long marvellous letters but kept none.

Law Like Love

Law, say the gardeners, is the sun,
Law is the one
All gardeners obey
To-morrow, yesterday, to-day.

Law is the wisdom of the old
The impotent grandfathers shrilly scold;
The grandchildren put out a treble tongue,
Law is the senses of the young.

Law, says the priest with a priestly look,
Expounding to an unpriestly people,
Law is the words in my priestly book,
Law is my pulpit and my steeple.

Law, says the judge as he looks down his nose,
Speaking clearly and most severely,
Law is as I've told you before,
Law is as you know I suppose,
Law is but let me explain once more,
Law is The Law.

Yet law-abiding scholars write;
Law is neither wrong nor right,
Law is only crimes
Punished by places and by times,
Law is the clothes men wear
Anytime, anywhere,
Law is Good morning and Good night.

Others say, Law is our Fate;
Others say, Law is our State;
Others say, others say,
Law is no more
Law has gone away.

And always the loud angry crowd
Very angry and very loud
Law is We,
And always the soft idiot softly Me.

If we, dear, know we know no more
Than they about the law,
If I no more than you
Know what we should and should not do
Except that all agree
Gladly or miserably
That the law is
And that all know this,
If therefore thinking it absurd
To identify Law with some other word,

Unlike so many men
I cannot say Law is again,
No more than they can we suppress
The universal wish to guess
Or slip out of our own position
Into an unconcerned condition.
Although I can at least confine
Your vanity and mine
To stating timidly
A timid similarity,
We shall boast anyway:
Like love I say.

Like love we don't know where or why
Like love we can't compel or fly
Like love we often weep
Like love we seldom keep.

Mundus et Infans

(For Arthur and Angelyn Stevens)

Kicking his mother until she let go of his soul
Has given him a healthy appetite: clearly, her rôle
    In the New Order must be
To supply and deliver his raw materials free;
    Should there be any shortage,
She will be held responsible; she also promises
To show him all such attentions as befit his age.
    Having dictated peace,

With one fist clenched behind his head, heel drawn up to
        thigh
The cocky little ogre dozes off, ready,
    Though, to take on the rest

Of the world at the drop of a hat or the mildest
    Nudge of the impossible,
Resolved, cost what it may, to seize supreme power and
Sworn to resist tyranny to the death with all
    Forces at his command.

A pantheist not a solipsist, he co-operates
With a universe of large and noisy feeling-states
    Without troubling to place
Them anywhere special, for, to his eyes, Funnyface
    Or Elephant as yet
Mean nothing. His distinction between Me and Us
Is a matter of taste; his seasons are Dry and Wet;
    He thinks as his mouth does.

Still his loud iniquity is still what only the
Greatest of saints become — someone who does not lie:
    He because he cannot
Stop the vivid present to think, they by having got
    Past reflection into
A passionate obedience in time. We have our Boy-
Meets-Girl era of mirrors and muddle to work through,
    Without rest, without joy.

Therefore we love him because his judgments are so
Frankly subjective that his abuse carries no
    Personal sting. We should
Never dare offer our helplessness as a good
    Bargain, without at least
Promising to overcome a misfortune we blame
History or Banks or the Weather for: but this beast
    Dares to exist without shame.

Let him praise our Creator with the top of his voice,
Then, and the motions of his bowels; let us rejoice
    That he lets us hope, for

He may never become a fashionable or
    Important personage:
However bad he may be, he has not yet gone mad;
Whoever we are now, we were no worse at his age;
    So of course we ought to be glad

When he bawls the house down. Has he not a perfect right
To remind us at every moment how we quite
    Rightly expect each other
To go upstairs or for a walk if we must cry over
    Spilt milk, such as our wish
That, since, apparently, we shall never be above
Either or both, we had never learned to distinguish
    Between hunger and love?

In Memory of W. B. Yeats

(d. January 1939)

I

He disappeared in the dead of winter:
The brooks were frozen, the airports almost deserted,
And snow disfigured the public statues;
The mercury sank in the mouth of the dying day.
O all the instruments agree
The day of his death was a dark cold day.

Far from his illness
The wolves ran on through the evergreen forests,
The peasant river was untempted by the fashionable quays;
By mourning tongues
The death of the poet was kept from his poems.

But for him it was his last afternoon as himself,
An afternoon of nurses and rumours;

The provinces of his body revolted,
The squares of his mind were empty,
Silence invaded the suburbs,
The current of his feeling failed: he became his admirers.

Now he is scattered among a hundred cities
And wholly given over to unfamiliar affections,
To find his happiness in another kind of wood
And be punished under a foreign code of conscience;
The words of a dead man
Are modified in the guts of the living.

But in the importance and noise of to-morrow
When the brokers are roaring like beasts on the floor of the
    Bourse,
And the poor have the sufferings to which they are fairly
    accustomed,
And each in the cell of himself is almost convinced of his
    freedom,
A few thousand will think of this day
As one thinks of a day when one did something slightly
    unusual.
O all the instruments agree
The day of his death was a dark cold day.

II

You were silly like us: your gift survived it all;
The parish of rich women, physical decay,
Yourself; mad Ireland hurt you into poetry.
Now Ireland has her madness and her weather still,
For poetry makes nothing happen: it survives
In the valley of its saying where executives
Would never want to tamper; it flows south
From ranches of isolation and the busy griefs,
Raw towns that we believe and die in; it survives,
A way of happening, a mouth.

Earth, receive an honoured guest;
William Yeats is laid to rest:
Let the Irish vessel lie
Emptied of its poetry.

Time that is intolerant
Of the brave and innocent,
And indifferent in a week
To a beautiful physique,

Worships language and forgives
Everyone by whom it lives;
Pardons cowardice, conceit,
Lays its honours at their feet.

Time that with this strange excuse
Pardoned Kipling and his views,
And will pardon Paul Claudel,
Pardons him for writing well.

In the nightmare of the dark
All the dogs of Europe bark,
And the living nations wait,
Each sequestered in its hate;

Intellectual disgrace
Stares from every human face,
And the seas of pity lie
Locked and frozen in each eye.

Follow, poet, follow right
To the bottom of the night,
With your unconstraining voice
Still persuade us to rejoice;

With the farming of a verse
Make a vineyard of the curse,

Sing of human unsuccess
In a rapture of distress;

In the deserts of the heart
Let the healing fountain start,
In the prison of his days
Teach the free man how to praise.

STEPHEN SPENDER (1909-   )

Stephen Spender was for many years associated in the minds of readers with Auden, so that the two were almost indistinguishable. But Spender is a poet of idealistic lyricism and of solemn moral statement, while Auden is a wit-poet, a writer of light verse with a serious purpose.

Spender was born of mixed Jewish, German, and English parents; his father was the well-known journalist, Harold Spender. At Oxford University and earlier the young poet operated his own press, printing labels to support himself and publishing his own and others' poetry in small editions. His early book *Nine Experiments* (1928) was produced in this way. *Twenty Poems* was published by Blackwell in 1930. But the mature poet appeared in *Poems* (1933), one of the books that ushered in the Thirties period in English poetry.

Spender was one of the leaders in a strong movement in poetry that aimed at social commitment and radical change as Europe, torn by unemployment and discontent, drifted towards war and revolution. His books, *Vienna* (1935), *The Still Centre* (1939), *Ruins and Visions* (1942), and in prose *The Destructive Element* (1935), are permanent records of an era. *Trial of a Judge* (1938) depicted the horror and brutality of Nazism in dramatic form.

After the Spanish Civil War and the outbreak of the Second World War, Spender turned to more personal themes in poetry, in *Poems of Dedication* (1947) and *The Edge of Being* (1949). He is one of the editors of *Encounter*, an important journal of literature and liberal ideas. His *Collected Poems* appeared in 1955.

'My parents kept me . . . '

My parents kept me from children who were rough
Who threw words like stones and who wore torn clothes.
Their thighs showed through rags. They ran in the street
And climbed cliffs and stripped by the country streams.

I feared more than tigers their muscles like iron
Their jerking hands and their knees tight on my arms.

I feared the salt coarse pointing of those boys
Who copied my lisp behind me on the road.

They were lithe, they sprang out behind hedges
Like dogs to bark at my world. They threw mud
While I looked the other way, pretending to smile.
I longed to forgive them, but they never smiled.

The Pylons

The secret of these hills was stone, and cottages
Of that stone made,
And crumbling roads
That turned on sudden hidden villages.

Now over these small hills, they have built the concrete
That trails black wire;
Pylons, those pillars
Bare like nude giant girls that have no secret.

The valley with its gilt and evening look
And the green chestnut
Of customary root,
Are mocked dry like the parched bed of a brook.

But far above and far as sight endures
Like whips of anger
With lightning's danger
There runs the quick perspective of the future.

This dwarfs our emerald country by its trek
So tall with prophecy:
Dreaming of cities
Where often clouds shall lean their swan-white neck.

The Express

After the first powerful, plain manifesto
The black statement of pistons, without more fuss
But gliding like a queen, she leaves the station.
Without bowing and with restrained unconcern
She passes the houses which humbly crowd outside,
The gasworks, and at last the heavy page
Of death, printed by gravestones in the cemetery.
Beyond the town, there lies the open country
Where, gathering speed, she acquires mystery,
The luminous self-possession of ships on ocean.
It is now she begins to sing — at first quite low
Then loud, and at last with a jazzy madness —
The song of her whistle screaming at curves,
Of deafening tunnels, brakes, innumerable bolts.
And always light, aerial, underneath,
Retreats the elate metre of her wheels.
Steaming through metal landscape on her lines,
She plunges new eras of white happiness,
Where speed throws up strange shapes, broad curves
And parallels clean like trajectories from guns.
At last, further than Edinburgh or Rome,
Beyond the crest of the world, she reaches night
Where only a low stream-line brightness
Of phosphorus on the tossing hills is light.
Ah, like a comet through flame, she moves entranced,
Wrapt in her music no bird song, no, nor bough
Breaking with honey buds, shall ever equal.

'He will watch the hawk . . . '

He will watch the hawk with an indifferent eye
   Or pitifully;

Nor on those eagles that so feared him, now
　　Will strain his brow;
Weapons men use, stone, sling and strong-thewed bow
　　He will not know.
This aristocrat, superb of all instinct,
　　With death close linked
Had paced the enormous cloud, almost had won
　　War on the sun;
Till now, like Icarus mid-ocean-drowned,
　　Hands, wings, are found.

'I think continually . . .'

I think continually of those who were truly great.
Who, from the womb, remembered the soul's history
Through corridors of light where the hours are suns,
Endless and singing. Whose lovely ambition
Was that their lips, still touched with fire,
Should tell of the Spirit, clothed from head to foot in song.
And who hoarded from the Spring branches
The desires falling across their bodies like blossoms.

What is precious, is never to forget
The essential delight of the blood drawn from ageless springs
Breaking through rocks in worlds before our earth.
Never to deny its pleasure in the morning simple light
Nor its grave evening demand for love.
Never to allow gradually the traffic to smother
With noise and fog, the flowering of the Spirit.

Near the snow, near the sun, in the highest fields,
See how these names are fêted by the waving grass
And by the streamers of white cloud

And whispers of wind in the listening sky.
The names of those who in their lives fought for life,
Who wore at their hearts the fire's centre.
Born of the sun, they travelled a short while toward the sun
And left the vivid air signed with their honour.

ROBINSON JEFFERS (1887-1962)

A poet of prophetic despair in his view of modern man, Robinson Jeffers lived most of his life in an austere private retreat overlooking the sea, near Carmel, on the coast of California. He was born in Pittsburgh in 1887, as a boy travelled widely in Europe with his parents, and later studied 'with faint interest' at a number of American universities. He married in 1913, after a stormy courtship, and intended to go to England, but the outbreak of war turned him back to California. There he settled permanently, building an observation tower with his own hands and writing poetry with the rugged, rocky coastal landscape for a background. Fame came to him suddenly with the publication of his third book, *Tamar and Other Poems*, in 1924.

He has been an isolated and lonely figure in twentieth-century poetry, violent and rhetorical in his prophecies of doom and his vivid conception of evil at the core of a mechanical, urban society, but at the same time large and serene in his evocation of nature's beauty as a timeless order, and classical in the austerity of his tragic vision.

The Answer

Then what is the answer? — Not to be deluded by dreams.
To know that great civilizations have broken down into
    violence, and their tyrants come, many times before.
When open violence appears, to avoid it with honor or choose
    the least ugly faction; these evils are essential.
To keep one's own integrity, be merciful and uncorrupted
    and not wish for evil; and not be duped
By dreams of universal justice or happiness. These dreams
    will not be fulfilled.
To know this, and know that however ugly the parts appear
    the whole remains beautiful. A severed hand
Is an ugly thing, and man dissevered from the earth and stars
    and his history ... for contemplation or in fact ...

Often appears atrociously ugly. Integrity is wholeness, the
    greatest beauty is
Organic wholeness, the wholeness of life and things, the
    divine beauty of the universe. Love that, not man
Apart from that, or else you will share man's pitiful confusions,
    or drown in despair when his days darken.

Shine, Perishing Republic

While this America settles in the mould of its vulgarity,
    heavily thickening to empire,
And protest, only a bubble in the molten mass, pops and
    sighs out, and the mass hardens,

I sadly smiling remember that the flower fades to make
    fruit, the fruit rots to make earth.
Out of the mother; and through the spring exultances,
    ripeness and decadence; and home to the mother.

You making haste haste on decay: not blameworthy; life
    is good, be it stubbornly long or suddenly
A mortal splendor: meteors are not needed less than
    mountains: shine, perishing republic.

But for my children, I would have them keep their distance
    from the thickening center; corruption
Never has been compulsory, when the cities lie at the
    monster's feet there are left the mountains.

And boys, be in nothing so moderate as in love of man,
    a clever servant, insufferable master.
There is the trap that catches noblest spirits, that
    caught — they say — God, when he walked on earth.

Triad

Science, that makes wheels turn, cities grow,
Moribund people live on, playthings increase,
But has fallen from hope to confusion at her own business
Of understanding the nature of things; — new Russia,
That stood a moment at dreadful cost half free,
Beholding the open, all the glades of the world
On both sides of the trap, and resolutely
Walked into the trap that has Europe and America; —
The poet, who wishes not to play games with words,
His affair being to awake dangerous images
And call the hawks; — they all feed the future, they serve
    God,
Who is very beautiful, but hardly a friend of humanity.

Blind Horses

The proletariat for your Messiah, the poor and many are
    to seize power and make the world new.
They cannot even conduct a strike without cunning leaders:
    if they make a revolution their leaders
Must take the power. The first duty of men in power:
    to defend their power. What men defend
To-day they will love to-morrow; it becomes theirs, their
    property. Lenin has served the revolution,
Stalin presently begins to betray it. Why? For the sake
    of power, the Party's power, the state's
Power, armed power, Stalin's power, Caesarean power.

                                              This is
    not quite a new world.
The old shepherd has been known before; great and
    progressive empires have flourished before; powerful
    bureaucracies

Apportioned food and labor and amusement; men have been
  massed and moulded, spies have gone here and there,
The old shepherd Caesar his vicious collies, watching the
  flock. Inevitable? Perhaps, but not new.
The ages like blind horses turning a mill tread their own
  hoofmarks. Whose corn's ground in that mill?

Natural Music

The old voice of the ocean, the bird-chatter of little rivers,
(Winter has given them gold for silver
To stain their water and bladed green for brown to line
  their banks)
From different throats intone one language.
So I believe if we were strong enough to listen without
Divisions of desire and terror
To the storm of the sick nations, the rage of the
  hunger-smitten cities,
Those voices also would be found
Clean as a child's; or like some girl's breathing who dances
  alone
By the ocean-shore, dreaming of lovers.

Fire on the Hills

The deer were bounding like blown leaves
Under the smoke in front of the roaring wave of the brush-fire;
I thought of the smaller lives that were caught.
Beauty is not always lovely; the fire was beautiful, the terror
Of the deer was beautiful; and when I returned
Down the black slopes after the fire had gone by, an eagle
Was perched on the jag of a burnt pine,

Insolent and gorged, cloaked in the folded storms of his
  shoulders.
He had come from far off for the good hunting
With fire for his beater to drive the game; the sky was
  merciless
Blue, and the hills merciless black,
The sombre-feathered great bird sleepily merciless between
  them.
I thought, painfully, but the whole mind,
The destruction that brings an eagle from heaven is better
  than mercy.

DYLAN THOMAS (1914-1953)

Dylan Thomas was born in Swansea, Wales, on October 27, 1914. He did not go beyond grammar school, but genius carried him to the heights of fame in a wild and turbulent career that ended in tragedy and death.

He appeared first in *18 Poems*, in 1934, when the leftist poetry of the Thirties was just gathering momentum; yet his own poetry was of a different cast entirely, destined to replace the rational assumptions of socialism with apocalyptic vision and magical rhetoric. (He was no less a socialist and radical for all that, but politics was not his theme, and reason applied to society and its ills was not a cure for his troubles.)

By the time he published *The World I Breathe* in 1939, a collection of his best poems, together with eleven stories, he was already recognized as a voice of powerful originality and imagination. His greatest triumph, however, and also the way to self-destruction, came with his lecture-tours in the United States. John Malcolm Brinnin, who acted as his agent and friend, gives a detailed and harrowing account of this period in his book *Dylan Thomas in America* (1955). Thomas was idolized, admired, and applauded by huge audiences who listened enraptured to his resounding bardic recitations. Distraught by strange environment, made tense by the academic company in which he found himself, he resorted to excessive drinking and irregular and sensational behaviour. He usually arrived drunk a few hours before a reading was scheduled, pulled himself together sufficiently to overwhelm the audience, and returned to the bars afterwards. He collapsed in New York on his thirty-ninth birthday, and died of encephalopathy, a disease of the brain caused by alcohol, on November 9, 1953.

But Dylan Thomas's stormy career should not distract us from the enduring qualities of his poetry. When he put pen to paper he wrote with the greatest sobriety, even at the end, and his poems are highly disciplined and carefully-structured designs. Perhaps to resist the maelstrom of chaos, he followed a traditional syllabic system in shaping the verses of his poems. The images develop by a series of contrasted opposites, the entire poem exploding with energy and violence. It is a poetry of ultimate things, of birth and death, and the eternal vision of life that passes between these poles, pregnant with colours of heaven and hell. 'My words are written for the love of man and the praise of God,' he once said, 'and I'd be a damned fool if they weren't.'

Fern Hill

Now as I was young and easy under the apple boughs
About the lilting house and happy as the grass was green,
   The night above the dingle starry,
     Time let me hail and climb
   Golden in the heydays of his eyes,
And honoured among wagons I was prince of the apple towns
And once below a time I lordly had the trees and leaves
     Trail with daisies and barley
   Down the rivers of the windfall light.

And as I was green and carefree, famous among the barns
About the happy yard and singing as the farm was home,
   In the sun that is young once only,
     Time let me play and be
   Golden in the mercy of his means,
And green and golden I was huntsman and herdsman, the
          calves
Sang to my horn, the foxes on the hills barked clear and cold,
    And the sabbath rang slowly
   In the pebbles of the holy streams.

All the sun long it was running, it was lovely, the hay-
Fields high as the house, the tunes from the chimneys, it was
       air
   And playing, lovely and watery
     And fire green as grass.
   And nightly under the simple stars
As I rode to sleep the owls were bearing the farm away,
All the moon long I heard, blessed among stables, the nightjars
   Flying with the ricks, and the horses
    Flashing into the dark.

And then to awake, and the farm, like a wanderer white
With the dew, come back, the cock on his shoulder; it was all

Shining, it was Adam and maiden,
　　The sky gathered again
　　And the sun grew round that very day.
So it must have been after the birth of the simple light
In the first, spinning place, the spellbound horses walking warm
　　Out of the whinnying green stable
　　　　On to the fields of praise.

And honoured among foxes and pheasants by the gay house
Under the new made clouds and happy as the heart was long,
　　In the sun born over and over,
　　　　I ran my heedless ways,
　　My wishes raced through the house-high hay
And nothing I cared, at my sky blue trades, that time allows
In all his tuneful turning so few and such morning songs
　　Before the children green and golden
　　　　Follow him out of grace,

Nothing I cared, in the lamb white days, that time would
　　　　take me
Up to the swallow thronged loft by the shadow of my hand,
　　In the moon that is always rising,
　　　　Nor that riding to sleep
　　I should hear him fly with the high fields
And wake to the farm forever fled from the childless land.
Oh as I was young and easy in the mercy of his means,
　　　　Time held me green and dying
　　Though I sang in my chains like the sea.

This Bread I break

　　　　This bread I break was once the oat,
　　　　This wine upon a foreign tree
　　　　Plunged in its fruit;

Man in the day or wind at night
Laid the crops low, broke the grape's joy.

Once in this wind the summer blood
Knocked in the flesh that decked the vine,
Once in this bread
The oat was merry in the wind;
Man broke the sun, pulled the wind down.

This flesh you break, this blood you let
Make desolation in the vein,
Were oat and grape
Born of the sensual root and sap;
My wine you drink, my bread you snap.

In My Craft or Sullen Art

In my craft or sullen art
Exercised in the still night
When only the moon rages
And the lovers lie abed
With all their griefs in their arms,
I labour by singing light
Not for ambition or bread
Or the strut and trade of charms
On the ivory stages
But for the common wages
Of their most secret heart.

Not for the proud man apart
From the raging moon I write
On these spindrift pages
Not for the towering dead
With their nightingales and psalms

But for the lovers, their arms
Round the griefs of the ages,
Who pay no praise or wages
Nor heed my craft or art.

Among those Killed in the Dawn Raid
was a Man Aged a Hundred

When the morning was waking over the war
He put on his clothes and stepped out and he died,
The locks yawned loose and a blast blew them wide,
He dropped where he loved on the burst pavement stone
And the funeral grains of the slaughtered floor.
Tell his street on its back he stopped a sun
And the craters of his eyes grew springshoots and fire
When all the keys shot from the locks, and rang.

Dig no more for the chains of his grey-haired heart.
The heavenly ambulance drawn by a wound
Assembling waits for the spades' ring on the cage.
O keep his bones away from that common cart,
The morning is flying on the wings of his age
And a hundred storks perch on the sun's right hand.

And Death shall have no Dominion

And death shall have no dominion.
Dead men naked they shall be one
With the man in the wind and the west moon;
When their bones are picked clean and the clean bones gone,
They shall have stars at elbow and foot;
Though they go mad they shall be sane,

Though they sink through the sea they shall rise again;
Though lovers be lost love shall not;
And death shall have no dominion.

And death shall have no dominion.
Under the windings of the sea
They lying long shall not die windily;
Twisting on racks when sinews give way,
Strapped to a wheel, yet they shall not break;
Faith in their hands shall snap in two,
And the unicorn evils run them through;
Split all ends up they shan't crack;
And death shall have no dominion.

And death shall have no dominion.
No more may gulls cry at their ears
Or waves break loud on the seashores;
Where blew a flower may a flower no more
Lift its head to the blows of the rain;
Though they be mad and dead as nails,
Heads of the characters hammer through daisies;
Break in the sun till the sun breaks down,
And death shall have no dominion.

KARL SHAPIRO (1913-   )

Karl Shapiro is a poet who soared into prominence in the midst of the Second World War. His experience in the South Pacific where he was stationed as an army sergeant provided the material for his first two books. When published in the United States without his assistance, they created an immediate impression and established him as the most representative voice of the new generation.

These books, *Person, Place and Thing* (1942) and *V-Letter and Other Poems* (1944), show a curious retreat from the experimental frontiers of modern poetry, a return to formal rhyme and metre, and an ironic worldly wisdom. The change was of course ushered in earlier by Auden. The new poetry was still entirely contemporary in subject matter, but the shift from tragic earnestness to tough worldliness produced an effect resembling light verse with a highly intelligent content. The analogy in English poetry of the past would be to neo-classicism. Karl Shapiro referred to 'the gigantic slapstick of modern war', and in several of his own poems he treated war with a detachment that only a soldier in the midst of war's ravages could afford. The poetry was not lacking in seriousness, or compassion, but its tone was that of a sobered sensibility.

In the last year of the war appeared *Essay on Rime* (1945), a versified analysis of 'the confusion in prosody, the confusion in language, and the confusion in belief'. Karl Shapiro has engaged with great zest in controversial criticism. In poetry he published *Trial of a Poet and Other Poems* (1947), *Poems 1940-1953*, and *Poems of a Jew* (1958). For a time Shapiro edited *Poetry* magazine in Chicago, and he has been currently employed in university teaching.

The Fly

O hideous little bat, the size of snot,
With polyhedral eye and shabby clothes,
To populate the stinking cat you walk
The promontory of the dead man's nose,
Climb with the fine leg of a Duncan-Phyfe
    The smoking mountains of my food

And in a comic mood
In mid-air take to bed a wife.

Riding and riding with your filth of hair
On gluey foot or wing, forever coy,
Hot from the compost and green sweet decay,
Sounding your buzzer like an urchin toy —
You dot all whiteness with diminutive stool,
In the tight belly of the dead
Burrow with hungry head
And inlay maggots like a jewel.

At your approach the great horse stomps and paws
Bringing the hurricane of his heavy tail;
Shod in disease you dare to kiss my hand
Which sweeps against you like an angry flail;
Still you return, return, trusting your wing
To draw you from the hunter's reach
That learns to kill to teach
Disorder to the tinier thing.

My peace is your disaster. For your death
Children like spiders cup their pretty hands
And wives resort to chemistry of war.
In fens of sticky paper and quicksands
You glue yourself to death. Where you are stuck
You struggle hideously and beg
You amputate your leg
Imbedded in the amber muck.

But I, a man, must swat you with my hate,
Slap you across the air and crush your flight,
Must mangle with my shoe and smear your blood,
Expose your little guts pasty and white,
Knock your head sideways like a drunkard's hat,
Pin your wings under like a crow's,

Tear off your flimsy clothes
And beat you as one beats a rat.

Then like Gargantua I stride among
The corpses strewn like raisins in the dust,
The broken bodies of the narrow dead
That catch the throat with fingers of disgust.
I sweep. One gyrates like a top and falls
  And stunned, stone blind, and deaf
    Buzzes its frightful F
  And dies between three cannibals.

The Dirty Word

The dirty word hops in the cage of the mind like the
Pondicherry vulture, stomping with its heavy left claw on the
sweet meat of the brain and tearing it with its vicious beak,
ripping and chopping the flesh. Terrified, the small boy bears
the big bird of the dirty word into the house, and grunting,
puffing, carries it up the stairs to his own room in the skull.
Bits of black feather cling to his clothes and his hair as he locks
the staring creature in the dark closet.

All day the small boy returns to the closet to examine and
feed the bird, to caress and kick the bird, that now snaps and
flaps its wings savagely whenever the door is opened. How
the boy trembles and delights at the sight of the white
excrement of the bird! How the bird leaps and rushes against
the walls of the skull, trying to escape from the zoo of the
vocabulary! How wildly snaps the sweet meat of the brain
in its rage.

And the bird outlives the man, being freed at the man's
death-funeral by a word from the rabbi.

(But I one morning went upstairs and opened the door and entered the closet and found in the cage of my mind the great bird dead. Softly I wept it and softly removed it and softly buried the body of the bird in the hollyhock garden of the house I lived in twenty years before. And out of the worn black feathers of the wing have I made these pens to write these elegies, for I have outlived the bird, and I have murdered it in my early manhood.)

Among the 'New Formalists' Richard Wilbur is perhaps the most finished craftsman. A writer of excellent smoothness and of exquisite detail, he deals with everyday objects and experiences and conveys them to us through the tinted glass of his idealism.

Though born in New York City, he was brought up in the country, 'among woods, orchards, corn-fields, horses, hogs, cows, and haywagons'. An attachment to nature has remained constant in his poetry. During the war he saw service on several fronts. After the war he proceeded to graduate studies at Harvard, and then like several other poets of the post-war generation entered upon a teaching career. His first book, *The Beautiful Changes* (1947), won immediate recognition among the select of poetry readers. It was followed by *Ceremony and Other Poems* (1950), *Things of This World* (1956), and *Advice to a Prophet and Other Poems* (1961). The second of these was awarded the Pulitzer Prize.

The Beautiful Changes

One wading a Fall meadow finds on all sides
The Queen Anne's Lace lying like lilies
On water; it glides
So from the walker, it turns
Dry grass to a lake, as the slightest shade of you
Valleys my mind in fabulous blue Lucernes.

The beautiful changes as a forest is changed
By a chameleon's tuning his skin to it;
As a mantis, arranged
On a green leaf, grows
Into it, makes the leaf leafier, and proves
Any greenness is deeper than anyone knows.

Your hands hold roses always in a way that says
They are not only yours; the beautiful changes

In such kind ways,
Wishing ever to sunder
Things and Things' selves for a second finding, to lose
For a moment all that it touches back to wonder.

Juggler

A ball will bounce, but less and less. It's not
A light-hearted thing, resents its own resilience.
Falling is what it loves, and the earth falls
So in our hearts from brilliance,
Settles and is forgot.
It takes a sky-blue juggler with five red balls

To shake our gravity up. Whee, in the air
The balls roll round, wheel on his wheeling hands,
Learning the ways of lightness, alter to spheres
Grazing his finger ends,
Cling to their courses there,
Swinging a small heaven about his ears.

But a heaven is easier made of nothing at all
Than the earth regained, and still and sole within
The spin of worlds, with a gesture sure and noble
He reels that heaven in,
Landing it ball by ball,
And trades it all for a broom, a plate, a table.

Oh, on his toe the table is turning, the broom's
Balancing up on his nose, and the plate whirls
On the tip of the broom! Damn, what a show, we cry:
The boys stamp, and the girls
Shriek, and the drum booms
And all comes down, and he bows and says good-bye.

If the juggler is tired now, if the broom stands
In the dust again, if the table starts to drop
Through the daily dark again, and though the plate
Lies flat on the table top,
For him we batter our hands
Who has won for once over the world's weight.

ROBERT LOWELL (1917-   )

Robert Lowell's great-grandfather was the brother of James Russell Lowell; his family on both his mother's and his father's side were distinguished Bostonians. The shadow of a great cultural tradition shudders over this outcast heir of New England aristocracy. But the tradition itself has been eroded by commercialism and vulgarized by the materialism of modern life, so that the poet's passion is spent in violent elegy and self-accusing rage.

A non-conformist in the tradition of New England Protestantism, Robert Lowell became a passionately convinced Roman Catholic. His poems written out of this faith are like no other religious poetry; they are violent expressions of religious revulsion against a world of temporal confusion. During the war he refused to reply to the draft and spent five months in prison as a conscientious objector. His first books, *Land of Unlikeness* (1944) and *Lord Weary's Castle* (1946), created a powerful impression by their explosive energy and packed metaphorical richness.

Clearly this poet owes as much to Dylan Thomas as Karl Shapiro owes to Auden; yet both Lowell and Shapiro are original voices translating a way of poetry to American needs. (Randall Jarrell, poet and critic, described Lowell's work as 'post- or anti-modernist poetry'.) Lowell's later books, *The Mills of the Kavanaghs* (1951) and *Life Studies* (1960), have continued to enlarge his reputation. *Life Studies* is highly autobiographical, fearlessly honest, and deeply moving in its record of suffering and personal struggle. It gained the National Book Award for 1960. *Imitations*, a book of virtuoso poems modelled on European writers, appeared in 1962.

Our Lady of Walsingham

(From *The Quaker Graveyard in Nantucket*)

There once the penitents took off their shoes
And then walked barefoot the remaining mile;
And the small trees, a stream and hedgerows file
Slowly along the munching English lane,
Like cows to the old shrine, until you lose

Track of your dragging pain.
The stream flows down under the druid tree,
Shiloah's whirlpools gurgle and make glad
The castle of God. Sailor, you were glad
And whistled Sion by that stream. But see:

Our Lady, too small for her canopy,
Sits near the altar. There's no comeliness
At all or charm in that expressionless
Face with its heavy eyelids. As before,
This face, for centuries a memory,
Non est species, neque decor,
Expressionless, expresses God: it goes
Past castled Sion. She knows what God knows,
Not Calvary's Cross nor crib at Bethlehem
Now, and the world shall come to Walsingham.

Colloquy in Black Rock

Here the jack-hammer jabs into the ocean;
My heart, you race and stagger and demand
More blood-gangs for your nigger-brass percussions,
Till I, the stunned machine of your devotion,
Clanging upon this cymbal of a hand,
Am rattled screw and footloose. All discussions

End in the mud-flat detritus of death.
My heart, beat faster, faster. In Black Mud
Hungarian workmen give their blood
For the martyre Stephen, who was stoned to death.

Black Mud, a name to conjure with: O mud
For watermelons gutted to the crust,
Mud for the mole-tide harbor, mud for mouse,

Mud for the armored Diesel fishing tubs that thud
A year and a day to wind and tide; the dust
Is on this skipping heart that shakes my house,

House of our Savior who was hanged till death.
My heart, beat faster, faster. In Black Mud
Stephen the martyre was broken down to blood:
Our ransom is the rubble of his death.

Christ walks on the black water. In Black Mud
Darts the kingfisher. On Corpus Christi, heart,
Over the drum-beat of St. Stephen's choir
I hear him, *Stupor Mundi*, and the mud
Flies from his hunching wings and beak — my heart,
The blue kingfisher dives on you in fire.

DAVID GASCOYNE (1916-   )

Among the British poets who emerged in the 1940s, David Gascoyne displays more than any other the apocalyptic and visionary qualities which characterized that period. No doubt the imposing presence of Dylan Thomas still haunts this poetry. But it is more open to the reader, more direct and hortatory than Thomas; and it allows the personal emotions of the poet to speak to the reader as Thomas rarely did.

For a time influenced by surrealism, Gascoyne wrote a book on the subject, *A Short Survey of Surrealism*. This important French movement in art and literature (it is the dominant source of much French poetry written in Canada) has had little direct influence in England; therefore it is especially interesting in this poet. He has lived in Paris and has written in French as well as in English. He has also translated the German romantic poet Hölderlin into English. The poem 'Ecce Homo' is taken from his collection *Poems: 1937-1942*, with illustrations by Graham Sutherland, published by *Poetry London* in 1943.

Ecce Homo

Whose is this horrifying face,
This putrid flesh, discoloured, flayed,
Fed on by flies, scorched by the sun?
Whose are those hollow red-filmed eyes
And thorn-spiked head and spear-stuck side?
Behold the Man: He is Man's Son.

Forget the legend, tear the decent veil
That cowardice or interest devised
To make their mortal enemy a friend,
To hide the bitter truth all His wounds tell,
Lest the great scandal be no more disguised:
He is in agony till the world's end,

And we must never sleep during that time!
He is suspended on the cross-tree now

And we are onlookers at the crime,
Callous contemporaries of the slow
Torture of God. Here is the hill
Made ghastly by His spattered blood.

Whereon He hangs and suffers still:
See, the centurions wear riding-boots,
Black shirts and badges and peaked caps,
Greet one another with raised-arm salutes;
They have cold eyes, unsmiling lips;
Yet these His brothers know not what they do.

And on his either side hang dead
A labourer and a factory hand,
Or one is maybe a lynched Jew
And one a Negro or a Red,
Coolie or Ethiopian, Irishman,
Spaniard or German democrat.

Behind His lolling head the sky
Glares like a fiery cataract
Red with the murders of two thousand years
Committed in His name and by
Crusaders, Christian warriors
Defending faith and property.

Amid the plain beneath His transfixed hands,
Exuding darkness as indelible
As guilty stains, fanned by funereal
And lurid airs, besieged by drifting sands
And clefted landslides our about-to-be
Bombed and abandoned cities stand.

He who wept for Jerusalem
Now sees His prophecy extend
Across the greatest cities of the world,
A guilty panic reason cannot stem

Rising to raze them all as He foretold;
And He must watch this drama to the end.

Though often named, He is unknown
To the dark kingdoms at His feet
Where everything disparages His words,
And each man bears the common guilt alone
And goes blindfolded to his fate,
And fear and greed are sovereign lords.

The turning point of history
Must come. Yet the complacent and the proud
And who exploit and kill, may be denied —
Christ of Revolution and of Poetry —
The resurrection and the life
Wrought by your spirit's blood.

Involved in their own sophistry
The black priest and the upright man
Faced by subversive truth shall be struck dumb,
Christ of Revolution and of Poetry,
While the rejected and condemned become
Agents of the divine.

Not from a monstrance silver-wrought
But from the tree of human pain
Redeem our sterile misery,
Christ of Revolution and of Poetry,
That man's long journey through the night
May not have been in vain.

ALEX COMFORT (1920-   )

Alex Comfort represents a direction of poetry in England since about 1940 described as neo-romantic, a reaction to the wit-poetry of W. H. Auden and to the traditional formalism which Auden brought back to poetry. New Romanticism in England corresponds in general to 'beat' poetry in America, just as the continuing Auden tradition corresponds to the formalism of Wilbur and others in America. (Of course these are only terms for general trends, not any organized movements; poets are individualists and do not submit to the rules of any school.) The chief influences upon New Romanticism are D. H. Lawrence, Dylan Thomas, and the novelist Henry Miller.

Alex Comfort was born in London, February 10, 1920. He was educated at Highgate and at Trinity College, Cambridge. A prolific writer, he has written a dozen books, including two bulky novels, several plays, and criticism, as well as books of poetry. *A Wreath for the Living* (1942) was his first book; *The Song of Lazarus* (1945) his most representative collection. In his work he appears as a non-conformist, a convinced pacifist, and a lyric poet of strong personal emotion. He is a practising physician and a lecturer in physiology.

Notes for My Son

(From *Song of Lazarus*)

Remember when you hear them beginning to say Freedom
Look carefully — see who it is that they want you to butcher.

Remember, when you say that the old trick would not have
fooled you for a moment
That every time it is the trick which seems new.

Remember that you will have to put in irons
Your better nature, if it will desert to them.

Remember, remember their faces — watch them carefully:
For every step you take is on somebody's body

And every cherry you plant for them is a gibbet
And every furrow you turn for them is a grave

Remember, the smell of burning will not sicken you
If they persuade you that it will thaw the world

Beware. The blood of a child does not smell so bitter
If you have shed it with a high moral purpose.

So that because the woodcutter disobeyed
they will not burn her today or any day

So that for lack of a joiner's obedience
The crucifixion will not now take place

So that when they come to sell you their bloody corruption
You will gather the spit of your chest
And plant it in their faces.

ALLEN GINSBERG (1926-)

Born in Paterson, New Jersey, on June 3, 1926, and educated at Columbia University, Allen Ginsberg emerged into prominence in 1956 with the publication of the long vehement poem *Howl*. It has symbolized a decade in American poetry just as T. S. Eliot's *Waste Land* did in the 1920s. Allen Ginsberg has described the composition of the poem in these words: 'I thought I wouldn't write a *poem*, but just write what I wanted to without fear, let my imagination go ... something I wouldn't be able to show anybody....' The result was a long episodic catalogue of desperate escapades, a list of excesses summarizing a generation. It was also a harangue of violent condemnation directed against a society.

Section Two of the poem depicts modern America as an inferno ruled by Moloch, the ancient god of the Phoenicians to whom human victims were sacrificed:

> Moloch! Solitude! Filth! Ugliness! Ashcans and unobtainable
>   dollars! Children screaming under the stairways! Boys sobbing
>   in armies! Old men weeping in the parks!
> Moloch! Moloch! Nightmare of Moloch! Moloch the loveless!
>   Mental Moloch! Moloch the heavy judger of men!
> Moloch the incomprehensible prison! Moloch the crossbone
>   soulless jailhouse and Congress of sorrows! Moloch whose
>   buildings are judgement! Moloch the vast stone of war! Moloch
>   the stunned governments!
> Moloch whose mind is pure machinery! Moloch whose blood
>   is running money! Moloch whose fingers are ten armies!
>   Moloch whose breast is a cannibal dynamo! Moloch whose ear
>   is a smoking tomb!

The power of this poetry derives from its intense emotion, a savage ardour for truth expressed with almost religious intensity. 'My poetry is Angelical Ravings,' Ginsberg has said, and the evangelist's (or prophet's) fervour is recognizable in both the language and its effect upon the hearer.

The long rhetorical line in which *Howl* is written and the epic catalogue it contains are indebted to Whitman. 'I realized at the time', Ginsberg has explained, 'that Whitman's form had rarely been further explored.' Even the religious overtones are an extension of Whitman's cosmic pantheism.

189

A continuing interest in Buddhism and in visionary experience, obtained sometimes through the use of drugs, has led this poet very far from the conventional paths of poetic experience. Since writing *Howl*, he has travelled in many parts of the world, in Europe and the Orient. He has also given highly successful poetry readings which have wellnigh mesmerized audiences of young people. In this respect the poetry of Allen Ginsberg represents a sociological phenomenon as much as a literary one. He is the central figure of the 'beat generation', if that term still has any meaning. In addition to *Howl and Other Poems*, he has published *Kaddish and Other Poems* (1960) and *Reality Sandwiches*, *1953-60*. A recording of a reading of *Howl* is available on Fantasy LP No. 7005.

A Supermarket in California

What thoughts I have of you tonight, Walt Whitman, for I walked down the sidestreets under the trees with a headache self-conscious looking at the full moon.

In my hungry fatigue, and shopping for images, I went into the neon fruit supermarket, dreaming of your enumerations!

What peaches and what penumbras! Whole families shopping at night! Aisles full of husbands! Wives in the avocados, babies in the tomatoes! — and you, Garcia Lorca, what were you doing down by the watermelons?

I saw you, Walt Whitman, childless, lonely old grubber, poking among the meats in the refrigerator and eyeing the grocery boys.

I heard you asking questions of each: Who killed the pork chops? What price bananas? Are you my Angel?

I wandered in and out of the brilliant stacks of cans following you, and followed in my imagination by the store detective.

We strode down the open corridors together in our solitary fancy tasting artichokes, possessing every frozen delicacy, and never passing the cashier.

Where are we going, Walt Whitman? The doors close in an hour. Which way does your beard point tonight?

(I touch your book and dream of our odyssey in the supermarket and feel absurd.)

Will we walk all night through solitary streets? The trees add shade to shade, lights out in the houses, we'll both be lonely.

Will we stroll dreaming of the lost America of love past blue automobiles in driveways, home to our silent cottage?

Ah, dear father, graybeard, lonely old courage-teacher, what America did you have when Charon quit poling his ferry and you got out on a smoking bank and stood watching the boat disappear on the black waters of Lethe?

LAWRENCE FERLINGHETTI (1919-   )

As publisher and bookseller, as well as poet, Lawrence Ferlinghetti has been a moving spirit in the 'far out' American poetry of the 1950s. Returning from Paris in 1951, he started 'the first all-paperbound bookstore in the U.S.' in San Francisco, City Lights Books, and there he soon began to publish some of the leading names in the new poetry movement.

Ferlinghetti, however, is also a poet with scholarly attainments. Born in Yonkers, New York, in 1919, he studied at the University of North Carolina and proceeded to an M.A. at Columbia University. After serving in the U.S. Navy during the war, he continued studies in Paris, completing a doctorate at the Sorbonne. His best-known books are *Pictures of the Gone World* (1955) and *A Coney Island of the Mind* (1958). He is also available on records (Fantasy LP recordings, Nos. 7002 and 7004).

'Constantly risking absurdity . . .'

(From *A Coney Island of the Mind*)

> Constantly risking absurdity
> > > > and death
> > > whenever he performs
> > > > above the heads
> > > > > of his audience
> > the poet like an acrobat
> > > > climbs on rime
> > > > > to a high wire of his own making
> and balancing on eyebeams
> > > > above a sea of faces
> > > paces his way
> > > > to the other side of day
> > performing entrechats
> > > > and sleight-of-foot tricks

and other high theatrics
                              and all without mistaking
                any thing
                              for what it may not be
      For he's the super realist
                              who must perforce perceive
                taut truth
                              before the taking of each stance or step
      in his supposed advance
                              toward that still higher perch
where Beauty stands and waits
                              with gravity
                              to start her death-defying leap
            And he
                a little charleychaplin man
                              who may or may not catch
                her fair eternal form
                              spreadeagled in the empty air
                of existence

Modern Canadian Poetry

The development of English-Canadian poetry in this century runs fairly parallel to British and American poetry, while the French examples, just as naturally, follow the course of things in France. The two are somewhat in contrast, yet are similarly related to modern life and to the problems of poetry after the romantic nineteenth century.

The mixture of tough realism and sentiment, the first phase of the break with Victorianism, is represented in Canada by such poets as Robert Service, Tom MacInnes, and E. J. Pratt. Robert Service, writing at the turn of the century, stated the theme:

> They have cradled you in custom, they have primed you
> with their preaching,
> They have soaked you in convention through and through;
> They have put you in a showcase; you're a credit
> to their teaching —
> But can't you hear the Wild? — it's calling you.

And Tom MacInnes achieved a similar iconoclastic attitude in many of his poems.

E. J. Pratt is a more complex figure, spanning the period from 1923 to 1964. His lifelong concern with the moral problem of destructive violence at the heart of nature springs from an awareness of modern science, especially of biology (and the drama of evolution), geology, and applied science or technology — especially in its military uses. (The work of Thomas Hardy contains much the same pattern of thought.) The mechanical vigour of Pratt's rhythms might well be compared with those of Kipling and Masefield.

Since modern poetry came late to Canada, at the end of the 1920s, our modern phase telescopes the developments in English poetry of the preceding two decades. F. R. Scott, A. J. M. Smith, and A. M. Klein employ ironic and experimental techniques similar to those of Eliot, Yeats, and Pound, yet they are at the same time poets of the Thirties, sharing the socialist leanings of the English poets Auden and Spender.

This early phase of Canadian modern poetry began in Montreal in the late 1920s, with Scott and Smith. Its development was somewhat hampered by the depression of the Thirties, but it grew into full vigour later. *New Provinces*, a small collection of the work of six poets, appeared in 1936; but it was not until 1940 that the poets of the Thirties began to bring out their first books. These combined with the first publications of Layton, Page, Dudek, Souster, and others to make the early 1940s a remarkable period of activity.

The French poets of Quebec begin from the same standpoint, but take a different course. Romanticism in France came into headlong conflict with reality in the poetry of Charles Baudelaire. (In England, Matthew Arnold reveals a similar dilemma in his stoical pessimism and concern with truth.) For Baudelaire the opposition between reality and the ideal is a central theme. This conflict may be sensed in the poetry of the French-Canadian Emile Nelligan, a tragic figure whose vessel of ideal striving was shattered on the rocks of reality. He was much influenced by Baudelaire. (A similar conflict between reality and idealism is reflected just before the turn of the century in Archibald Lampman, who on his side is indebted to Matthew Arnold.) In both French and English, therefore, we have inherited the problem of reconciling romantic idealism with the requirements of truth and actuality.

But whereas in the poetry of F. R. Scott, Klein, Layton, Souster, and others English-Canadian writing is clearly following the path into reality in trying to resolve this problem, French-Canadian poetry has followed the inward path of spirituality, subjectivity, and idealism, without being any less aware of the problems of reality that produce this poetry. This is in line with the course of modern poetry in France, which has proceeded after Baudelaire to Mallarmé and Valéry, poets of extreme inwardness and aesthetic purity (that is, purity free of the coarse elements of reality).

In France, the central movement in this development is surrealism, the elaboration of the dream-world as a subject for art; and the best French poetry written in Canada has been described as 'post-surrealist', that is, a refinement of the poetry of inward vision. In this direction we find Saint-Denys Garneau and Anne Hébert, poets of aesthetic contemplation and symbolic vision. The more recent poets of French Canada bring their symbolic and visionary art to an explosive state of tension as their awareness of uncongenial reality presses upon them.

Saint-Denys Garneau's *Regards et jeux dans l'espace* appeared in 1937. This was followed by Anne Hébert's *Les Songes en équilibre* in 1942. The work of these two poets begins modern French-Canadian poetry in much the same way as that of F. R. Scott and A. J. M. Smith on the English side. The French movement began a little later, but it has had an equally rich development. A considerable number of talents now exist in French Canada and the literature is in the midst of a development that corresponds to the 1940s and '50s in English-Canadian poetry.

In English Canada, the path of realism is followed after the 1930s by poets like Birney, Souster, Layton, Purdy, and Nowlan. But the opposing strain of imaginative or ideal aspiration, which is the groundwork of modern poetry, is always present. It may be seen in the development of any particular poet, and it is present in the conflict of poets, movements, and schools of criticism.

The two principal branches of English-Canadian poetry since the Second World War have been described as the 'mythopoeic' and the 'realistic'. The mythopoeic branch is related to the critical writings of Northrop Frye, who represents in Canada the school of critical thought that places myth or symbolic imagination at the centre of the poetic process. The poets who most clearly display this in their writing, whether through the influence of Dr. Frye or by natural inclination, are James Reaney, Jay Macpherson, and Eli Mandel.

Outside these somewhat artificial categories — which are only useful if they help us to observe the finer differences — there are poets who illustrate various spontaneous mixtures of whatever is possible in art or experience. These may actually parallel the New Romanticism of post-war British poetry, or the 'beat' style of the United States. But poets like Leonard Cohen, Gilles Vigneault, D. G. Jones, and Eldon Grier are beyond classification, individual, and independent of any school. Perhaps this freedom of mind and reliance on the opportunity of experience, without preconceptions, is the keynote of present poetry. And it is a good note to end with, just as it is a good beginning for whatever is still to come.

E. J. PRATT (1883-1964)

A wide-ranging writer and the foremost Canadian poet of this century, E. J. Pratt published sixteen books during his lifetime, in addition to two editions of his *Collected Poems*. Described by one critic as 'a Christian humanist', he affirms human courage and compassion against the ruthless elements of nature, yet the drama of his poetry turns on the constant possibility of a lapse from humanity and a reversion to nature's primitive violence:

> The snarl Neanderthal is worn
> Close to the smiling Aryan lips,
> The civil polish of the horn
> Gleams from our praying finger tips.

Born in Newfoundland, he was first educated there and followed in his father's footsteps as a Methodist preacher. In 1907 he went to Toronto to continue his studies, at first in theology, then in psychology and literature. He was given a doctoral degree in 1916, but after a stint of teaching psychology he turned to teaching literature, his destined career. He remained at the University of Toronto until his retirement.

His first books, *Rachel* (1917) and *Newfoundland Verse* (1923), were followed by *The Witches' Brew* (1925), a comic poem exploring the effect of alcohol upon the aquatic mind, and by *Titans*, which appeared in 1926, poems about monsters of the deep and their battles with man and nature. His later works include *The Titanic* (1935), *Brébeuf and His Brethren* (1940), and *Dunkirk* (1941). Pratt died in 1964 after a prolonged illness, honoured by the many Canadians who had loved and enjoyed his poetry.

The Child and the Wren

(To Claire)

It took three weeks to make them friends —
The wren in fear the maid molest
Those six white eggs within the nest
She built up at the gable-end.

What fearful language might be heard
(If only English she could speak)
On every day of the first week,
All from the throat of that small bird!

The scolding died away, and then
The fear was followed by surprise
At such sky-blue within the eyes,
That travelled from the girl to wren.

But that third week! I do not know —
It's neither yours to tell nor mine —
Some understanding glance or sign
Had passed between them to and fro;

For never was her face so flushed,
Never so brilliant blue her eye
At any gift that I could buy,
As at the news when in she rushed

To tell us that the wren had come,
With flutter and hop and gurgling sound,
From gable to tree, to shrub, to ground,
Right to her hand to get a crumb.

Cherries

'I'll never speak to Jamie again' —
Cried Jennie, 'let alone wed,
No, not till blackbirds' wings grow white,
And crab-apple trees grow cherries for spite,
But I'll marry Percy instead.'

But Jamie met her that self-same day,
Where crab-apple trees outspread,

And poured out his heart like a man insane,
And argued until he became profane,
That he never meant what he said.

Now strange as it seems, the truth must be told,
So wildly Jamie pled,
That cherries came out where the crab-apples grew,
And snow-winged blackbirds came down from the blue,
And feasted overhead.

The Dying Eagle

A light had gone out from his vanquished eyes;
His head was cupped within the hunch of his shoulders;
His feathers were dull and bedraggled; the tips
Of his wings sprawled down to the edge of his tail.
He was old, yet it was not his age
Which made him roost on the crags
Like a rain-drenched raven
On the branch of an oak in November.
Nor was it the night, for there was an hour
To go before sunset. An iron had entered
His soul which bereft him of pride and of realm,
Had struck him today; for up to noon
That crag had been his throne.
Space was his empire, bounded only
By forest and sky and the flowing horizons.
He had outfought, outlived all his rivals,
And the eagles that now were poised over glaciers
Or charting the coastal outlines of clouds
Were his by descent: they had been tumbled
Out of their rocky nests by his mate,
In the first trial of their fledgeling spins.

Only this morning the eyes of the monarch
Were held in arrest by a silver flash
Shining between two peaks of the ranges —
A sight which galvanized his back,
Bristled the feathers on his neck,
And shot little runnels of dust where his talons
Dug recesses in the granite.
Partridge? Heron? Falcon? Eagle?
Game or foe? He would reconnoitre.

Catapulting from the ledge,
He flew at first with rapid beat,
Level, direct: then with his grasp
Of spiral strategy in fight,
He climbed the orbit
With swift and easy undulations,
And reached position where he might
Survey the bird — for bird it was;
But such a bird as never flew
Between the heavens and the earth
Since pterodactyls, long before
The birth of condors, learned to kill
And drag their carrion up the Andes.

The eagle stared at the invader,
Marked the strange bat-like shadow moving
In leagues over the roofs of the world,
Across the passes and moraines,
Darkening the vitriol blue of the mountain lakes.
Was it a flying dragon? Head,
Body and wings, a tail fan-spread
And taut like his own before the strike;
And there in front two whirling eyes
That took unshuttered
The full blaze of the meridian.
The eagle never yet had known

202

A rival that he would not grapple,
But something in this fellow's length
Of back, his plated glistening shoulders,
Had given him pause. And did that thunder
Somewhere in his throat not argue
Lightning in his claws? And then
The speed — was it not double his own?
But what disturbed him most, angered
And disgraced him was the unconcern
With which this supercilious bird
Cut through the aquiline dominion,
Snubbing the ancient suzerain
With extra-territorial insolence,
And disappeared.

So evening found him on the crags again,
This time with sloven shoulders
And nerveless claws.
Dusk had outridden the sunset by an hour
To haunt his unhorizoned eyes.
And soon his flock flushed with the chase
Would be returning, threading their glorious curves
Up through the crimson archipelagoes
Only to find him there —
Deaf to the mighty symphony of wings,
And brooding
Over the lost empire of the peaks.

EMILE NELLIGAN (1879-1941)

A great and tragic figure in French-Canadian poetry, Emile Nelligan wrote all his poetry before he had reached the age of twenty. Mental illness ended his brief career and he lived the rest of his life a patient in a hospital near Montreal.

His father was Irish, his mother French. He was a lagging student, failing several times to pass his grades and obliged to give up his studies without finishing his classical course. As a young man he joined 'l'Ecole littéraire de Montréal', a literary society which met regularly at the historic Château de Ramezay to read from manuscript and discuss poetry. Here, on the memorable night of May 26, 1899, Nelligan recited his great poem 'Romance du vin'. His famous sonnet 'Le Vaisseau d'Or' is known to every schoolboy in Quebec as a poem that expresses his tragic fate in a single memorable image.

Nelligan's poetry was published in 1903, with a preface by Louis Dantin. It has since been reprinted in many editions and several critical studies exist of this important poet. English translations are available in P. F. Widdows' *Selected Poems of Emile Nelligan* (1960).

Le Vaisseau d'Or

Ce fut un grand Vaisseau taillé dans l'or massif:
Ses mâts touchaient l'azur, sur des mers inconnues;
La Cyprine d'amour, cheveux épars, chairs nues,
S'étalait à sa proue, au soleil excessif.

Mais il vint une nuit frapper le grand écueil
Dans l'Océan trompeur où chantait la Sirène,
Et le naufrage horrible inclina sa carène
Aux profondeurs du Gouffre, immuable cercueil.

Ce fut un Vaisseau d'Or, dont les flancs diaphanes
Révélaient des trésors que les marins profanes,
Dégoût, Haine et Névrose, entre eux ont disputés.

Que reste-t-il de lui dans la tempête brève?
Qu'est devenu mon coeur, navire déserté?
Hélas! Il a sombré dans l'abîme du Rêve!

The Golden Ship

(Translation by P. F. Widdows)

There was a fine Ship, carved from solid gold,
With azure-reaching masts, on seas unknown.
Spreadeagled Venus, naked, hair back-thrown,
Stood at the prow. The sun blazed uncontrolled.

But on the treacherous Ocean in the gloom
She struck the great reef where the Sirens chant.
Appalling shipwreck plunged her keel aslant
To the Gulf's depths, that unrelenting tomb.

She was a Golden Ship: but there showed through
Translucent sides treasures the blasphemous crew,
Hatred, Disgust and Madness, fought to share.

How much survives after the storm's brief race?
Where is my heart, that empty ship, oh where?
Alas, in Dream's abyss sunk without trace.

F. R. SCOTT (1899-   )

A first mover of Canadian poetry, F. R. Scott edited the *McGill Fortnightly Review* with A. J. M. Smith from 1925 to 1927, and was one of the editors of *The Canadian Mercury* (1928-9) and later of the magazine *Preview* (1942-5). In this way he initiated the new poetry of the 'Montreal school' and he has remained its enterprising spirit ever since.

Born in Quebec City, the son of Archdeacon F. G. Scott, he was educated at Bishop's College, Lennoxville, Quebec, and at Oxford, where he was distinguished as a Rhodes scholar. Later he entered the Law School at McGill University, and after graduation joined the McGill faculty. (He was appointed Dean of Law at McGill in 1961.) A distinguished lawyer and teacher, he has argued several important civil-liberties cases before the Supreme Court of Canada and other courts: the *Lady Chatterley* case, the repeal of the 'Padlock Law' in Quebec, and the plea of Roncarelli against the premier of the province.

His first poems appeared in *New Provinces* (1936), a collection of six poets of the modern school. *Overture* (1945), his first separate publication, displayed the full range of his satirical and reflective poetry. A variety of publications followed: *Events and Signals* (1954), *The Blasted Pine* (1957), which is an anthology of satire compiled jointly with A. J. M. Smith, *The Eye of the Needle* (1957), *Signature* (1964), and *St.-Denys Garneau, Anne Hébert: Translations* (1962).

F. R. Scott is a democrat, a socialist by conviction (he was National Chairman of the C.C.F. party from 1942 to 1950). A thirst after righteousness evoked into poetry characterizes his work. And a scientific outlook that sometimes conflicts with deeper emotions makes for a poetry of sharp wit and striking irony.

Old Song

> far voices
> and fretting leaves
> this music the
> hillside gives

but in the deep
Laurentian river
an elemental song
for ever

a quiet calling
of no mind
out of long aeons
when dust was blind
and ice hid sound

only a moving
with no note
granite lips
a stone throat

Tourist Time

This fat woman in canvas knickers
Gapes seriously at everything.
We might be a city of the dead
Or cave men
Instead of simple town folk.
We have nothing to show
That cannot be seen better somewhere else,
Yet for this woman the wonder does not cease.

Madam, the most extraordinary thing in this town
Is the shape of your legs.

O communication!
O rapid transit!

Summer Camp

(From *Social Notes*)

Here is a lovely little camp
Built among the Laurentian hills
By a Children's Welfare Society,
Which is entirely supported by voluntary contributions.
All summer long underprivileged children scamper about
And it is astonishing how soon they look happy and well.
Two weeks here in the sun and air
Through the charity of our wealthy citizens
Will be a wonderful help to the little tots
When they return for a winter in the slums.

Christmas Shopping

It is so nice for people to give things at Christmas
That the stores stay open every evening till ten,
And the shop-girls celebrate the coming of Christ
By standing on their feet fourteen hours a day.

Conflict

When I see the falling bombs
Then I see defended homes.
Men above and men below
Die to save the good they know.

Through the wrong the bullets prove
Shows the bravery of love.
Pro and con have single stem
Half a truth dividing them.

Between the dagger and the breast
The bond is stronger than the beast.
Prison, ghetto, flag and gun
Mark the craving for the One.

Persecution's cruel mouth
Shows a twisted love of truth.
Deeper than the rack and rope
Lies the double human hope.

My good, your good, good we seek
Though we turn no other cheek.
He who slays and he who's slain
Like in purpose, like in pain.

Who shall bend to single plan
The narrow sacrifice of man?
Find the central human urge
To make a thousand roads converge?

A. J. M. SMITH (1902-)

Our chief anthologist and *accoucheur* of modern poetry, A. J. M. Smith founded the *McGill Fortnightly Review* (1925-7) jointly with F. R. Scott and co-edited *New Provinces* in 1936. In 1943, on a Guggenheim Fellowship, he edited *The Book of Canadian Poetry*, the standard comprehensive anthology of Canadian poetry and one that for the first time showed the poetry of this century as a clear departure from the tradition of Bliss Carman and Archibald Lampman.

A. J. M. Smith was born in Montreal, educated at McGill University and Edinburgh University (Ph.D., 1931). Since 1936, an expatriate Canadian, he has been teaching at Michigan State University, but he has kept in contact with literary life in Canada. His first book, *News of the Phoenix*, appeared in 1943. *A Sort of Ecstasy* followed after a lapse of eleven years, in 1954. And a book of *Collected Poems* in 1962.

A. J. M. Smith is a perfectionist for whom the work of art, independently of its subject matter, is the main concern. Yet his poetry is deeply rooted in the conflict between Platonic absolutes — the unchanging essence of things — and the affirmation of sensuous real experience. Christianity in his poetry is often associated with the absolutes of the spirit, while images of lust or of contemporary reality serve as opposing counters.

In addition to his own poetry, he has edited *Seven Centuries of Verse* (1947), *The Worldly Muse* (1951), *The Blasted Pine* (1959, jointly with Scott), *Masks of Fiction* (1961), *Masks of Poetry* (1962), and *The Oxford Book of Canadian Verse* (1960). In 1965 he edited *A Pageant of Canadian Prose, Vol. I*. A second volume is in preparation.

The Lonely Land

> Cedar and jagged fir
> uplift sharp barbs
> against the gray
> and cloud-piled sky;
> and in the bay
> blown spume and windrift

and thin, bitter spray
snap
at the whirling sky;
and the pine trees
lean one way.

A wild duck calls
to her mate,
and the ragged
and passionate tones
stagger and fall,
and recover,
and stagger and fall,
on these stones —
are lost
in the lapping of water
on smooth, flat stones.

This is a beauty
of dissonance,
this resonance
of stony strand,
this smoky cry
curled over a black pine
like a broken
and wind-battered branch
when the wind
bends the tops of the pines
and curdles the sky
from the north.

This is the beauty
of strength
broken by strength
and still strong.

News of the Phoenix

They say the Phoenix is dying, some say dead.
Dead without issue is what one message said,
But that has been suppressed, officially denied.

I think myself the man who sent it lied.
In any case, I'm told, he has been shot,
As a precautionary measure, whether he did or not.

Beside One Dead

This is the sheath,
   the sword drawn,
These are the lips,
   the word spoken.
This is Calvary
   toward dawn;
And this is the
   third-day token —
The opened tomb
   and the Lord gone:
Something whole
   that was broken.

A. M. KLEIN (1909-   )

A member of the first modernist generation in Canada, A. M. Klein entered McGill University when Scott and Smith were editing the *McGill Fortnightly*. He did not appear in that magazine, but his first published poem came out in *The Canadian Mercury* which followed soon after. He was a frequent contributor to *The Canadian Forum* and other periodicals in the 1930s. His first book, *Hath Not a Jew*, appeared in 1940, and *Poems* in 1944.

Klein continued with law studies at the University of Montreal (Montreal's French-speaking university) after completing his work at McGill, and became a practising lawyer in 1933. His knowledge of French-Canadian life resulted in the book *The Rocking Chair and Other Poems* (1948). Here he departs from the exclusively Jewish themes he had previously pursued and adopts a satirical documentary style akin to that of Karl Shapiro in American poetry. *The Second Scroll* (1951), a blending of prose and poetry, is a parable of the return of the Jewish people to Israel and the search for a lost identity.

In addition to poetry, Klein has written an elaborate critical explication of James Joyce's *Ulysses*. Only parts of this criticism have as yet appeared. For some years serious illness has incapacitated him for further writing.

The Rocking Chair

It seconds the crickets of the province. Heard
in the clean lamplit farmhouses of Quebec, —
wooden, — it is no less a national bird;
and rivals, in its cage, the mere stuttering clock.
To its time, the evenings are rolled away;
and in its peace the pensive mother knits
contentment to be worn by her family,
grown-up, but still cradled by the chair in which she sits.

It is also the old man's pet, pair to his pipe,
the two aids of his arithmetic and plans,

plans rocking and puffing into market-shape;
and it is the toddler's game and dangerous dance.
Moved to the verandah, on summer Sundays, it is,
among the hanging plants, the girls, the boy-friends,
sabbatical and clumsy, like the white haloes
dangling above the blue serge suits of the young men.

It has a personality of its own;
is a character (like that old drunk Lacoste,
exhaling amber, and toppling on his pins);
it is alive; individual; and no less
an identity than those about it. And
it is tradition. Centuries have been flicked
from its arcs, alternately flicked and pinned.
It rolls with the gait of St. Malo. It is act

and symbol, symbol of this static folk
which moves in segments, and returns to base, —
a sunken pendulum; *invoke, revoke*;
loosed yon, leashed hither, motion on no space.
O, like some Anjou ballad, all refrain,
which turns about its longing, and seems to move
to make a pleasure out of repeated pain,
its music moves, as if always back to a first love.

Lookout: Mount Royal

Remembering boyhood, it is always here
the boy in blouse and kneepants on the road
trailing his stick over the hopscotched sun;
or here, upon the suddenly moving hill;
or at the turned tap its cold white mandarin mustaches;
or at the lookout, finally,
breathing easy, standing still

to click the eye on motion forever stopped:
the photographer's tripod and his sudden faces
buoyed up by water on his magnet caught
still smiling as if under water still;
the exclamatory tourists descending the caleches;
the maids in starch; the ladies in white gloves;
other kids of other slums and races;
and on the bridle-paths
the horsemen on their horses like the tops of f's:

or from the parapet make out
beneath the green marine
the discovered road, the hospital's romantic
gables and roofs, and all the civic Euclid
running through sunken parallels and lolling
in diamond and square, then proud-pedantical
with spire and dome
making its way to the sought point, his home.

home recognized: there: to be returned to —

lets the full birdseye circle to the river,
its singsong bridges, its mapmaker curves, its
island with the two shades of green, meadow and wood;
and circles round that water-tower'd coast;
then, to the remote rhapsodic mountains; then,
— and to be lost —
to clouds like white slow friendly animals
which all the afternoon across his eyes
will move their paced spaced footfalls.

SAINT-DENYS GARNEAU (1912-1943)

The French-Canadian poet of this century most widely discussed and admired, Saint-Denys Garneau died at the age of thirty-one. He had published only one book, *Regards et jeux dans l'espace* (1937), which remains a turning-point in the development of French-Canadian poetry. After his death, additional poems were gathered together to form the *Poésies complètes* (1949) and an important *Journal*, covering the years from 1935 to 1939, was published in 1954.

Hector de Saint-Denys Garneau was a descendant of a distinguished family. Among his forebears were the historian François-Xavier Garneau, author of a notable *Histoire du Canada*, and Alfred Garneau the poet. As a young man, Saint-Denys Garneau was active, athletic, and exuberant. But a heart lesion in his twenty-second year, while he was still a student, cut short his active career and he went into meditative retirement at Sainte-Catherine-de-Fossambault, a small village north of Quebec City. Here he wrote his last poems and his famous journal.

The poetry of Saint-Denys Garneau is deeply reflective, concerned with the ultimate questions of reality and spiritual illumination. The world of men appears tenuous and unreal to this religious sensibility groping in a shadow-land on the verge of the unknown. Yet he depicts the human condition, in its spiritual state of deprivation, with great fidelity and insight. It is an example that other poets in our time were to follow.

English versions of Saint-Denys Garneau are available in F. R. Scott's *St.-Denys Garneau, Anne Hébert: Translations* (1962).

Cage d'oiseau

Je suis une cage d'oiseau
Une cage d'os
Avec un oiseau

L'oiseau dans sa cage d'os
C'est la mort qui fait son nid

Lorsque rien n'arrive
On entend froisser ses ailes

Et quand on a ri beaucoup
Si l'on cesse tout à coup
On l'entend qui roucoule
Au fond
Comme un grelot

C'est un oiseau tenu captif
La mort dans ma cage d'os

Voudrait-il pas s'envoler
Est-ce vous qui le retiendrez
Est-ce moi
Qu'est-ce que c'est

Il ne pourra s'en aller
Qu'après avoir tout mangé
Mon coeur
La source du sang
Avec la vie dedans

Il aura mon âme au bec.

Bird Cage

(Translation by F. R. Scott)

I am a bird cage
A cage of bone
With a bird

The bird in the cage of bone
Is death building his nest

When nothing is happening
One can hear him ruffle his wings

And when one has laughed a lot
If one suddenly stops
One hears him cooing
Far down
Like a small bell

It is a bird held captive
This death in my cage of bone

Would he not like to fly away
Is it you who will hold him back
Is it I
What is it

He cannot fly away
Until he has eaten all
My heart
The source of blood
With my life inside

He will have my soul in his beak.

Accompagnement

Je marche à côté d'une joie
D'une joie qui n'est pas à moi
D'une joie que je ne puis pas prendre

Je marche à côté de moi en joie
J'entends mon pas en joie qui marche à côté de moi
Mais je ne puis changer de place sur le trottoir
Je ne puis pas mettre mes pieds dans ces pas-là
　　　　　et dire voilà c'est moi

Je me contente pour le moment de cette compagnie
Mais je machine en secret des échanges

Par toutes sortes d'opérations, des alchimies,
Par des transfusions de sang
Des déménagements d'atomes
                par des jeux d'équilibre

Afin qu'un jour, transposé,
Je sois porté par la danse de ces pas de joie
Avec le bruit décroissant de mon pas à côté de moi
Avec la perte de mon pas perdu
                s'étiolant à ma gauche
Sous les pieds d'un étranger
                qui prend une rue transversale.

Accompaniment

(Translation by F. R. Scott)

I walk beside a joy
Beside a joy that is not mine
A joy of mine which I cannot take

I walk beside myself in joy
I hear my footsteps in joy marching beside me
But I cannot change places on the sidewalk
I cannot put my feet in those steps and say
                Look it is I

For the moment I am content with this company
But secretly I plot an exchange
By all sorts of devices, by alchemies,
By blood transfusions
Displacement of atoms
        by balancing tricks

So that one day, transposed,
I may be carried along by the dance of those steps of joy

With the noise of my footstep dying away beside me
With the fall of my own lost step
              fading to my left
Under the feet of a stranger
         who turns down a side street.

Portrait

C'est un drôle d'enfant
C'est un oiseau
Il n'est plus là

Il s'agit de le trouver
De le chercher
Quand il est là

Il s'agit de ne pas lui faire peur
C'est un oiseau
C'est un colimaçon.

Il ne regarde que pour vous embrasser
Autrement il ne sait pas quoi faire
                              avec ses yeux

Où les poser
Il les tracasse comme un paysan sa casquette

Il lui faut aller vers vous
Et quand il s'arrête
Et s'il arrive
Il n'est plus là

Alors il faut le voir venir
Et l'aimer durant son voyage.

Portrait

(Translation by Louis Dudek)

He's such a funny kid
He's just like a bird
Already gone

You've got to find him
To seek him out
Once he's there

You've got to mind you don't scare him
He's just like a bird
Or he's like a snail

He only looks at you to give you a kind of hug
Otherwise he does not know what to do
                              with his eyes

Or where to put them
He shuffles them as a peasant shuffles his cap

He has to come toward you
And when he comes to a stop
And if he comes near you
He is no longer there

So it's important to watch him coming
And to love him while he's on the way.

Patricia K. Page was very active in the poetry movement in Montreal in the 1940s — she was one of the editors of the little magazine *Preview* — but she has abandoned poetry since and has turned to painting and drawing as a means of expression.

Born in England, she was brought to Canada as a child and was educated in Calgary, Alberta. Later she met Alan Crawley, editor of the Vancouver magazine *Contemporary Verse* (1941-51), who encouraged her interest in modern verse. She joined the *Preview* group in Montreal and contributed some of her most memorable poems to that magazine. *Unit of Five* (1944) contained a group of her poems. *As Ten as Twenty* appeared in 1946. Under a pseudonym, Judith Cape, she published a novel, *The Sun and the Moon*. After a lapse of ten years, a second book of poems, *The Metal and the Flower*, appeared in 1954.

The Bands and the Beautiful Children

Band makes a tunnel of the open street
at first, hearing it;
seeing it, band becomes
high; brasses ascending on the strings of sun
build their own auditorium of light,
windows from cornets
and a dome of drums.

And always attendant on bands, the beautiful children,
white with running and innocence;
and the arthritic old
who, patient behind their windows
are no longer split by the quick yellow of imagination
or carried beyond their angular limits of distance.

But the children move
in the trembling building of sound,

sure as a choir
until band breaks and scatters,
crumbles about them and is made of men
tired and grumbling
on the straggling grass.

And the children, lost, lost,
in an open space,
remember the certainty of the anchored home
and cry on the unknown edge of their own city
their lips stiff from an imaginary trumpet.

The Permanent Tourists

Somnolent through landscapes and by trees
nondescript, almost anonymous,
they alter as they enter foreign cities —
the terrible tourists with their empty eyes
longing to be filled with monuments.

Verge upon statues in the public squares
remembering the promise of memorials
yet never enter the entire event
as dogs, abroad in any kind of weather,
move perfectly within their rainy climate.

Lock themselves into snapshots on the steps
of monolithic bronze as if suspecting
the subtle mourning of the photograph
might, later, conjure in the memory
all they are now incapable of feeling.

And track all heroes down: the boy who gave
his life to save a town: the stolid queen;
forgotten politicians minus names;

the plunging war dead, permanently brave,
forever and ever going down to death.

Look, you can see them nude in any café
reading their histories from the bill of fare,
creating futures from a foreign teacup.
Philosophies like ferns bloom from the fable
that travel is broadening at the café table.

Yet, somehow beautiful, they stamp the plaza.
Classic in their anxiety they call
all the memorials of naked stone
into their passive eyes, as placid rivers
are always calling to the ruined columns.

ANNE WILKINSON (1910-1961)

A descendant of the Osler family, born in Toronto, Anne Wilkinson was educated in schools in the United States and abroad. She attracted notice as a poet in 1951 with the publication of *Counterpoint to Sleep*. This was a First Statement book, produced by John Sutherland, who was then editor of *Northern Review* (1945-56), the chief outlet of the new poetry in Montreal. *The Hangman Ties the Holly* followed in 1955, and a prose history of the Osler family, *Lions in the Way*, appeared in 1956. *Swann and Daphne* (1960) is an imaginative book for young readers.

Anne Wilkinson's poetry is witty, swift, brittle, and highly charged with individual sensibility. She reveals a love of life that is touched with sadness, with a premonition of death, like the poetry of Saint-Denys Garneau. Her poems were written under the shadow of an illness that caused her death in the winter of 1961.

Alleluia

No fanfare of flowers
But an almost inaudible
Clatter of bells
As the last icicle falls
And rivers ride again
And warn their banks
To warn the woods
And the waking worm

Of the coming Passion of our Soil,
An oratorio rehearsed by treble birds
But bursting bass from earth. O hear
The vegetable kingdom swell
And life explode,
The sound upheaved about our ears
By cabbages and cauliflower

And the gangly stalks of fresh risen corn
And radishes newborn
And row on row of cheering lettuces
Proclaiming their authentic green.

On a Bench in a Park

On a bench in a park
Where I went walking
A boy and girl,
Their new hearts breaking,
Sat side by side
And miles apart
And they wept most bitterly.

'Why do you mourn,'
I asked,
'You, who are barely born?'

'For gold that is gone,'
Said the girl,
'I weep distractedly.'

I turned to the youth,
'And you?'
'For what I have not gained,' he cried,
'Possessing her
I lost myself and died.'

And so we sat, a trio
Tuned to sobs,
And miles to go
And miles and miles apart

Till they, amazed
That one as old as I

Had juice enough for tears,
Dried their streaming eyes
To ask the cause of mine.

I told of the grit I'd found
In a grain of truth,
Mentioned an aching tooth
Decayed with fears
And the sum of all I'd lost
In the increased tax on years.

They yawned and rose
And walked away. I moved
To go but death sat down.
His cunning hand
Explored my skeleton.

I Am So Tired

I am so tired I do not think
Sleep in death can rest me

So line my two eternal yards
With softest moss
Then lengths of bone won't splinter
As they toss
Or pierce their wooden box
To winter

Do not let the children
Pass my way alone
Lest these shaking bones
Rattle out their fright
At waking in the night

EARLE BIRNEY (1904-   )

A prolific writer of the same generation as F. R. Scott and A. J. M. Smith, Earle Birney as a Westerner was for some time cut off from the centre of Canadian literary activity. His first book, *David and Other Poems*, appeared in 1942 and immediately placed him in the forefront of modern poetry.

Born in Calgary, he was brought up in Alberta. Later he studied at the University of British Columbia and at Toronto. He then taught in various colleges in the United States, but he returned to Canada to complete a doctoral degree at Toronto in 1936. He was literary editor of *The Canadian Forum* for the next five years while lecturing at the University of Toronto, and later for two years edited the *Canadian Poetry Magazine*. During the war he served overseas as a personnel officer. His second book, *Now Is Time*, appeared at the close of the war, in 1945.

For a time Birney acted as supervisor of foreign-language broadcasts for the CBC in Montreal, an experience which contributed to his next book, *The Strait of Anian* (1948). His comic war novel *Turvey* (1949) was hugely popular with a wide audience of readers. *Trial of a City* (1952) is a verse play in the style of Archibald MacLeish, displaying further his range of humour and satire. Birney has edited an anthology, *Twentieth-Century Canadian Poetry* (1953), and has published a second novel, *Down the Long Table* (1955). *Ice Cod Bell or Stone* (1962) is a collection of experimental and highly entertaining verse as well as poems of serious intent. His most recent book is *Near False Creek Mouth* (1964).

Like other poets of the Thirties generation, Birney has been strongly committed to themes of social realism. He has been described by Desmond Pacey as a 'chronicler of Canadian life' in the post-war period, a tribute to his range and documentary style. But he is also a reflective poet and a craftsman on a superior scale. Like Archibald MacLeish he is a professional writer who has mastered his materials and techniques and writes with deliberate skill. He is also one of the few poets among us who has won a certain recognition in the United States and abroad.

David

David and I that summer cut trails on the Survey,
All week in the valley for wages, in air that was steeped
In the wail of mosquitoes, but over the sunalive week-
    ends
We climbed, to get from the ruck of the camp, the surly

Poker, the wrangling, the snoring under the fetid
Tents, and because we had joy in our lengthening
    coltish
Muscles, and mountains for David were made to see
    over,
Stairs from the valleys and steps to the sun's retreats.

II

Our first was Mount Gleam. We hiked in the long
    afternoon
To a curling lake and lost the lure of the faceted
Cone in the swell of its sprawling shoulders. Past
The inlet we grilled our bacon, the strips festooned

On a poplar prong, in the hurrying slant of the sunset.
Then the two of us rolled in the blanket while around us
    the cold
Pines thrust at the stars. The dawn was a floating
Of mists till we reached to the slopes above timber,
    and won

To snow like fire in the sunlight. The peak was
    upthrust
Like a fist in a frozen ocean of rock that swirled
Into valleys the moon could be rolled in. Remotely
    unfurling
Eastward the alien prairie glittered. Down through
    the dusty

229

Skree on the west we descended, and David showed me
How to use the give of shale for giant incredible
Strides. I remember, before the larches' edge,
That I jumped a long green surf of juniper flowing

Away from the wind, and landed in gentian and saxifrage
Spilled on the moss. Then the darkening firs
And the sudden whirring of water that knifed down a
    fern-hidden
Cliff and splashed unseen into mist in the shadows.

III

One Sunday on Rampart's arête a rainsquall caught us,
And passed, and we clung by our blueing fingers and
    bootnails
An endless hour in the sun, not daring to move
Till the ice had steamed from the slate. And David
    taught me

How time on a knife-edge can pass with the guessing of
    fragments
Remembered from poets, the naming of strata beside
    one,
And matching of stories from schooldays. . . . We
    crawled astride
The peak to feast on the marching ranges flagged

By the fading shreds of the shattered stormcloud.
    Lingering
There it was David who spied to the south, remote,
And unmapped, a sunlit spire on Sawback, an overhang
Crooked like a talon. David named it the Finger.

That day we chanced on the skull and the splayed
    white ribs
Of a mountain goat underneath a cliff-face, caught

On a rock. Around were the silken feathers of hawks.
And that was the first I knew that a goat could slip.

IV

And then Inglismaldie. Now I remember only
The long ascent of the lonely valley, the live
Pine spirally scarred by lightning, the slicing pipe
Of invisible pika, and great prints, by the lowest

Snow, of a grizzly. There it was too that David
Taught me to read the scroll of coral in limestone
And the beetle-seal in the shale of ghostly trilobites,
Letters delivered to man from the Cambrian waves.

V

On Sundance we tried from the col and the going was
    hard.
The air howled from our feet to the smudged rocks
And the papery lake below. At an outthrust we balked
Till David clung with his left to a dint in the scarp,

Lobbed the iceaxe over the rocky lip,
Slipped from his holds and hung by the quivering pick,
Twisted his long legs up into space and kicked
To the crest. Then grinning, he reached with his
    freckled wrist

And drew me up after. We set a new time for that
    climb.
That day returning we found a robin gyrating
In grass, wing-broken. I caught it to tame but David
Took and killed it, and said, 'Could you teach it to
    fly?'

VI

In August, the second attempt, we ascended The
    Fortress.

By the forks of the Spray we caught five trout and fried
    them
Over a balsam fire. The woods were alive
With the vaulting of mule-deer and drenched with
    clouds all the morning,

Till we burst at noon to the flashing and floating round
Of the peaks. Coming down we picked in our hats the
    bright
And sunhot raspberries, eating them under a mighty
Spruce, while a marten moving like quicksilver scouted
    us.

VII

But always we talked of the Finger on Sawback,
    unknown
And hooked, till the first afternoon in September we
    slogged
Through the musky woods, past a swamp that quivered
    with frog-song,
And camped by a bottle-green lake. But under the cold

Breath of the glacier sleep would not come, the moon-
    light
Etching the Finger. We rose and trod past the
    feathery
Larch, while the stars went out, and the quiet heather
Flushed, and the skyline pulsed with the surging bloom

Of incredible dawn in the Rockies. David spotted
Bighorns across the moraine and sent them leaping
With yodels the ramparts redoubled and rolled to the
    peaks,
And the peaks to the sun. The ice in the morning thaw

Was a gurgling world of crystal and cold blue chasms,
And seracs that shone like frozen saltgreen waves.

At the base of the Finger we tried once and failed.
    Then David
Edged to the west and discovered the chimney; the last

Hundred feet we fought the rock and shouldered and
    kneed
Our way for an hour and made it. Unroping we formed
A cairn on the rotting tip. Then I turned to look north
At the glistening wedge of giant Assiniboine, heedless

Of handhold. And one foot gave. I swayed and
    shouted.
David turned sharp and reached out his arm and
    steadied me,
Turning again with a grin and his lips ready
To jest. But the strain crumbled his foothold. Without

A gasp he was gone. I froze to the sound of grating
Edge-nails and fingers, the slither of stones, the lone
Second of silence, the nightmare thud. Then only
The wind and the muted beat of unknowing cascades.

VIII

Somehow I worked down the fifty impossible feet
To the ledge, calling and getting no answer but echoes
Released in the cirque, and trying not to reflect
What an answer would mean. He lay still, with his
    lean

Young face upturned and strangely unmarred, but his
    legs
Splayed beneath him, beside the final drop,
Six hundred feet sheer to the ice. My throat stopped
When I reached him, for he was alive. He opened his
    grey

Straight eyes and brokenly murmured 'over . . . over.'
And I, feeling beneath him a cruel fang

Of the ledge thrust in his back, but not understanding,
Mumbled stupidly, 'Best not to move,' and spoke

Of his pain. But he said, 'I can't move . . . If only I felt
Some pain.' Then my shame stung the tears to my
    eyes
As I crouched, and I cursed myself, but he cried,
Louder, 'No, Bobbie! Don't ever blame yourself.

I didn't test my foothold.' He shut the lids
Of his eyes to the stare of the sky, while I moistened his
    lips
From our water flask and tearing my shirt into strips
I swabbed the shredded hands. But the blood slid

From his side and stained the stone and the thirsting
    lichens,
And yet I dared not lift him up from the gore
Of the rock. Then he whispered, 'Bob, I want to go
    over!'
This time I knew what he meant and I grasped for a lie

And said, 'I'll be back here by midnight with ropes
And men from the camp and we'll cradle you out.'
    But I knew
That the day and the night must pass and the cold dews
Of another morning before such men unknowing

The ways of mountains could win to the chimney's top.
And then, how long? And he knew . . . and the hell
    of hours
After that, if he lived till we came, roping him out.
But I curled beside him and whispered, 'The bleeding
    will stop.

You can last.' He said only, 'Perhaps . . . For
    what? A wheelchair,

Bob?' His eyes brightening with fever upbraided me.
I could not look at him more and said, 'Then I'll stay
With you.' But he did not speak, for the clouding
    fever.

I lay dazed and stared at the long valley,
The glistening hair of a creek on the rug stretched
By the firs, while the sun leaned round and flooded the
    ledge,
The moss, and David still as a broken doll.

I hunched to my knees to leave, but he called and his
    voice
Now was sharpened with fear. 'For Christ's sake push
    me over!
If I could move . . . Or die . . . ' The sweat ran from
    his forehead,
But only his eyes moved. A hawk was buoying

Blackly its wings over the wrinkled ice.
The purr of a waterfall rose and sank with the wind.
Above us climbed the last joint of the Finger
Beckoning bleakly the wide indifferent sky.

Even then in the sun it grew cold lying there . . . And
    I knew
He had tested his holds. It was I who had not . . . I
    looked
At the blood on the ledge, and the far valley. I looked
At last in his eyes. He breathed, 'I'd do it for you, Bob.'

IX

I will not remember how nor why I could twist
Up the wind-devilled peak, and down through the
    chimney's empty
Horror, and over the traverse alone. I remember
Only the pounding fear I would stumble on It

When I came to the grave-cold maw of the bergschrund
    . . . reeling
Over the sun-cankered snowbridge, shying the caves
In the névé . . . the fear, and the need to make sure
    It was there
On the ice, the running and falling and running,
    leaping

Of gaping greenthroated crevasses, alone and pursued
By the Finger's lengthening shadow. At last through
    the fanged
And blinding seracs I slid to the milky wrangling
Falls at the glacier's snout, through the rocks piled huge

On the humped moraine, and into the spectral larches,
Alone. By the glooming lake I sank and chilled
My mouth but I could not rest and stumbled still
To the valley, losing my way in the ragged marsh.

I was glad of the mire that covered the stains, on my
    ripped
Boots, of his blood, but panic was on me, the reek
Of the bog, the purple glimmer of toadstools obscene
In the twilight. I staggered clear to a firewaste,
    tripped

And fell with a shriek on my shoulder. It somehow
    eased
My heart to know I was hurt, but I did not faint
And I could not stop while over me hung the range
Of the Sawback. In blackness I searched for the trail
    by the creek

And found it . . . My feet squelched a slug and
    horror
Rose again in my nostrils. I hurled myself

Down the path. In the woods behind some animal
    yelped.
Then I saw the glimmer of tents and babbled my story.

I said that he fell straight to the ice where they found
    him.
And none but the sun and incurious clouds have
    lingered
Around the marks of that day on the ledge of the
    Finger,
That day, the last of my youth, on the last of our
    mountains.

Status quo

Now every spraying syllable
    veneering private gain
shall gloss another farmboy for
    the toy-display of pain.

For ten lies from a radio
    and twenty on a page
a hundred thousand charming eyes
    will aim the atom's rage.

For every nose despised,
    for each dishonoured skin,
steelpelted herds of elephants
    will trumpet out our sin.

The boundaries of nations
    wrinkle the heart of man
and rats in history's basement gnaw
    the half-deciphered plan.

The slumgirl locked from life,
 the lane where hate leans tall,
maintain a world of gallant growth
 blocked by the bullet's wall.

This mouth we teach to speak
 first of itself alone
will conjure back the Belsen breath
 and raise a town of bone.

Time-bomb

In this friend's face I know
 the grizzly still, and in the mirror;
lay my ear to the radio's conch
 and hear the atom's terror.

In each high stalk of wheat
 I watch osmotic rise of blood;
through nightsky see new firedrakes hosed
 with light and lead.

Within the politician's ribs,
 within my own, the time-bombs tick.
O men be swift to be mankind
 or let the grizzly take.

For George Lamming

To you
 I can risk words about this

Mastering them you know
 they are dull
  servants

who say less
    and worse
            than we feel

That party above Kingston Town
        we stood   five (six?) couples
linked singing
        more than rum happy
I was giddy
        from sudden friendship
        wanted   undeserved
        black tulip faces
self swaying forgotten
        laughter in dance

Suddenly on a wall mirror
        my face assaulted me
stunned to see itself
        like a white snail
        in the supple dark flowers
Always now
        I move grateful
                to all of you
who let me walk thoughtless
        and unchallenged
in the gardens
        in the castles
                of your skins

ROY DANIELLS (1902-   )

A formalist, a writer of quiet measured lines, Roy Daniells is a scholar, Head of the English Department at the University of British Columbia, and author of two books of poetry, *Deeper into the Forest* (1948) and *The Chequered Shade* (1963). He has also written a book on John Milton and edited the sermons of Thomas Traherne.

An expert with the sonnet, he has written in his poetry about modern man's moral predicament, about the human past, and about the struggle to build a future in Canada. Primarily a poet in the older tradition, he may be compared with poets such as Robert Graves, Edwin Muir, or Richard Wilbur in England and America.

Psalm 23

My enemies were certain I was starving,
It must have given them a fearful shock
Through the binoculars to see me carving
A roast of beef up on the barren rock.
And when I moved upon them down a byway,
Bathed and anointed, sweet with oil of rose,
They blanched for they had left me on the highway
Covered with blood and with a broken nose.
The landlord, in the arbour where I'm seated,
Has brimmed the bowl with wine, the bubbles wink.
It's time my gasping enemies were treated,
Do tell them to come in and have a drink.
And any day they like they may appear;
Thanks to the landlord, I'll be living here.

All Through the 'Thirties

All through the 'thirties, south of Saskatoon,
A farmer farmed a farm without a crop.
Dust filled the air, the lamp was lit at noon,
And never blade of wheat that formed a top.
One New Year's to the hired man he said,
'I have no money. You must take the deeds.
And I will be the hired man instead,
To shovel snow and fork the tumbleweeds.'
So it was done. And when the next year came,
'Take back the farm,' the other had to say.
And year by year, alternate, just the same
Till the War came and took them both away.
With such superb resource and self-possession
Canada made it through the long depression.

For many years unpublished in book form, the poems of Margaret Avison were only available in scattered periodicals and in a few anthologies. Yet her reputation in Canada was firmly established by this occasional appearance. The publication of *Winter Sun* in 1960 immediately placed her work among her peers on the select shelf of Canadian poets of this century.

Born in Galt, Ontario, she was educated at the University of Toronto. She is a librarian by occupation, and her poetry is both learned and directly related to experience. The images are usually concrete and clear, but the detail of observation is so closely packed that reading her poems requires close attention. A ready comparison would be with the poetry of Marianne Moore, among the American poets; or with Emily Dickinson, for the moral and religious implications. It is, in any case, a feminine sensibility that she displays, and one of a high poetic order. The best study of Margaret Avison is an article by Milton Wilson in *Canadian Literature* (Autumn, 1959).

Hiatus

The weedy light through the uncurtained glass
Finds foreign space where the piano was,
And mournful airs from the propped-open door
Follow forlorn shreds of excelsior.
Though the towel droops with sad significance
All else is gone; one last reviewing glance,
One last misplacing, finding of the key,
And the last steps echo, and fade, and die.

　　　Then wanderer, with a hundred things to see to,
Scores of decisions waiting on your veto,
Or worse, being made at random till you come
So weeks will pass before you feel at home,
Mover unmoved, how can you choose this hour

To prowl at large around a hardware store?
When you have purchased the superfluous wrench
You wander still, and watch the late sun drench
The fruit-stalls, pavements, shoppers, cars, as though
All were invisible and safe but you.
    But in your mind's ear now resounds the din
Of friends who've come to help you settle in,
And your thoughts fumble, as you start the car,
On whether somebody marked the barrel where the glasses
    are.

JOHN GLASSCO (1909-   )

John Glassco was a 'sleeper' in Canadian poetry until the publication of his book *The Deficit Made Flesh* in 1958. He had contributed to the *McGill Fortnightly* and to the European little magazines *Transition* and *This Quarter* in the 1920s, but he had not published a separate book. An expert horseman, Glassco has long been a breeder of hackney ponies at Foster, Quebec; in 1951 he started the Foster Horse Show, an annual event famous in that region. His poetry deals largely with country life, but it is rural in the real sense, never sentimental; and the tone and technique belong to the twentieth century. As a translator, he has done *The Journal of Saint-Denys Garneau*, and he is working on a translation of the complete poetry of this poet.

Quebec Farmhouse

Admire the face of plastered stone,
 The roof descending like a song
  Over the washed and anointed walls,
Over the house that hugs the earth
Like a feudal souvenir: oh see
The sweet submissive fortress of itself
  That the landscape owns!

And inside is the night, the airless dark
 Of the race so conquered it has made
  Perpetual conquest of itself,
Upon desertion's ruin piling
The inward desert of surrender,
Drawing in all its powers, puffing its soul,
  Raising its arms to God.

This is the closed, enclosing house
 That set its flinty face against
  The rebel children dowered with speech

To break it open, to make it live
And flower in the cathedral beauty
Of a pure heaven of Canadian blue —
        The larks so maimed

They still must hark and hurry back
    To the paradisal place of gray,
    The clash of keys, the click of beads,
    The sisters walking leglessly,
    While under the wealth and weight of stone
All the bright demons of forbidden joy
        Shriek on, year after year.

R. G. EVERSON (1903-   )

Educated for the law, and formerly a practising lawyer, R. G. Everson is head of a public-relations firm in Montreal but a serious poet by avocation. His poems have appeared frequently in the *Atlantic Monthly*, *Poetry* (Chicago), *Saturday Review*, and other well-known journals. They contain an astringent, pithy quality that is vastly informed and canny about the ways of life, yet humane and wittily at odds with cruelty and unkindness. A quiet, reflective poetry is his forte.

Born in Oshawa, Ontario, he is 'a seventh-generation Canadian', strongly conscious of Canada's history. His published books are *Three Dozen Poems* (1957), *A Lattice for Momos* (1958), *Blind Man's Holiday* (1963), and *Wrestle with an Angel* (1965).

Greeks Had Nothing Else To Do

An ancient Greek awoke at dawn,
shook loose his blanket which he then put on,
draped it elegantly around him for a cloak.
Unhindered by TV, radio, books, newspaper
or breakfast, which he did not have, he went out

against no traffic. In a caper
an Athenian reached work, which was right there
near home. When he returned at night
the classic soil, stripped bare, classic light,
did not impose on him lawn-mowing.
Also, Greeks didn't go in for woman-wooing.

Nothing else to do, even I might romp,
inventing choral odes, all literature
and thought, engaging in a footrace or a war
against my city's state of Persian pomp.

Credo

Passionate human love, the scenes of nature,
agony of bringing into life
child, or thought, or sound, or shaped colour
— these triumph over our lives' horror. Power
    and vanity go raging out of mind.

Even Science, Paul of our age,
circuit-riding among the gentile suns,
is no lord of this blotpage
cheerfully ballpointing nine lines.

RALPH GUSTAFSON (1909-   )

A skilful technician with both the plain and the arcane word ('Wenk-chemna' is a small valley in the Rockies, not to be found in many gazetteers), Ralph Gustafson was a professional writer for many years in New York, an anthologist, and a contributor to CBC dramatic pro-grams. An expert musicologist, he has also presented his rare-record col-lections on the air. He now teaches literature at Bishop's University in Lennoxville, Quebec.

Among his books of poetry are *The Golden Chalice* (1935), *Alfred the Great* (1937), a verse play, *Epithalamium in Time of War* (1941), *Lyrics Unromantic* (1942), *Flight into Darkness* (1946), *Rivers among Rocks* (1960), and *Rocky Mountain Poems* (1960). He has also pub-lished a book of short stories, *Summer Storm* (1958), and he has edited three Penguin anthologies of Canadian writing.

Essentially an experimentalist, he writes poems that must be carefully studied to be enjoyed. Like Hopkins, his frequent model, he wrenches words from their usual positions and gives them special point by line-breaks (enjambments) and pauses that create a modern music of excep-tional timbre.

In the Valley of Wenkchemna

> Spunsilkengreen,
> It hovered,
> Bit the flower;
> And went.
> There was snow
> Nearby,
> But it was summer;
> Glacial snow,
> Patchwhites of it
> On northsides
> Of boulder
> And cirque.

This was high
In the mountains
Of hemlock
And rushing
Marbled,
Rockflour creeks,
But clear lakes
Made from it,
High
In the mountains.
You had
Sweatersweat
To get to them,
Climbing through
Darkwork
Where forests were,
And near
Glaciers,
Rottenstone.
You sweated from branch-
And stone-work,
Rewarded
In the valley
With the sight
Of snownear
Green hummingbird.

More widely read and discussed than any other Canadian poet in recent years, Irving Layton represents a thorough break with Canada's genteel, conformist traditions. Robert Service had already chanted 'the ancient outworn puritanic traditions of right and of wrong', but Layton has belaboured conformity, Calvinism, prudery, and plain dullness with a direct fury and passion unequalled by any Canadian past or present.

Born in Romania, Layton arrived in Canada at the age of twelve months and has been protesting ever since. Reputedly a good street-fighter as a boy, he was educated in schools in the tough Main Street sector of Montreal, which he has described vividly in poetry. Later he studied agriculture at Macdonald College and political science at McGill University. He was a teacher at a small school in Montreal for many years, and recently he has been lecturing at Sir George Williams University in that city.

Layton is the author of some fourteen books of poetry. The first of these was *Here and Now* in 1945. After many years of moderate productivity, he became a prolific writer, starting with *The Black Huntsmen* in 1951. Nine books followed in the next five years, among them *Love the Conqueror Worm* (1952), *In the Midst of My Fever* (1954), and *The Cold Green Element* (1955). Layton's collected poetry is available under the title *Collected Poems* (1965).

First Snow: Lake Achigan

No noise of rowlocks, no ecstasy of hands,
No sound of crickets in the inextricable air:
But a Roman silence for a lone drummer's call.

Now noiseless as a transaction, a brown hare
Breaks from the cold fields, bounds ahead;
Now slowly slowly the season unwinters
On its spool of white thread.

Lonely and fleshed with hates, who here
Would be God's angry man, a thundering Paul
When December, a toga'd Cato, slow to anger,
At last speaks the word that condemns us all.

From Colony to Nation

A dull people,
but the rivers of this country
are wide and beautiful

A dull people
enamoured of childish games,
but food is easily come by
and plentiful

Some with a priest's voice
in their cage of ribs: but
on high mountain-tops and in thunderstorms
the chirping is not heard

Deferring to beadle and censor;
not ashamed for this,
but given over to horseplay,
and making of money

A dull people, without charm
or ideas,
settling into the clean empty look
of a Mountie or dairy farmer
as into a legacy

One can ignore them
(the silences, the vast distances help)
and suppose them at the bottom
of one of the meaner lakes,
their bones not even picked for souvenirs.

Anglo-Canadian

A native of Kingston, Ont.
— two grandparents Canadian
and still living

His complexion florid
as a maple leaf in late autumn,
for three years he attended
Oxford

Now his accent
makes even Englishmen
wince, and feel
unspeakably colonial.

RAYMOND SOUSTER (1921-   )

Raymond Souster is a Toronto poet with a unique directness of style and a gift for observation that make him the most representative of the poets of the 1940s in Canada. Associated with the Montreal group of *First Statement* and *Northern Review*, later himself the editor of *Contact* magazine and an editor of Contact Press (the outlet for much *avant-garde* poetry in Canada since 1952), he has been at the centre of the literary movement stemming from Montreal and he has enriched our poetry with currents from abroad.

He was born in Toronto and briefly educated there. During the war he served in the R.C.A.F. overseas, an experience that has contributed much to his poetry. After the war, he returned to Toronto to resume work in a bank, where he now holds a responsible post as custodian and accountant.

Souster first appeared in *Unit of Five* (1944), a collection containing five young poets. His first separate book was *When We Are Young* (1946). Later titles reveal an increasing disenchantment: *Go To Sleep World* (1947), *Shake Hands with the Hangman* (1953), *A Dream That Is Dying* (1954). But in his recent poetry he has recorded a delight in simple experience that is the reward of patient waiting and devotion to art. *The Selected Poems of Raymond Souster*, now out of print, was for many years the standard collection. Now his collected poetry is available in *The Colour of the Times* (1964).

I Watched a Bird

> I watched a bird blown in the sky
> like some poor thing without control,
> dipping and swerving here and there
> with wings spread wide and motionless.
>
> I watched a bird tossed down the wind
> that never fought or uttered cry,
> surrendered to that boundless air,
> caught up in that great mystery.

The Lilac Poem

Before the lilacs are over and they are only
shrunken stalks at the ends of drooping branches,
I want to write a poem about them and their beauty
brief and star-shining as a young girl's promise.

Because there is so much made of strength and wealth
    and power,
because the little things are lost in this world,
I write this poem about lilacs knowing that both
are this day's only: tomorrow they will lie forgotten.

Lagoons, Hanlan's Point

Mornings
before the sun's liquid
spilled gradually, flooding
the island's cool cellar,
there was the boat
and the still lagoons,
with the sound of my oars
the only intrusion
over cries of birds
in the marshy shallows
or the loud thrashing
of the startled crane
rushing the air.

And in one strange
dark, tree-hung entrance,
I followed the sound
of my heart all the way
to the reed-blocked ending,

with the pads of the lily
thick as green-shining film
covering the water.

And in another
where the sun came
to probe the depths
through a shaft of branches,
I saw the skeletons
of brown ships rotting
far below in their burial-ground,
and wondered what strange fish
with what strange colours
swam through these palaces
under the water ...

A small boy
with a flat-bottomed punt
and an old pair of oars
moving with wonder
through the antechamber
of a waking world.

The Penny Flute

On the side street as we came along it in the darkness
an old man, hat beside him on the pavement, was playing
    a penny flute.
The sound was small and sweet, a whisper beside the machinery
of the cloth factory across the street (almost as if he wasn't
    playing
for an audience, only for himself).
                    I wondered
who he was, how long he'd been standing there

piping that thin string of music.
                                    But we were late
        for where we were going
and young and impatient: we didn't have time for old men
        and thin lonely tunes,
especially tunes played on a penny flute.

The Man Who Finds His Son
Has Become a Thief

Coming into the store at first angry
at the accusation, believing
the word of his boy who has told him,
I didn't steal anything, honest . . .

Then becoming calmer, seeing that anger
won't help in the business, listening patiently
as the other's evidence unfolds, so painfully slow.

Then seeing gradually that evidence
almost as if slowly tightening around the neck
of his son, at first circumstantial, then gathering damage,
until there's present guilt's sure odour seeping
into the mind, laying its poison.
                                    Suddenly feeling
sick and alone and afraid, as if
an unseen hand had slapped him in the face
for no reason whatsoever; wanting to get out
into the street, the night, the darkness, anywhere to hide
the pain that must show to these strangers, the fear.

It must be like this.
It could not be otherwise.

LOUIS DUDEK (1918-   )

An active figure in Canadian poetry, Louis Dudek was first a part of the poetry movement in Montreal in the early 1940s, and has written in a variety of styles since then. Of Polish descent, he was born in the French east end of Montreal, the setting of his first separate book, *East of the City* (1946). He was educated at McGill University, where he now lectures on modern poetry.

Dudek initially appeared with Raymond Souster, P. K. Page, and others in *Unit of Five* (1944). Some ten books of his own followed, among them *Europe* (1955), *The Transparent Sea* (1956), *En México* (1958), and *Laughing Stalks* (1958). He is also the author of a prose work on the history of printing and publishing, *Literature and the Press* (1960), and he edits *Delta* magazine from Montreal. As an editor of Contact Press he has done much to encourage young poets. His long poem, *Atlantis*, is scheduled for publication in 1966.

Tree in a Street

Why will not that tree adapt itself to our tempo?
We have lopped off several branches,
cut her skin to the white bone,
run wires through her body and her loins,
yet she will not change.
Ignorant of traffic, of dynamos and steel,
as uncontemporary
as bloomers and bustles
she stands there like a green cliché.

Midnight Train

Falling pell-mell in a torrent past my eyes
telegraph posts and homes

run into the infinite bag of night,
the past behind us,
in which enclosed, as from a nightmare
we have hidden within our artifice of train,
the capsule, in which all objects seem both real and whole.
But I would break through and escape from this lie
and face the night of which I am impatient, yet afraid;
I wish and wait for the sun to rise in blood
to halt the falling trees and homes,
stand all things again on their roots
and make the world turn in a great horizontal wheel,
or a road splayed up the mountain like a hand on fire.

In Spring

In spring, the air is magnetic,
wherever girls and boys meet
the eyes are north and south poles
oscillating in unison.

In spring the young are especially graceful —
six-year-olds tumble like sweet potatoes,
boys of eight get rapacious,
girls go dreamy.

And the wreck of fire-escapes seems blacker
in the shining morning;
and the black bean of the sick, shaven slum child
in the iron seems entangled.

Yet love insists on being important:
youth and sweet-sixteen lean on the doorpost
at evening —
Clark Gable and Lana Turner.

The stars melt like snowdrops.
A warm wind erases
the rising vapour of the city from view,
and even the refuse in the streets
looks romantic.

News

He fell from the roof
    of the dock-shed onto the wharf
hitting it with his knees —
                one of the boys
diving all day into the deep water
and climbing on odd corners, to do it,
    I saw him
lying on the fish-cart,
his legs tied up in a towel,
and his arms terribly shaking, the eyes closed;
            it comes like that
some little accident to prove
the genial power over us
      that death preserves:
the mourning sister so beautiful,
the silent bathers,
and the pale lips of the boy.
The ocean cannot come near to it, in magnificence,
nor can we degrade it
      by using it for our pleasure.

ALAIN GRANDBOIS (1900-   )

The importance of Alain Grandbois in modern French-Canadian literature springs from his un-Canadian character, his extreme cosmopol-
itanism and sense of the world. He brought the spirit of modern
French poetry — its vast incantatory rhetoric and surrealist imagination —
to Canada with the publication of *Les Iles de la nuit* in 1944, and French
poetry in Canada has never been the same since.

Born of a well-to-do family at Saint-Casimir (Portneuf), educated at
the Séminaire de Québec and at St. Dunstan's University in Prince
Edward Island, Grandbois left Canada to study literature at the Sorbonne. He later divided his time between residence in Paris and travels
to the four corners of the world, to Italy, Spain, Austria, Russia, Africa,
India, China, and Japan. The result was two books on famous travellers
whose footsteps he had traced, Jolliet in *Né à Québec* (1933) and Marco
Polo in *Les Voyages de Marco Polo* (1942). Three volumes of poetry
followed, *Les Iles de la nuit* (1944), *Rivages de l'homme* (1948), and
L'Etoile pourpre (1957).

Grandbois's poetry is difficult, but it also falls into a recognizable pattern. An anguished idealism at odds with the world is expressed in a
language of symbolism and visionary ecstasy. Sound and colour are as
essential to this poetry as they are to modern abstract painting, where the
question 'What is it?' no longer has relevant meaning. Comparison with
the English poetry of Dylan Thomas, Edith Sitwell, Hart Crane, and
Robert Lowell will show the differences and variations in this romantic
poetry of the twentieth century.

Grandbois's collected poems are available under the title *Poèmes*
(1963), and English translations in Peter Miller's *Alain Grandbois:
Selected Poems* (1964).

Ce qui reste

> Ce qui reste de la nuit
> Dévastant les étoiles
> Recréant lentement
> Le contour des prés et des bois
> Des lacs des rivages de la mer

Marquant la fin
Du balancement des somnambules
Aux toits perdus des gratte-ciel

La fin du poème du poète
La fin des grands silences bénis
La fin des dernières agonies
La mort du juste et du pécheur
Ce qui reste de l'ombre épaisse
Prépare le jour et la joie
La danse frissonnante du soleil

Les chemins de l'aurore
Se retrouvent avec difficultés
La nuit trop lourde
Noie l'homme du destin
Ce qu'il exigeait
Ce qu'il réclamait
L'étrangle dans sa propre épouvante

'What remains . . .'

(Translation by Peter Miller)

What remains of the night
Laying waste the stars
Recreating slowly
The contour of fields and woods
Of lakes and shores of the sea
Marking the end
Of the swaying of sleepwalkers
On the lost roofs of skyscrapers

The end of the poet's poem
The end of the great blessed silences

The end of the last agonies
The death of just man and sinner
What remains of the dense dark
Prepares day and joy
And the shivering dance of the sun

The roads of dawn
Are refound with difficulties
The too heavy night
Drowns the man of destiny
What he exacted
What he demanded
Strangles him in his own fright

L'Enfance oubliée

Ces cloches de haute basilique
Enfant torturé d'espoir
Mes yeux étaient remplis
Des belles merveilles pourpres
Du lent secret des astres
Et je voyais parfois
Sous mes paupières
Le grand triomphe extraordinaire
Des archanges de neige tendre
Et j'entends parfois encore
Au seuil de mon ombre
Le son de ce violon
Qui ne jouait pour personne

Forgotten Childhood

(Translation by Peter Miller)

Those high basilica bells
Child tortured with hope
My eyes were filled
With the fine purple marvels
Of the slow secret of the stars
And I saw sometimes
Under my eyelids
The great extraordinary triumph
Of the archangels of tender snow
And I hear sometimes still
At the threshold of my shadow
The sound of that violin
Which played for no one

C'est à vous tous . . .

C'est à vous tous que je fais appel
O beaux Visages de mon passé
C'est à vous tous et à chacun de vous
Je sais que vous entendrez ma voix de
    pierre sourde
Je sais que ma voix ébranlera les voiles
    de plomb
Je sais que vous surgirez de l'ombre aux
    destins engloutis
Je sais que vous secouerez les cendres de
    vos chevelures mortes
Je sais que vos ardentes prunelles viendront
    incendier mes ultimes nuits

Je fais appel à vous tous du fond de mon
   exil
Je ne vous avais trahis que pour une
   nouvelle blessure
Je ne vous avais trahis qu'une fois
Je ne vous avais trahis que pour une
   cicatrice ancienne
Mais plus que vous j'ai saigné de mes
   abandons
Et cette dure faim d'un plus mortel plongeon
Je l'ai nourrie des mille mains de mon
   épouvante

O mes beaux Visages avec un sourire triste
O vous tous ensevelis derrière les murs
   des chambres vides
Vous tous qui pleuriez les larmes de ferveur
Vous avez cette musique d'ombre émerveillée
Vous séparés du jour comme l'étoile
O Vous tous sur ce chemin perdu de mon
   passé
Je fais appel à vous de toutes mes blessures
   ouvertes
Et même si vous ne répondiez pas
Tout votre silence se dresserait soudain comme
   un grand cri emplissant ma nuit

'It is to all of you . . .'

(Translation by Peter Miller)

It is to all of you that I appeal
O beautiful Faces of my past

It is to all of you and to each of you
I know that you will hear my voice of dull stone
I know that my voice will shake the leaden sails
I know that you will arise from shadows to the engulfed fates
I know that you will shake the ashes from your dead hair
I know that your burning eyes will come to kindle my last
nights

I appeal to you all from the depths of my exile
I betrayed you only for a new wound
I betrayed you only the one time
I betrayed you only for an old scar
But more than you I bled from my abandonments
And as to that hard hunger of a more mortal plunge
I fed it with the thousand hands of my terror

O my beautiful Faces with a sad smile
O all of you shrouded behind the walls of empty rooms
All of you who wept tears of fervor
You with that music of an astonished shadow
You detached from the day like a star
O all of You on that lost road of my past
I appeal to you all with all my open wounds
And even if you did not reply
Your whole silence would rise suddenly like a great cry
filling my night

ANNE HEBERT (1916-   )

Like Saint-Denys Garneau, to whom she is related, Anne Hébert writes allusive poetry in the French Symbolist tradition, a poetry in which explicit meaning is irrelevant and 'the essence of things' is communicated through the music and the connotation of words. But the human side of such poetry is nevertheless possible to grasp. Its quality of feeling is conveyed to the reader directly, even if the sense and the images remain vague and uncertain.

Born in Sainte-Catherine-de-Fossambault, the manorial home of the family, Anne Hébert was brought up in relative seclusion and privately educated at home. Her first book, *Les Songes en équilibre*, appeared in 1942 and made an immediate impression. *Le Tombeau des rois* followed in 1953. Both books are long out of print, but a select collection is available under the title *Poèmes* (1960). English translations of some of her poems may be found in F. R. Scott's *St.-Denys Garneau, Anne Hébert: Translations* (1962).

In addition to poetry, Anne Hébert has published short stories in *Le Torrent* (1950, 1963) and a novel, *Les Chambres de bois* (1958). She has also published two plays, *La Mercière assassinée* and *Le Temps sauvage*, available in the series Ecrits du Canada Français.

Neige

La neige nous met en rêve sur de vastes plaines,
sans traces ni couleur

Veille mon coeur, la neige nous met en selle sur
des coursiers d'écume

Sonne l'enfance couronnée, la neige nous sacre en
haute mer, plein songe, toutes voiles dehors

La neige nous met en magie, blancheur étale, plumes
gonflées où perce l'oeil rouge de cet oiseau

Mon coeur; trait de feu sous des palmes de gel file
le sang qui s'émerveille.

Snow

(Translation by Peter Miller)

*The snow sets us in dream on vast plains, without
tracks or color*

*Keep watch, my heart, the snow sets us in the saddle
on chargers of foam*

*Ring out, crowned childhood, the snow hallows us on the
high sea, full fancy, all sails flying*

*The snow sets us in magic, becalmed whiteness, swollen
plumage pierced by the red eye of this bird*

*My heart; flash of fire under the palms of frost,
flows the marvelling blood.*

Une Petite Morte

Une petite morte
    s'est couchée en travers de la porte.

Nous l'avons trouvée au matin, abattue
                sur notre seuil
Comme un arbre de fougère plein de gel.

Nous n'osons plus sortir depuis qu'elle est là
C'est une enfant blanche dans ses jupes mousseuses
D'où rayonne une étrange nuit laiteuse.

Nous nous efforçons de vivre à l'intérieur
Sans faire de bruit
Balayer la chambre
Et ranger l'ennui

267

Laisser les gestes se balancer tout seuls
Au bout d'un fil invisible
A même nos veines ouvertes.

Nous menons une vie si minuscule et tranquille
Que pas un de nos mouvements lents
Ne dépasse l'envers de ce miroir limpide
Où cette soeur que nous avons
Se baigne bleue sous la lune
Tandis que croît son odeur capiteuse.

A Little Corpse

(Translation by Peter Miller)

A little corpse
        lies across the doorway.

We found her in the morning, fallen
                    on our threshold
Like a bough of bracken full of frost.

We have not dared to go out since she arrived
She is a white child in her foaming skirts
From which shines a strange milky night.

We try our best to live inside
Without making any noise
Sweeping the room
And tidying the boredom
Letting the gestures dangle on their own
At the end of an invisible thread
Flush with our open veins.

We lead a life so tiny and quiet
That not one of our slow movements

Goes past the back of this clear mirror
Where that sister of ours
Bathes blue under the moon
While her heady odor grows.

La Fille maigre

Je suis une fille maigre
Et j'ai de beaux os.

J'ai pour eux des soins attentifs
Et d'étranges pitiés

Je les polis sans cesse
Comme de vieux métaux.

Les bijoux et les fleurs
Sont hors de saison.

Un jour je saisirai mon amant
Pour m'en faire un reliquaire d'argent

Je me pendrai
A la place de son coeur absent.

Espace comblé,
Quel est soudain en toi cet hôte sans fièvre?

Tu marches
Tu remues;
Chacun de tes gestes
Pare d'effroi la mort enclose.

Je reçois ton tremblement
Comme un don.

Et parfois
En ta poitrine, fixée,
J'entrouvre
Mes prunelles liquides

Et bougent
Comme une eau verte
Des songes bizarres et enfantins.

The Lean Girl

(Translation by F. R. Scott)

I am a lean girl
And I have beautiful bones.

I tend them with great care
And feel strange pity for them.

I continually polish them
As though they were old metal.

Now jewels and flowers
Are out of season.

One day I shall clasp my lover
And make of him a silver shrine.

I shall hang myself
In the place of his absent heart.

O well-filled space,
What is this cold guest suddenly in you?

You walk,
You move;
Each one of your gestures
Adorns with fear the enclosed death.

I receive your trembling
As a gift.

And sometimes
Fastened in your breast,
I half open
My liquid eyes

As strange and childish dreams
Swirl
Like green water.

JAMES REANEY (1926-   )

One of the most original and surprising poets on the Canadian scene, James Reaney won immediate recognition with his book *The Red Heart* in 1949. The edition was exhausted within a few weeks and has remained a treasured item since then. The poems, fanciful, humorous, painfully disenchanted, yet childlike in their affection for innocence betrayed, moved and delighted many readers. The book received the Governor General's Award.

Since then, Reaney has had a prolific career. *A Suit of Nettles* (1958), his second book of poetry, contains a sequence of twelve pastorals for the twelve months of the year, and deals with the fate of geese on an Ontario farm, from the hatchery to the chopping-block. The dialogues are allegorical, providing scope for satirical thrusts and for philosophical disquisitions on the absurdity and vanity of human wishes.

Twelve Letters to a Small Town followed in 1962, and *The Dance of Death at London Ontario* in 1963. Reaney has written a number of plays, published under the title *The Killdeer and Other Plays* (1962). He has also published short stories and has completed a novel (unpublished). He is now working on a second novel. A graduate of the University of Toronto, Reaney teaches literature at the University of Western Ontario and edits the valuable magazine, *Alphabet*.

The Katzenjammer Kids

With porcupine locks
And faces which, when
More closely examined,
Are composed of measle-pink specks,
These two dwarf imps,
The Katzenjammer Kids,
Flitter through their Desert Island world.
Sometimes they get so out of hand
That a blue Captain
With stiff whiskers of black wicker

And an orange Inspector
With a black telescope
Pursue them to spank them
All through that land
Where cannibals cut out of brown paper
In cardboard jungles feast and caper,
Where the sea's sharp waves continually
Waver against the shore faithfully
And the yellow sun above is thin and flat
With a collar of black spikes and spines
To tell the innocent childish heart that
It shines
And warms (see where she stands and stammers)
The dear fat mother of the Katzenjammers.
Oh, for years and years she has stood
At the window and kept fairly good
Guard over the fat pies that she bakes
For her two children, those dancing heartaches.
Oh, the blue skies of that funny paper weather!
The distant birds like two eyebrows close together!
And the rustling paper roar
Of the waves
Against the paper sands of the paper shore!

The School Globe

Sometimes when I hold
Our faded old globe
That we used at school
To see where oceans were
And the five continents,
The lines of latitude and longitude,
The North Pole, the Equator and the South Pole —

Sometimes when I hold this
Wrecked blue cardboard pumpkin
I think: here in my hands
Rest the fair fields and lands
Of my childhood
Where still lie or still wander
Old games, tops and pets;
A house where I was little
And afraid to swear
Because God might hear and
Send a bear
To eat me up;
Rooms where I was as old
As I was high;
Where I loved the pink clenches,
The white, red and pink fists
Of roses; where I watched the rain
That Heaven's clouds threw down
In puddles and rutfuls
And irregular mirrors
Of soft brown glass upon the ground.
This school globe is a parcel of my past,
A basket of pluperfect things.
And here I stand with it
Sometime in the summertime
All alone in an empty schoolroom
Where about me hang
Old maps, an abacus, pictures,
Blackboards, empty desks.
If I raise my hand
No tall teacher will demand
What I want.
But if someone in authority
Were here, I'd say
Give me this old world back

274

Whose husk I clasp
And I'll give you in exchange
The great sad real one
That's filled
Not with a child's remembered and pleasant skies
But with blood, pus, horror, death, stepmothers, and lies.

JAY MACPHERSON (1931-   )

Jay Macpherson had already published two small books — *Nineteen Poems* (1952) and *O Earth Return* (1954) — when her impressive third book, *The Boatman* (1957), established her as one of Canada's leading poets and won her the Governor General's Award. With James Reaney and Eli Mandel she represents a branch of Canadian poetry strongly influenced by the fertile ideas of Northrop Frye, making use of myth as a profound source of universal poetic meaning.

Jay Macpherson was born in England, and came to Canada at the age of nine. She studied at Carleton College, Ottawa, and later at the University of Toronto. Since the publication of *The Boatman* she has been much occupied in research and in teaching. She has written an excellent book on classical mythology for young readers, *Four Ages of Man* (1962).

Although her poetry is gnomic and difficult, attached to mythological references and ideas which are very specialized, there is a quality of conviction and personal involvement in her work which gives it unusual power. She has been much admired for her pithy oracular lyrics and her mastery of traditional forms.

Coral

A living tree that harbours
No singing-birds, no flowers,
Offers no shady arbours,
No comfortable bowers
For man's inactive hours.

The sea's untended gardens
And waving meadows bear
— A tree of flesh that hardens
In our destroying air
And stands petrific there.

It shelters shiny fishes
And leggy crustacee,
Welcomes whatever wishes,
And shines a perfect tree
Of coral in the sea.

ELI MANDEL (1922-   )

Eli Mandel's first publication was in the book *Trio* (1954), with Gael Turnbull and Phyllis Webb. There he already showed a capacity for complex rhetorical handling of classical myths as a way of expressing contemporary reality. The mixture of contemporary realism — even social realism — with the mythopoeic method distinguishes him from other poets of this school.

Eli Mandel was born in Estevan, Saskatchewan. He served in the Royal Canadian Army Medical Corps overseas during the war and later studied for his doctorate at the University of Toronto. Here he was affected by the poetry of Blake and came into contact with Northrop Frye's stimulating criticism. He subsequently taught at the Collège Militaire in St-Jean, Quebec, and is now teaching at the University of Alberta in Edmonton.

Mandel's first separate book was *Fuseli Poems*, published in 1960. His most recent book is *Black and Secret Man* (1964). He has also edited, with Jean-Guy Pilon, an anthology of current Canadian poetry, *Poetry 62*; and he is a frequent contributor of articles and reviews to Canadian literary magazines.

Day of Atonement: Standing

My Lord, how stands it with me now
Who, standing here before you
(who, fierce as you are, are also just),
Cannot bow down. You order this.
Why, therefore, I must break
If bend I will not, yet bend I must.

But I address myself to you thus,
Covered and alert, and will not bare
My self. Then I must bear you,
Heavy as you are.

This is the time
The bare tree bends in the fierce wind
And stripped, my God, springs to the sky.

The Anarchist-Poets

Step carefully through this rubble of words.
Can you really say which wrecks were once poems,
which weapons?
                    Who once ran havoc
through these cities of language
scattering flowers of darkness,
black bursts of unmeaning?
                    What guerrillas
frantic for peace, love, home, nation,
government, even for death itself?

D. G. JONES (1929-   )

Douglas G. Jones was a student in Montreal in the late 1940s where he met John Sutherland, Patrick Anderson, F. R. Scott, and other poets of that active period. The clear, imagistic lines of his own poetry and the crisp definiteness of his language have come out of that experience. He writes reflective poetry of a very genuine, personal kind.

His first book was *Frost on the Sun* (1957), a Contact Press book. This has been followed by *The Sun Is Axeman* (1961), published by the University of Toronto Press. A graduate of McGill and Queen's, D. G. Jones has taught at Ontario Agricultural College and at Bishop's University. He is now at the University of Sherbrooke.

On the 24th of May

Six cows
lie
or kneel
in the green grass —
like badly built tents.
They flap
an ear
or tail
to keep off the flies.
They are indeed
obsolete structures.
They look out
from unnecessarily
large eyes
at the bright
automobiles
driving northward,
and are profoundly
unmoved.

LEONARD COHEN (1934-   )

Leonard Cohen is a young poet widely admired for his lyrical verve, his spontaneous frankness, the engaging personality he displays as a poet, a poetry-reader, and a narrator. He belongs to the new generation which includes the beats, the Beatles, and the *boîtes à chanson*.

Born in Montreal, he studied at McGill and at Columbia University. His first book, published in the McGill Poetry Series, was *Let Us Compare Mythologies* (1956). It was sold out within a month of publication. *The Spice-Box of Earth* followed in 1961. He has since written a novel in a poetic, autobiographical vein, *The Favourite Game* (1963). His most recent book is *Flowers for Hitler* (1964).

Les Vieux

Northeastern Lunch,
        with rotting noses and tweed caps,
huddling in thick coats
and mumbling confidential songs
to ancient friends —
        the public men of Montreal;

and in parks
        with strange children
who listen to sad lies
in exchange for whistles
        carved from wet maple branches;

in Phillips Square,
        on newspaper-covered benches,
unaware of Ste. Catherine Street
or grey and green pigeons
        inquiring between their boots —

public men,
        letters of reference crumbling in wallets,
speaking all the languages of Montreal.

Prayer for Sunset

The sun is tangled
        in black branches,
raving like Absalom
        between sky and water,
struggling through the dark terebinth
to commit its daily suicide.

Now, slowly, the sea consumes it,
leaving a glistening wound
        on the water,
        a red scar on the horizon;
in darkness
        I set out for home,
terrified by the clash of wind on grass,
and the victory cry of weeds and water.

Is there no Joab for tomorrow night,
        with three darts
        and a great heap of stones?

The Bus

I was the last passenger of the day,
I was alone on the bus,
I was glad they were spending all that money
just getting me up Eighth Avenue.
Driver! I shouted, it's you and me tonight,
let's run away from this big city
to a smaller city more suitable to the heart,
let's drive past the swimming pools of Miami Beach,
you in the driver's seat, me several seats back,
but in the racial cities we'll change places

so as to show how well you've done up North,
and let us find ourselves some tiny American fishing village
in unknown Florida
and park right at the edge of the sand,
a huge bus pointing out,
metallic, painted, solitary,
with New York plates.

GILLES VIGNEAULT (1928-   )

A poet of a different stamp from all others in this book, Gilles Vigneault is a troubadour, a popular singer who writes poetry and also the words and the music of his own songs. He is called 'un chansonnier' in his own province of Quebec, a singer-composer of what is known as 'la chanson canadienne'. These songs are similar to popular songs in France, and some of the Canadian singers — for example, Félix Leclerc — have achieved fame in France. But Gilles Vigneault, at present the chief name among the *chansonniers*, is also something apart as a poet and artist. He seems to be a reincarnation of the medieval troubadour in the haunting beauty of his quieter melodies, in his far-away echoes of old romanticism, in the poetry of his love songs, which are like the love songs of all ages.

Born in Natashquan, a little fishing village on the Gulf of St. Lawrence north of Quebec, he sings and writes much out of his early memories. It is indeed a far-away world, and one that is changing or disappearing quickly. For a time he was a school-teacher, then for some years simply a poet, before he took to composing songs. In recent years in Quebec many a tennis club, garage, or abandoned shop has been turned into a café or *boîte à chanson* with a small stage for singing. Out of this bohemian movement Gilles Vigneault has sprung. But though he is a singing star, he still writes serious poetry and stories and publishes his work in the Editions de l'Arc. His recent books are *Etraves* (1959), *Balises* (1964), and *Contes sur la pointe des pieds* (1961). His songs on record are available on Columbia FL 292, FL 298, and FL 312.

Quand vous mourrez de nos amours

Quand vous mourrez de nos amours
J'irai planter dans le jardin
Fleur à fleurir de beau matin
Moitié métal moitié papier
Pour me blesser un peu le pied
Mourez de mort très douce
Qu'une fleur pousse

Quand vous mourrez de nos amours
J'en ferai sur l'air de ce temps
Chanson chanteuse pour sept ans
Vous l'entendrez, vous l'apprendrez
Et vos lèvres m'en sauront gré
Mourez de mort très lasse
Que je la fasse

Quand vous mourrez de nos amours
J'en ferai deux livres si beaux
Qu'ils vous serviront de tombeau
Et m'y coucherai à mon tour
Car je mourrai le même jour
Mourez de mort très tendre
A les attendre

Quand vous mourrez de nos amours
J'irai me pendre avec la clef
Au crochet des bonheurs bâclés
Et les chemins par nous conquis
Nul ne saura jamais par qui
Mourez de mort exquise
Que je les dise

Quand vous mourrez de nos amours
Si trop peu vous reste de moi
Ne me demandez pas pourquoi
Dans les mensonges qui suivraient
Nous ne serions ni beaux ni vrais
Mourez de mort très vive
Que je vous suive

When You Die of All Our Loves

(Translation by Louis Dudek)

When you die of all our loves
I shall go and plant in the garden
A flower to bloom some fine morning
Half of metal and half of paper
To hurt my foot just a trifle
So you may die a death most sweet
That a flower might blossom

When you die of all our loves
I shall make in the fashion of that time
A song to be sung for seven years
You will hear it, you will learn it
And your lips will thank me for it
And you may die a death most easy
So that I may do so

When you die of all our loves
I shall make of it two beautiful books
That they may serve you for a tomb
And I shall lie there in my turn
For I shall die on that same day
O you may die a death most gentle
In waiting for them

When you die of all our loves
I shall go and hang myself with the key
From the hasp of all our ruined joys
And the many roads conquered by us
Though no one will ever know by whom
And you may die a death most exquisite
So that I may tell them

When you die of all our loves
If too little of me remains with you
Then do not ask me why
In all the falsehoods that would ensue
We would be neither beautiful nor true
But you may die a death most gay
So that I might follow you

'A des oiseaux d'ailleurs . . .'

A des oiseaux d'ailleurs à des roses nouvelles
Ma mie allez conter de la lèvre et du doigt
Quelles sont mes chansons et quel est mon patois
Quand je cause de vous au temps qui nous nivelle

Il est temps que vos mains et votre voix révèlent
A des roses d'ailleurs, aux oiseaux de ces bois
Caresse de mes mains et chansons de ma voix
Avant que la rumeur ou le vent ne s'en mêlent

Contez que vous aimez et si cela n'est point
Assez pour que les fleurs se fanent un peu moins
Et pour que les oiseaux viennent sur votre épaule

Dites leur le secret des âmes qui se frôlent
Et les oiseaux iront dans les jeux du matin
Fêter la rose neuve et l'automne au jardin

'To the birds from afar . . .'

(Translation by Louis Dudek)

To the birds from afar and the roses new-blown
My love, go tell with your fingers and lips

What my songs are, what my native speech is
When my talk is of you while time wears us down

It is time your hands and your voice should show
To the roses afar and the wood-birds about
The caress of my hands and the songs of my throat
Before rumour or wind are mingled with those

Tell them you love, and if that does not much
To make the flowers fade somewhat less
Or the birds to come down to your shoulder to rest

Tell them the secret of souls that can touch
Then the birds will join in the morning hours
To praise the new rose and the autumn flowers

Si les bateaux

Si les bateaux que nous avons bâtis
Prennent la mer avant que je revienne
Cargue ta voile, aussi la mienne
Fais comme si . . . fais comme si
Nous en étions toujours les capitaines
Nous en étions toujours les capitaines

Profond comme au large de l'île
Doux comme une aile d'istorlet
Loin comme l'Angleterre
Je t'aimerai
Je t'aimerai

Si les trésors dont nous avions la clé
Le plan la carte et la belle aventure
N'étaient que rêve et qu'imposture
Evoque-les . . . évoque-les
Par des drapeaux de plus dans les mâtures
Par des drapeaux de plus dans les mâtures

Profond comme au large de l'île
Doux comme une aile d'istorlet
Loin comme l'Angleterre
Je t'aimerai
Je t'aimerai

Si je me fais facteur ou jardinier
Ne me viens plus parler de contrebande
Mais si tu veux que je me pende
Au grand hunier ... au grand hunier
Raconte-moi que tu as vu l'Irlande
Raconte-moi que tu as vu l'Irlande

Profond comme au large de l'île
Doux comme une aile d'istorlet
Loin comme l'Angleterre
Je t'aimerai
Je t'aimerai

'If all the ships . . .'

(Translation by Louis Dudek)

If all the ships that we have built together
Take to the sea before I shall return
Clew up your sail, and also mine
Try to pretend ... try to pretend
That we are still the captains sailing them
That we are still the captains sailing them

Deep as the open water off the island
Soft as the wing of a starling
As far away as England
I shall love you
I shall love you

If the treasures to which we had the key
The plan the map and the lovely adventure
Should only prove a dream and an imposture
Think of them still . . . think of them still
By adding more flags to sail at the masthead
By adding more flags to sail at the masthead

Deep as the open water off the island
Soft as the wing of a starling
As far away as England
I shall love you
I shall love you

If I should become an agent or a gardener
Don't come to tell me of forbidden traffic
But if you should want me to hang myself
From the great topsail . . . from the great topsail
Tell me that you have sailed and seen Ireland
Tell me that you have sailed and seen Ireland

Deep as the open water off the island
Soft as the wing of a starling
As far away as England
I shall love you
I shall love you

JEAN-GUY PILON (1930-   )

A representative of the group of exciting young poets who have appeared in the renaissance of French Canada since 1950, Jean-Guy Pilon is both a poet committed to public responsibility and a conscientious personal artist. For some years he has helped organize the annual conferences of French poets in Quebec. He is an editor and founder of the magazine *Liberté* and he was one of the moving spirits of Les Editions de l'Hexagone, the most important French outlet for new poetry in recent years. He is also supervisor of cultural programs on the French network of the CBC.

His first book, *La Fiancée du matin*, appeared in 1953. Since then he has published several small volumes of highly-polished poetry: *Les Cloîtres de l'été* (1955), *L'Homme et le jour* (1957), *La Mouette et le large* (1960), *Recours au pays* (1961), and *Pour saluer une ville* (1963). His poetry is marked by a sensitive moral concern and a search for thoughtful resolutions to complex political problems. The form of these poems is free but the language is chaste, like the thought and the ethical sense to which these correspond.

Noces

Des noms se heurtent
Dans ma mémoire menacée
Noms de villes noms de femmes
Places et chambres
Jouissances et ruines
Tous ces éclairs sur ma route indécise
Toutes ces louanges
Seules prières de mon corps
Qui sait maintenant
Son appartenance irréductible à la terre
A tous les climats du monde
Aux lumières et aux brouillards

Mon hérédité est immense
Et je la devine à peine
Enfouie dans tous les replis de la planète
Ma patrie orgueilleuse et sans fin

Je me souviens d'un affreux matin à Santiago
D'une indienne endormie dans une chambre froide
Je me rappelle les promesses d'Amsterdam
La baie vertigineuse de Rio
L'émouvante naïade de Copenhague
Et les nuits du monde
Ajoutées aux bonheurs
Des jours sans pareil
Affirmés et possédés

Debout
Sur cette terre brûlée d'espérance
Malgré les jungles et les guerres
Je réinvente l'amour
Qui crie dans les villes du monde
Au bout des mains tremblantes
De femmes aimées

Par-dessus les jours et les nausées
Les océans et les faiblesses
Les capitales et l'ennui
J'affirme l'opiniâtreté de mon sang
Et je ne sais plus qu'un mot
Pour saluer ma maison
Et les vies qu'elle protège
Seules raisons de ma propre vie

OUI

A Wedding

(Translation by Louis Dudek)

Names clash
In my memory filled with menace
Names of cities and of women
Places and rooms
Pleasures and ruins
All those flashes on the road of my stumbling advance
All those words of praise
Solitary prayers my body makes
O who can now affirm
His certain kinship to the earth
To all the weathers of the world
To the qualities of light and the rain-mists

My heredity is immense
And I can hardly measure it at all
Absorbed in all the folds of the planet
My country proud without end

I remember a horrible morning in Santiago
And an Indian woman asleep in a cold room
I remember Amsterdam with its promise
And the vertiginous bay of Rio
The amazing naiad of Copenhagen
And the nights of the world
Added to the pleasures
Of days without equal
Affirmed and possessed

Standing erect
On this burned earth of hope
Despite the jungles and the wars
I re-invent love

Which cries through the cities of the world
Held at the end of trembling hands
Of women loved

Above the days and the nauseas
The oceans and weaknesses
The capitals and the boredom
I assert the obstinacy of my blood
And I know only one word
With which to salute my home
And the lives it protects
Who are my sole reasons for living

YES

'L'Exigence du pays! . . .'

(From *Recours au pays*)

L'exigence du pays!

Qui suis-je donc pour affronter pareilles étendues, pour comprendre cent mille lacs, soixante-quinze fleuves, dix chaînes de montagnes, trois océans, le pôle nord et le soleil qui ne se couche jamais sur mon pays?

Où planter ma maison dans cette infinitude et ces grands vents? De quel côté placer le potager? Comment dire, en dépit des saisons, les mots quotidiens, les mots de la vie: femme, pain, vin?

Il y a des pays pour les enfants, d'autres pour les hommes, quelques-uns pour les géants . . .

Avant de savoir les mots pour vivre, il est déjà temps d'apprendre à mourir.

'The needs of the land! . . .'

(From *Recours au pays*, translation by Louis Dudek)

The needs of the land!

Who am I then to take on such expanses of space, to comprehend a hundred thousand lakes, seventy-five rivers, ten chains of mountains, three oceans, the North Pole and the sun that never sets on my country?

Where shall I plant my home in this infinitude and these great winds? In what corner place the vegetable garden? How shall I say, in despite of the seasons, those everyday words, the words of life: woman, bread, wine?

There are countries for children, and others for men, some few only for giants . . .

Before we can learn the words necessary to live, it is already time to learn to die.

ALFRED PURDY (1918-   )

Alfred Purdy is one of several vigorous iconoclastic poets who have appeared in Canada in the last ten years. Some of these, Milton Acorn, John Newlove, George Bowering, have written powerful poems of love and anger. Purdy is a representative voice of this new generation.

Born near Wooler, Ontario, he attended Albert College but left without graduating. Later he worked in Vancouver, travelled across Canada, and briefly visited Europe. He has been writing occasionally for CBC radio and contributing to Canadian literary magazines.

Purdy has already published six books. The first of these, *The Enchanted Echo* (1944), was conventional poetry in the traditional metric. *Pressed on Sand* (1955), his first book in the modern vein, began to explore the possibilities of free verse and of realistic subject matter. Purdy has not yet resolved the problem of looseness and incongruity which this mixture of materials has forced on his poetry. But he has dredged up more reality than any other recent poet. *The Crafte So Longe To Lerne* (1959) testifies to his conscious progress. His recent books are *Poems for All the Annettes* (1962), *The Blur in Between* (1963), and *The Cariboo Horses* (1965).

Negroes on St. Antoine

Here there's a blackness under the sun
where tracks cross and glum groceries are molars
set in slums that no forceps budge —
rooted deep in the continental jawbone.

Here their peculiar lankiness flaunts
exaggerated curves
                    repressed by the dwarfish
architecture into black goldfish:
a girl fumbling with being a woman,
unaccustomed to having breasts and being
looked at: here
                    on holidays come black New Yorkers,

jazz combos and beat musicians,
the clean pride of Jomo Kenyatta
dulled on the face of a C.N.R. porter:
in front of a kilted Scottish girl
on a billboard praising cigarettes a
swaying boy forgets
                    what century
                    it is and dances —

I have stood on the sweep of Mount Royal,
thinking of Israeli gunners
on the Sinai Peninsula,
farmers with rifles in the Negev
                              Spartacus
waiting for ships to come and staring
alone across the Straits of Messina,
Lumumba dead in coppery Katanga province
            (a janitor on St. Antoine
                    picked up for questioning):
how human history is meaningless
on the non-involved mountain
in the admirable stillness called
death high
            over the stopped city
permitting
            no human heartbeat to reach
this hilltop —
from the cruciform building in Place Ville Marie
            no noise of riveters —

Scarcities

I dreamed your hair was
on fire and you ran —
its bright scarf
flung back
to the wind.
And once at your side
while you slept
I looked at whiteness
enough for fields
of level snow —
and there were no fences.
Today in April
snow is scarce,
but I found some
in nearby woods,
a rare inch or so
covered with a leaf —

ALDEN NOWLAN (1933-   )

Alden Nowlan writes of small-town life with the same harshness and ironic stress that other poets apply to the big city. He lives in Hartland, New Brunswick, where he has worked on a newspaper and gathered much of the material for his poems. A somewhat surrealistic imagination plays over his compact formal lines, and the sense of horror he sometimes communicates derives from a vision of reality charged with dissatisfaction and prophetic ire. (His most recent book, *The Things Which Are*, takes its title from the Revelation of St. John.)

Born in Windsor, Nova Scotia, Nowlan left school at an early age. He has read widely, however, and his work shows poetic skill as well as a wide range of knowledge. He has published four books, beginning with *The Rose and the Puritan* in 1958. His poems are also included in *Five New Brunswick Poets* (1962) and his prose in *A Book of Canadian Stories* (1962), edited by Desmond Pacey.

The Bull Moose

Down from the purple mist of trees on the mountain,
lurching through forests of white spruce and cedar,
stumbling through tamarack swamps,
came the bull moose
to be stopped at last by a pole-fenced pasture.

Too tired to turn or, perhaps, aware
there was no place left to go, he stood with the cattle.
They, scenting the musk of death, seeing his great head
like the ritual mask of a blood god, moved to the other end
of the field, and waited.

The neighbours heard of it, and by afternoon
cars lined the road. The children teased him
with alder switches and he gazed at them
like an old, tolerant collie. The women asked
if he could have escaped from a Fair.

The oldest man in the parish remembered seeing
a gelded moose yoked with an ox for plowing.
The young men snickered and tried to pour beer
down his throat, while their girl friends took their pictures.

And the bull moose let them stroke his tick-ravaged flanks,
let them pry open his jaws with bottles, let a giggling girl
plant a little purple cap
of thistles on his head.
When the wardens came, everyone agreed it was a shame
to shoot anything so shaggy and cuddlesome.
He looked like the kind of pet
women put to bed with their sons.

So they held their fire. But just as the sun dropped in the river
the bull moose gathered his strength
like a scaffolded king, straightened and lifted his horns
so that even the wardens backed away as they raised their rifles.
When he roared, people ran to their cars. All the young men
leaned on their automobile horns as he toppled.

The Execution

On the night of the execution
a man at the door
mistook me for the coroner.
'Press,' I said.

But he didn't understand. He led me
into the wrong room
where the sheriff greeted me:
'You're late, Padre.'

'You're wrong,' I told him. 'I'm Press.'
'Yes, of course, Reverend Press.
We went down a stairway.

'Ah, Mr. Ellis,' said the Deputy.
'Press!' I shouted. But he shoved me
through a black curtain.
The lights were so bright
I couldn't see the faces
of the men sitting
opposite. But, thank God, I thought
they can see me!

'Look!' I cried. 'Look at my face!
Doesn't anybody know me?'

Then a hood covered my head.
'Don't make it harder for us,' the hangman whispered.

ELDON GRIER (1917-   )

A painter as well as a poet, Eldon Grier has lived in Spain and in Mexico. He has described the process of writing poetry as 'meaning arrived at through feeling', a conception which explains the flowing impressionist quality of his work and its tentative approaches to direct thought and statement.

Born in London, England, of Canadian parents, Eldon Grier was educated in Montreal, Ottawa, and Aurora, Ontario. He has studied painting under John Lyman in Canada and Diego Rivera in Mexico, and has taught art classes in the Montreal Museum of Fine Arts. He has published five books of poetry, *A Morning from Scraps* (1955), *Poems* (1956), *Manzillo and Other Poems* (1957), *The Ring of Ice* (1957), and *A Friction of Lights* (1963).

'English poetry never went crazy'

(From *An Ecstasy*)

English poetry never went crazy, a Frenchman said.
It was not a compliment.

Our poets must give themselves to a kind
of unsensible madness;
they must hear music not meaning as they write.

Words must be clear bells,
or sound gravely along like horns.
They should detonate, explode like lightning
                              under the sea,
be silver wire, silk thread suspended,

sardonyx,

layers of white alternated with sard.

There are words that are the incomparable beasts
of our imagination.

Sound them.
Revel in the extravagance.

Study Aids

Almost all the poems in this book can be interesting at a first reading. However, there are many fine points that you will discover by going over these study aids. The questions are not designed to stump you, or really as a test, but to help you discover interesting details that only close reading can reveal and thus to enhance your enjoyment of the poetry.

Some of the questions will not have a single correct answer; they are asked so that a few of the possible answers will be elicited in reading and discussion. And remember that when you have 'understood' a poem the essential part may be still to come, namely a genuine response of feeling to all that it contains.

Walt Whitman

pages 22-3

'THE LITTLE ONE SLEEPS IN ITS CRADLE': *1*. In the first six lines of the poem, the images relating to good and evil are moving in a particular direction. What is this direction? *2. Song of Myself* is a long poem. Whitman says in another section:

> What blurt is this about virtue and about vice
> Evil propels me and reform of evil propels me, I stand indifferent,
> My gait is no fault-finder's or rejector's gait,
> I moisten the roots of all that has grown.

Point out the elements of 'evil' and of 'good' in the selection studied. Which of the two predominates? What is Whitman saying about reality? *3*. This extract is an entire section from *Song of Myself*. As a single poem, or unit in itself, is it well organized?

Gerard Manley Hopkins

pages 24-6

SPRING: *1*. What is the poet saying in the first eight lines? To what does he turn his attention in the concluding six? What form of poem has the poet created? What is the rhyme scheme? Notice the irregularity of rhythm and the varying length of line. Do not try to systematize it; enjoy the sound and bounce of it. *2*. Is the spring *all* of perfection — Eden — or only a part of it? Does this explain the urgency at the end? How? *3*. Who is being addressed in the closing lines of the poem? What is the object of the verbs 'have, get'? *4*. What, then, is the relation between 'spring' and youthful innocence?

SPRING AND FALL: *1*. Why is Margaret 'grieving' at the beginning of the poem? *2*. Will she grieve for the same thing in later life? *3*. What will she grieve for in later life? *4*. Hopkins says that the two kinds of grief are the same: that is, the 'leaves' represent her own life to the little girl. What, then, is 'the blight man was born for'?

'NO WORST, THERE IS NONE': *1*. This is a poem of agony and near-despair. What are the two meanings of 'pitch' here? How do pains increase, in the second line? Is there any limit to pain? *2*. *Comforter* is a recognized name for the Holy Spirit. Do you think Hopkins is doubting, or rejecting faith? What moment in the New Testament is suggested by lines 3 and 4? *3*. Hopkins does not tell us the cause of his suffering, but he describes it as a 'main' woe, a 'chief woe', a 'world-sorrow', an 'age-old' sorrow. What kinds of grief would fit such a description? *4*. Does your answer help to interpret the last line? Why does the word 'all' hang suspended at the end of the line?

Emily Dickinson

pages 27-9

'A NARROW FELLOW IN THE GRASS': *1*. Is Emily Dickinson afraid of snakes? What is her attitude towards the snake in the first three verses? How does her attitude relate to verse six? *2*. Why are the following words especially suitable: rides, comb, shaft, wrinkled, zero? *3*. Is there possibly some big idea suggested by 'whip-lash/unbraiding'? Has it any connection with fear? What is the traditional association of 'snake' that may possibly lurk behind this?

'I DIED FOR BEAUTY': *1*. What famous line of John Keats is recalled by the poem? (If you do not know, look up the opening of *Endymion*.) *2*. Why are the following words particularly meaningful: adjusted, adjoining, failed? *3*. The rhymes in verses two and three are imperfect. Is this deliberate? (Try a substitute word for 'said' in verse two. Is it easy to find a perfect rhyme? Try a substitute for 'names' in verse three, to rhyme with 'rooms'.) Could there be a pleasure (and purpose) in imperfect harmony? *4.* Is the union of truth and beauty permanent? Explain.

'SOME KEEP THE SABBATH GOING TO CHURCH': *1.* Do you think Emily Dickinson is being irreligious? Explain your opinion. If nature is a church, how is our view of nature affected; and our view of the church? *2.* Who might the 'sexton' be? (Look up the word in a good dictionary and you may find an answer.) *3.* Judging from the last two lines, how does Emily's way of life differ from that of other people? In what way do you think that God 'preaches' to her?

'I TASTE A LIQUOR NEVER BREWED': *1.* Imagine a cup made of a scooped-out pearl. What is the 'liquor' that Emily drinks from such a cup? Where are the 'inns'? *2.* Who are her competitors and companions in drink? *3.* She is going home 'drunk' at the end. What do 'seraphs' and 'saints' add to the meaning?

A. E. Housman
pages 30-1

TO AN ATHLETE DYING YOUNG: *1.* When he won the race, the athlete was brought home on the shoulders of friends. In the second stanza, how is he being brought home a second time? What is the 'threshold' and the 'stiller town'? *2.* The laurel is the crown of victory, while the rose is beauty. Why does he say the laurel fades more quickly? *3.* In stanza four, 'the record cut' may mean that the athlete's record is beaten. What other sense of 'cut' is possible in the same context? *4.* Does the poem say it is better to live – or to die young? 'The strengthless dead' are spirits of the dead as represented in Greek and Latin literature (Housman was a classical scholar). The 'garland' is the athlete's crown of victory again. Why does the comparison with a young girl strike us as particularly touching?

'INTO MY HEART AN AIR THAT KILLS': *1.* There is a 'far country' for which the poet longs. The second verse tells us what that far country is. Why does the air from that place 'kill'? What is 'air'? *2.* Would you say that such regret is a universal human emotion? Is it the same in all of us? What kind of person feels it most? Who feels it least?

Thomas Hardy
pages 32-4

THE DARKLING THRUSH: *1*. A *coppice* is a thicket; *bine* means the same as vine; *evensong* is an evening prayer or song. Do these words tell you anything about the nationality of the writer? *2*. There are about ten details in the first two stanzas that give a picture of desolation. Point out a half-dozen of these. *3*. What 'century' does Hardy refer to (the poem is dated 31 December 1900)? There were many inspired and joyful poems about bird-songs and singing maidens in that century: 'The Skylark', 'To A Skylark', 'The Solitary Reaper'. What may be the significance here? *4*. Try to estimate how far Hardy is convinced that there is some hidden joy being communicated to him, and how far he doubts that joy is possible. *5*. *Darkling* has several dictionary meanings: in the dark, deeply shadowed, uncannily dark, dim, obscure, gloomy. Which of these applies here? Is the meaning 'gloomy' possible in the present context?

WHERE THE PICNIC WAS: *1*. Study the rhyme scheme of the poem. How many stressed syllables do you find in each line? The meter is called *dimeter*. *2*. What contrast does Hardy explicitly make between the two friends who have dispersed and himself? Is such a contrast more relevant to the poetry of the past than to our own time? What additional thoughts do we have by considering *three* different places — country, city, and death?

Edwin Arlington Robinson
pages 35-6

RICHARD CORY: *1*. In this dramatic poem, what are the two aspects of Richard Cory's good fortune in the eyes of the world? Why have they been selected (various reasons may be given)? *2*. What are the two features attributed to the rest of 'us'? *3*. How does 'waited for the light' bear especially on the fate of Richard Cory? Did he have any light? *4*. If the poem states the truth about Richard Cory, who seemed so fortunate, what is the implication about the state of other men?

Rudyard Kipling

pages 37-41

L'ENVOI TO *THE SEVEN SEAS*: *1*. 'Envoi' is pronounced *en-voy*; it means postscript or final poem. The metaphor of painting pictures is used in the poem. With what is this equated? *2*. In the afterlife we shall do our work more perfectly. What is wrong with the way we work in this world (see stanza three)? *3*. What is the formula for perfect happiness in our work? State it in your own words.

GUNGA DIN: *1*. *Aldershot it* means 'had an easy time at Aldershot military academy'; *bhisti* is water carrier; *slippery hitherao* means 'Come over here!'; *Panee lao* means 'bring water quick'; *Harry By* is 'O brother'; *juldee* is speed; *marrow you* is 'hit you'; *mussick* is water skin; *plugged me* means stopped the wound; *dooli* is a litter for carrying the wounded. *2*. What is implied in the phrase 'Injia's sunny clime'? *3*. In the last stanza, what is 'the place where 'e is gone'? Why? How does he see himself? ('Lazarushian-leather' is a nonce-word from lazarus meaning a leprous beggar and leather referring to Gunga Din's skin.) *4*. What is the position of Gunga Din on the social scale? What does 'race' have to do with it? What is the attitude of the speaker toward him? What is the effect of the poem on these relations?

John Masefield

pages 42-7

THE FIGHT: *1*. Pick out, in this poem, at least a dozen examples of sub-standard English; also some vulgar expressions that would not be acceptable in normal conversation. What justification is there for these? (Such usage has been common since Chaucer's day. He justified it by saying that 'Christ spoke himself full broad in Holy Writ'.) *2*. Masefield is deliberately giving us a picture of brutal reality. Apart from the language, what features in the story serve his purpose? *3*. Saul Kane is suffering from a sense of guilt. Show where his guilt appears in his account of the fight. (Later in the story he turns to religion and reforms. Some time you might want to read the entire poem — it's an old best-seller.)

William Butler Yeats

pages 48-52

HE THINKS OF THOSE WHO HAVE SPOKEN EVIL OF HIS BELOVED: *1*. Is this a realistic poem? Why not? What makes it a somewhat 'highfalutin pose'? Do you agree that it is beautiful nevertheless? *2*. Yeats evokes an imaginary world in which great lovers and the realities are opposed. Is there any truth behind this fiction? (Discuss.)

HE WISHES FOR THE CLOTHS OF HEAVEN: *1*. The same questions may be asked of this poem as of the preceding one. What do the 'cloths of heaven' represent? What do 'dreams' represent; that is, in what form has the poet expressed them? *2*. What, then, is the meaning of 'tread softly ... on my dreams'?

THE COMING OF WISDOM WITH TIME: *1*. The poem was written in the middle period of Yeats's life. The two preceding poems are typical of his early poetry. Does the idea expressed here have any relation to these earlier poems? *2*. What are 'leaves' here? If the 'root' is one, what does that imply for the future? What will you look for in the later poems?

ADAM'S CURSE: *1*. Do you see a difference in the language and attitude here, as compared with the two earlier poems of Yeats? (The poem was written some years after these early poems.) How would you describe the change? *2*. With what is the writing of the poem compared in the first two stanzas? Notice that these comparisons evoke a strong sense of reality. *3*. How do women 'labour to be beautiful'? What does the poet next describe as requiring labour? *4*. In verse four, Yeats refers to the tradition of courtly love, developed in the Middle Ages, in which the art of addressing a lady was highly studied and perfected. (Think of the words 'courting' and 'to pay court'.) In almost everything we do today we apply an opposite formula, well expressed in Irving Berlin's hit song 'Doin' What Comes Natur'lly'. What is Yeats's opinion on this matter? *5*. What is 'Adam's curse'? What did God say to Adam when He sent him out of Eden?

THE SECOND COMING: *1*. If beauty or poetry, and love, seem to have lost their value (as we see in the preceding poem), the poet finds himself in conflict with his age. In 'The Second Coming', written in the mid 1920s, Yeats goes further. What kind of new age is being born? *2*. A *gyre* (pronounced with a hard *g*, as in *guide*) is a spiral form. If our world is falling apart because 'the falcon' over the centuries has moved out of earshot of 'the falconer' — what is the falconer? What is it that originally held our civilization together? What relation has that cohesive force to the end of the poem? *3*. *Mere* means, absolute, unmixed, an old meaning of the word. Try to expand the meaning of 'ceremony of innocence'. Also, give some examples of 'the worst / Are full of passionate intensity'. *4*. Christ was expected to return to earth, in a 'second coming'. Here the Spirit of the World (Spiritus Mundi) produces a dream of monstrous birth. Was Yeats's prophetic vision realized in the 1930s and '40s? Do you think the prophecy is now complete, or is more still to come?

ON BEING ASKED FOR A WAR POEM: *1*. Would you say, after reading the other poems of Yeats represented here, that his view in this poem is justified? Why? *2*. Is poetry important if it can do the two things described in the last two lines?

Carl Sandburg
pages 53-60

CHICAGO: *1*. This famous poem made Carl Sandburg's reputation when it appeared in *Poetry* magazine in Chicago in 1914. Can you see why? What are the elements of stark realism that would shock the reader accustomed to romantic nature poetry? *2*. Sandburg is addressing the city. He finds evil in it, but seems to accept it. Compare 'Chicago' to the poem by Walt Whitman at the beginning of this book. Does Sandburg really approve of evil? *3*. What are the virtues that Sandburg celebrates in the lines beginning 'Come and show me . . .'? What does he praise?

COOL TOMBS: *1*. A *copperhead* was a northerner who sympathized with the South in the Civil War. Sandburg is a great admirer of Abraham Lincoln. Yet is there something shocking in the way he speaks of him? What is his purpose in so speaking? What does death have to do with it? *2*. Ulysses Grant was the general who received Lee's surrender and later became President himself. Why are his problems with finance introduced into the poem? What is the relation to modern life? *3*. In turn, what does Pocahontas seem to represent? Does this point to the conclusion of the poem? Are the final theme and the 'tombs' naturally related?

GONE: *1.* The poem sounds very much like a folk-song. In what way is this effect achieved? (Carl Sandburg is a collector and singer of folk-songs.) Do you know any other songs or poems that have the same theme? *2.* Is the wistful image of Chick Lorimer vividly evoked? What particular words produce this image? *3.* If the poem has a certain down-to-earth quality, despite the romantic feeling, what are the social conditions you can imagine as a background?

WORKING GIRLS: *1.* What is being contrasted in the lines beginning 'Green and gray . . .'? *2.* What does the comparison at the beginning of the poem add to the picture of working girls? *3.* Is the poem primarily a feeling, or an idea? Is it a good poem? (Discuss.)

HAPPINESS: *1.* Why does Sandburg compare 'professors' 'famous executives' , and 'Hungarians'? To what do we relate each of these? *2.* What is happiness, according to the poem? Is there any truth in this view?

THE SHOVEL MAN: *1.* If Sandburg celebrates the working-man, why does he use the word 'dago' — an insulting word for Italian? *2.* Why is the long line beginning 'And a dark-eyed woman . . .' contrasted to all that went before? What is Sandburg's purpose in this contrast?

' "DO TELL!" . . . "I WANT TO KNOW!" ': *1.* Who speaks in most of this poem? Could almost anyone write another like it? What has Sandburg contributed by arrangement and selection? *2.* What is the view we get of 'the people'? What qualities do 'the people' have? *3.* Does the poem give a true picture of mankind in the mass? Does that matter in evaluating the poetry? To what extent? What is valuable in Sandburg's feeling for 'the people'?

Edgar Lee Masters
pages 61-7

SETH COMPTON: *1.* The point of the poem is, of course, stated in the last four lines. But what kind of poetry or art results when

only 'what is good' is considered? Can you think of any examples —
especially in popular art and decoration? *2.* Why do some people
object to art that presents 'what is evil' as well as what is good? This
is a far-reaching question. How can these people be answered?
3. Faust sold his soul to the devil. *Evangeline* is a sentimentally-
treated love-story. Joseph Butler's *Analogy of Religion* (1736) was
a conservative defence of Christianity, directed against deists or
rationalists. Count de Volney's *Les Ruines ou Méditations sur les
révolutions des empires* (1791) was a sceptical book, expounding
political equality and religious agnosticism. What sort of circulat-
ing-library business did Mr. Compton have in Spoon River? Was
his bookstore popular? Who patronized it?

MINERVA JONES: *1.* What is the irony, or conflict of opposites,
contained in Minerva Jones's fate? What relation does the poem
have to the preceding one? Is the problem here something more
than to 'know' good and evil? How is society responsible for this
problem? (The poet here is indicting a society, not individuals.)
2. What is the emotion evoked by the last four lines? (Distinguish
between the emotion of Minerva's outcry and our emotion in hearing the story.)

DOCTOR MEYERS: *1.* Why was Doctor Meyers indicted and
disgraced? What he committed was an illegal act; yet why do we
feel so strongly that he was innocent and suffered an unjust fate?
2. How are the people of Spoon River responsible for this tragedy
of life?

DAISY FRASER: *1.* What two classes of people does Daisy Fraser
choose to castigate with her ironic comment? Why? *2.* If Daisy
Fraser is 'evil', what is the point that Masters is making in the closing
lines? How does the equation apply to the citizens she mentions?
Are we being enlightened or confused as to the nature of good and
evil?

JUDGE SOMERS: *1.* Why is 'Nature' introduced into the poem?
Is the ironic reversal possibly justified? What virtues did the Judge
possess? Does Masters seem to admire him or not? Does he dis-
approve of Chase Henry? *2.* What does the poem suggest about
our true merits and deserts?

EMILY SPARKS: *1*. How does the teacher visualize her favourite pupil? Do you think she had a good judgment of him? *2*. What is the teacher's nature? Is she realistic or sentimental, religious or sceptical, cynical or idealistic? Which terms apply?

REUBEN PANTIER: *1*. How is the discovery in this poem, about the sordid life of Reuben Pantier, implicit in the preceding poem? *2*. A *cocotte* is a woman of loose morals. Is Reuben Pantier's life unredeemed, a life of evil? Examine the poem carefully. What does the 'new vision' suggest?

FIDDLER JONES: *1*. What point is made in the two opening lines? How does it relate to Fiddler Jones? *2*. In line 5, which word should be emphasized? Various preferences are then described, examples of what people find most valuable in life. List them. *3*. Cooney Potter had a special talent. What was it? What was it that looked like 'Red-Head Sammy' to Fiddler Jones? *4*. He heard music in his ears when certain sounds ('only these' – nothing more) reached his ears. What sounds? *5*. What makes the last four lines memorable?

Robert Frost

pages 68-72

THE PASTURE: *1*. This poem stands at the beginning of Frost's *Collected Poems*, as a kind of preface. In view of this, what is it really inviting us to do? *2*. Along such a line of thought, what would 'clean the pasture spring' mean, as a metaphor for something else? Will Frost spend much time over it? What would we see in 'clear water'? Is he urging us to come with him? Does he consider his labour very important? Unimportant? *3*. How does the subject of verse two differ from that of verse one? What is Frost's feeling in the second verse? What is the effect of the repetition of the refrain?

MOWING: *1*. In Shakespeare's *Cymbeline* there is a dirge that begins with this verse: 'Fear no more the heat o' the sun, / Nor the furious winter's rages; / Thou thy worldly task hast done, / Home art gone and ta'en thy wages: / Golden lads and girls all must, / As chimney-sweepers, come to dust.' Can you find a point of connection between this dirge and Frost's sonnet? *2*. Following this lead, examine closely the meaning of this sonnet. What is the relevance of 'scythe', 'the lack of sound', the word 'whispered', the 'spikes of flowers' and the 'bright green snake'? Try to interpret these without insisting too dogmatically on a particular meaning. *3*. Discuss the meaning of the ninth line and show by example what it means. If the poem is about the truth contained in poetry, what does he mean by saying he 'left the hay to make'?

'OUT, OUT – ': *1*. Do you see the significance of the 'five mountain ranges'? In the description of the saw, what is the contrast between the words 'snarled and rattled' on the one hand, and 'stovelength . . . sweet-scented' wood on the other? What is the reason for such contrast? *2*. What does the presence of the sister add to the narrative? *3*. The boy is doing necessary work for a living. Where do we learn this? How does it relate to the tragedy? *4*. Why do you think the last two lines are so abrupt? Why do the people not grieve longer? What attitude to life's tragedies is indicated here? Do you think Frost is being cruel? What does he feel for the boy? *5*. Relate the title to *Macbeth*, Act V, Scene *5*.

A CONSIDERABLE SPECK: *1*. This little poem is filled with ideas. Note the line about 'collectivistic regimenting love'. What kinds of things does it refer to? *2*. What is the tiny creature's attitude to what Frost is writing, that is, toward his poetry? Whom does the creature represent? What attitudes, successively, does Frost have toward the tiny thing? *3*. How would too much general compassion for every individual be 'collectivistic regimenting love'? What would it neglect? Does Frost imply that we should judge people severely? When? Why does the insignificant mite deserve respect?

Ezra Pound
pages 73-82

THE RIVER-MERCHANT'S WIFE: A LETTER: *1*. Rihaku is the Japanese name for Li Po, a famous Chinese poet who lived about 750 A.D. during the T'ang dynasty. The poem is a translation, or adaptation, from the Chinese. *2*. About what age are the two people in the first passage? *3*. Is timidity alone, or something more, implied in the second strophe? *4*. What change occurs in the third strophe? Why do you think the man went away? What feelings and thoughts are aroused by mosses, monkeys, early autumn, and butterflies, in the context of the poem? Do we need to know where Cho-fu-Sa is located?

N.Y.: *1.* The poetic fiction of attributing feeling or life to inanimate objects was described by Ruskin as 'the pathetic fallacy' (*pathetic* here meaning 'pertaining to feeling', from the Greek *pathein* – to suffer). How is this fallacy illustrated in the present poem? What kind of character does the poet assume in the first three lines? *2.* What is the shift in the next four lines? What point of view has he now taken? *3.* Why does he return to the fiction in the last six lines? How would you interpret such vacillation? What does it say about poetry?

THE STUDY IN AESTHETICS: *1.* The Italian words in line 4 mean 'Look! Look!' What a beauty!' *Sta fermo* means 'Keep still!' What is the contrast between the children and their aesthetic response – i.e., why is it surprising to hear this from these particular children? Later, what is the contrast between the second incident and the first? *2.* Why are the Dantes and Catulli mentioned? Why should the poet be 'abashed' (i.e., humbled and confused)? What is the lesson we get from this study in aesthetics?

MEDITATIO: *1.* A witty poem that is no less artfully constructed than the preceding ones – like the lowly sardines, it too can be admired. Can you imagine the 'curious habits of dogs'? (Mention these in as polite terms as the poet has done by effective understatement.) The first three lines say that man is civilized, as compared to the dog. The last two leave the matter in question. In what ways does man lack taste, reasonableness, culture, civilization – i.e., in what ways does he display bad habits?

SALUTATION I: *1.* In the poem four degrees of happiness are mentioned. What are these? Which are the two extreme opposites? Place the four in order of rank, as to happiness. What does this reveal about the poet? *2.* Try to explain why 'smugness' is the reverse of freedom. (Look up the word *smug* for all its connotations.)

THE REST: *1.* Pound is an American who, as an artist, had to leave his country but achieved fame abroad. What is the position of the artist in society described in this poem? Examine every detail.

2. By using himself as an example, what does Pound achieve dramatically for other artists? Finally, how true is the poem? Also, how important is such a consideration to the success of the poem? (Both these are very interesting and debatable questions.)

COMMISSION: *1. Mortmain* – literally *dead hand* – is a legal term signifying inalienable tenure or possession: here it means tradition, custom, hereditary oppression in general. The poem is a declaration of rights for all those oppressed by society and custom. If you agree with it, you will probably like it that much more. Is this usually true of art? Does our admiration always depend on agreement? Or is more involved? *2.* Examine the individual phrases in this poem. Which are particularly trenchant? Which are most sharply ironic? *3.* To whom is the poem addressed, and what does this contribute to the poem's effectiveness?

'THESE FOUGHT IN ANY CASE' and 'THERE DIED A MYRIAD': *1.* These are two sections of a longer poem. These two sections deal with the First World War. Examine, in the first poem, each of the reasons given for going to war. Is any of these a good reason? *2.* The quotation referred to is *dulce et decorum est pro patria mori* – 'pleasant and fitting it is to die for one's country'. What does Pound think of this slogan? But was there virtue in the young men who died? Point out these virtues. *3.* How do the last three lines of Section IV differ from what precedes? *4.* In the second poem Pound enlarges his condemnation to the entire civilization which produced the war. Discuss his view of it as a decaying civilization. Why is there a special bitterness for Pound in the last two lines?

'WHAT THOU LOVEST WELL REMAINS . . . ': *1.* The poem is an extract from Pound's huge book-length poem, or epic, *The Cantos*, dealing with history, economics, morality, the decline of civilization, and the value of the arts. Here he affirms the good of what each man loves, against the general flood of destruction and barbarism released in the Second World War: 'Elysium, though it were in the halls of hell'. Give some examples of what is meant by 'What thou lovest well'. *2.* What is the point about the ant? Who was it 'made courage . . . order . . . grace'? Does the poem tell us? *3.* Paquin is the name of a fashion designer in Paris. How does this reference relate to the theme of the poem? *4.* At the time of writing, Pound, an aging man of sixty, had been imprisoned in a wire cage, accused of treason to his country. Where in the poem is this reflected? He had also been charged with anti-Semitism and fascist leanings. Can you find the lines that might bear on the accusation? *5. Rathe* is an obsolete word meaning prompt. Blunt is the poet William Scawen Blunt; Pound seems to be referring to an actual incident. The *fine old eye* is someone possessing seasoned taste (perhaps Yeats, who admired Pound's poetry).

T. S. Eliot
pages 83-98

PRELUDES: *1.* The 'cab-horse' and the 'lighting of the lamps' place the poem at the beginning of our century. Does it then sound dated? If not, what features make it still a vivid image of city life? *2.* Eliot does not find things beautiful, as might have been expected from a poet. Show how he brings out the negative elements of reality. *3.* What does 'masquerades / That time resumes' say about this reality? How does it relate to Eliot's dissatisfaction with the world he describes? *4.* Are all 'souls' constituted of 'sordid images'? By using the word *souls*, what else is suggested? *5.* Is a man or a woman being addressed in Prelude III? *6.* What various experiences (six in number) does the man's 'soul' suffer in Prelude IV? Do the Preludes contain any example of an 'infinitely gentle / Infinitely suffering thing'? How does this image relate to the others in the poem? *7.* The last two lines summarize in a single image the feeling of these preludes. Name several aspects of life expressed by the image.

MORNING AT THE WINDOW: *1.* The images of a poem can be taken as vehicles for emotions and attitudes. Look closely at each image in this short poem and decide what feelings it conveys.

PORTRAIT OF A LADY: *1.* To what social class does the lady belong? How is her class revealed by the language of the speaker? What is the chief quality of character, or rather the characteristic weakness, that the poet brings out about the lady? Show this in detail. *2.* Why is 'Juliet's tomb' mentioned? What associations are thus brought to the poem? What is the relation between the lady and the speaker of the poem? (See the middle of Section II and middle of Section III.) What is the lady's approximate age? and the man's? *3*. What is the time of year described in each section? What does this tell us? *4*. What is the speaker's frame of mind? Examine each section for evidence. Why does he feel so? Is it just the lady, or possibly something more general?

A GAME OF CHESS: *1*. This poem is the second part of T. S. Eliot's poem *The Waste Land*, which describes contemporary life as an arid desert through which the individual wanders in search of redeeming faith. The imagery of the poem represents an ordeal like that of the medieval knight in quest of the Holy Grail, travel through a wilderness (which is the modern world), temptations, fears and hallucinations, ending in the so-called Chapel Perilous where ultimate questions are to be answered. The answers to these questions, in Eliot's poem, are: Give. Sympathize. Control. This is expressed in Sanskrit, a language that modern man cannot understand. In the opening passage of this section, up to line 34, how many examples can you find of fluids and liquids which are unpalatable? *2*. A number of literary allusions appear in the passage: the opening recalls Shakespeare's *Antony and Cleopatra* ('The barge she sat in, like a burnish'd throne, / Burn'd on the water . . .'); the 'Chair', capitalized, refers to the constellation of Cassiopeia, who was punished for boasting of her beauty; a *Cupidon* is a decorative representation of the god of love; the 'sevenbranched candelabra' refers to the Pleiades, seven maidens who were pursued by Orion and who were turned into a constellation; the 'laquearia', or coffered ceiling, refers to Virgil's story of Dido, who was abandoned by Aeneas and afterwards committed suicide; 'the sylvan scene' refers to Milton's description of Adam and Eve in the garden of Eden, a scene of idyllic innocence before the fall of man; 'the change of Philomel' refers to the story of King Tereus, his wife Procne, and Philomela. Tereus did violence to his wife's sister Philomela, then cut out her tongue and imprisoned her in a hut in a forest; she was able to send a message to her sister, however, and together they avenged themselves on Tereus by killing his son and serving his flesh to the father. Philomela turned into a nightingale and Procne into a swallow as they were pursued by Tereus. A song by John Lyly which has the phrase ' "jug, jug, tereu," she cries' refers to the story of Philomela. How do all these allusions bear on the description of a nerve-wracked modern woman in her boudoir, sitting before a mirror? *3*. In the conversation between the man and the lady in question, which follows, make clear who is speaking at each point. What is the state of mind of each speaker? There is a reference to Shakespeare's *Tempest* ('Those are pearls that were his eyes'), a play in which the famous words occur when Miranda sees noble human beings for the first time: 'O wonder! / How many goodly creatures are there here! / How beauteous mankind is! O brave new world, / That has such people in't!' How does this apply to the present context? The phrase 'a game of chess', Eliot tells us, refers to a play by Thomas Middleton, *Women beware Women*, in which Bianca, a married woman, is seduced in the balcony while her chaperon is entertained below at a game of chess. This idea of brutal seduction and betrayal gives unity to this part of Eliot's *Waste Land* entitled 'A Game of Chess'. How does it relate also to the ending, 'Good night, sweet ladies', which alludes to Ophelia's sad raving after the death of her father in *Hamlet*? Ophelia, of course, drowned herself. 4. The passage beginning 'When Lil's husband got demobbed ...' presents a scene in a London pub. The capitalized words are spoken by the barman, and mean literally 'It's closing time'; but here they have an ominous and even terrifying effect. Why? Go over the conversation carefully, to distinguish who is speaking at each point, and then describe the situation and character of Lil and Albert, that is, all that you can tell about them. 5. *Demobbed* means demobilized or discharged from the army. Can you date the poem from this? 'Them pills I took' refers to an abortion, part of Eliot's picture of 'love and marriage' in modern life. A *hot gammon* is a ham. What is the effect of the word 'beauty' here? Point out examples of sub-standard English in the passage. What impression does it make on the reader? How does such use of English relate to Eliot's main purpose?

DEATH BY WATER: *1.* This poem is Section IV of *The Waste Land*. It is at the same time both contemporary and ancient. Which are the words that suggest a modern setting? What suggests something of the early days of the Christian era? What is achieved by such ambiguity? *2.* What values of life are criticized by the poem? What else is advised as preferable? *3.* Is the shape of the poem loose, disorganized? or beautiful, pleasing? Examine the movement of the words for their rhythmic and emotional effect. Notice what happens at the ends of lines when there is no punctuation. Relate all these rhythmic effects to the meaning conveyed.

JOURNEY OF THE MAGI: *1.* You may want to read the second chapter of Matthew in the New Testament as background for this poem. Who is speaking in the poem? (The opening words are in quotation-marks because Eliot is quoting a seventeenth-century sermon by Lancelot Andrewes.) 2. What is the sense of 'regretted' in line 8? How does the language manage to suggest that it is all happening today? Is there a purpose in this? Are we seeking the truth, just like the wise men of the east? Interpret the entire poem, in detail, according to this view. 3. For 'white horse' see Revelations, chapter six. What meaning may be contained in 'three trees'? (If you cannot guess, look up Acts v.30.) Similarly, what do 'pieces of silver' recall? More difficult, what may 'running stream' suggest? (Think of the whole story of Jesus.) These allusions surrounding the birth of Christ bring to mind the later events, and they are presented in modern terms as almost unrecognizable. Do you think there is a purpose in this? 4. How might 'birth' and 'death' be the same, in terms of Christian faith? In what sense do we live in 'the old dispensation'?

CHORUSES FROM 'THE ROCK': 1. *The Rock* is a liturgical play, dated 1933. *Lobelias* are flowers common in English suburban gardens. A *cavie* is a chicken coop; a *marmot* is a rodent, like the Canadian ground-hog. The poem is not difficult to understand – it is direct as a sermon. Compare it with Ezra Pound's 'Commission' and discuss the questions raised in the first part of the study notes on that poem. 2. The Introduction to the present anthology states that 'Poetry does not persuade; it makes us feel and perceive.' How could that statement be reconciled with the present poem or with Ezra Pound's 'Commission'?

D. H. Lawrence
pages 99-104

SNAKE: 1. The effect of the poem turns on the way that Lawrence communicates to us his intimate personal feelings for an animal creature, the snake, and makes this deeply significant. Trace, point by point, the poet's changing feelings toward the snake. 2. What are the two opposing influences working on the poet, two ways of life between which he is divided? The first – the voices – is easier to understand; the other must be partly illustrated by the poem – its full description would lead us far into the ideas of D. H. Lawrence. Relate the snake, at least, to 'the earth' and to so-called 'nature'. What relation does Lawrence desire with these things? 3. Notice the phrase 'bowels of the earth'. In actuality the snake probably went under some rocks, about six inches deep; the phrase 'bowels of the earth' is therefore symbolic rather than literal. 'Bowels', of course, suggest the procreative body and the sources of sexuality. Which of the attitudes expressed in the poem would apply as attitudes toward the sexual instinct? 4. Do you recognize the allusion to 'albatross'? What is the idea, then, in the three lines following the albatross couplet?

GREEN: 1. The interest of this poem derives very much from the chiming rhyme. Listen first to the effect of the rhyme sounds. 2. Point out four qualities of 'green' that occur in the poem. (Incidentally, a 'green wine' is possible – as a liqueur at least.) 3. What is the connection between what happens in line 1 and in line 4?

A YOUNG WIFE: 1. It is best if we assume that the young wife is speaking in the poem. In the second verse, 'fear' and 'darkness' are associated with the one she loves. This is because, for Lawrence, love is not merely carnal enjoyment but a profound and awful principle in nature. It is, also, inseparable from union in marriage, about which Lawrence had deep convictions: he believed in chastity, monogamy, and reverence for the sexual reality. What is the paradox, then, in lines 7 and 8? 2. The tree in verse four looks at its own shadow (a dark side of things) as something newly discovered. What is said here about all nature as well as about human love? (*The cup* is of course innocence and virginity, which is now changed.) 3. The air is filled with a new dark knowledge; and then it becomes identified with death. Is this step logical? What is the relation between death and marriage? 4. Despite these sombre meanings, is the poem depressing or is it filled with light and joy? Explain why.

AFTER THE OPERA: 1. What do we know about the opera that has just been performed? Why is 'wreckage' mentioned? What opinion does Lawrence have of the way the ladies have responded to the opera? Is there a difference between the 'girls' and the 'ladies' in their response? Distinguish carefully. 2. What does the barman have to do with the subject? And where do we assume that Lawrence 'came from'?

322

William Carlos Williams

pages 105-10

LOVE SONG: *1*. The theme is life (or love) and death. What are the qualities of life in which Williams delights? What are the two aspects of it contained in the phrase 'a burst of fragrance'? *2*. Why is the word 'loaves' extremely apt? (You buy only one loaf of bread, usually; but where do 'loaves' come from?)

THE ACT: *1*. What two facts of life are the subject of this poem, represented by 'roses' and the action of cutting them? *2*. What point of view does the speaker represent? What is the opposed view, expressed by the feminine voice? Which is stronger? What mixture of emotions does this strength and decision express?

COMPLAINT: *1*. Here we see Williams, in his medical role, on his early-morning rounds. What is the feeling implied in using the words 'Joy! Joy!' (Look at the context preceding.) *2*. What feeling is conveyed by the reference to night ... lovers ... and the morning sun? Does it have to do with the old woman? What is in the mind of the good doctor? Is he sympathetic to the sick lady? What is the shift in the three closing lines?

THE RED WHEELBARROW: *1*. This poem is one of the most famous in Williams's repertoire, and one of the shortest. The first reaction is, 'How simple can you get?' Yet the simplicity of the poem is combined with an extreme formal organization. Notice the mathematical arrangement of the words. *2*. At first sight the poem says very little. After the four opening words, all we have is a picture of the wheelbarrow (an example of *Imagism*, a school of poetry started in 1912, which aimed at presenting a clear perception, or image, in a short poem). What are the qualities of the image of a wheelbarrow? If you have this right, you will discover an important statement about life contained in the four opening words. Can you express the statement in your own way?

YOUNG WOMAN AT A WINDOW: *1*. Here the chain-like connection of the words provides additional order to the formal arrangement. The poem presents grief and compassion with great economy. *2*. Is there a possible idea in the items being linked together in the poem? How is the link in each case emphasized by the arrangement of words?

323

POEM: *1*. If you 'weighed' the lines in this poem, you would find them about equal. Yet the poem is not metrical, it is free verse. The arrangement again is formal and precise. The poem is an experiment in kinetic effect, action. *2*. What factors in the placing of words make it easy to see the cat going through these motions? Notice such things as words at the ends of lines, or phrases divided by the line endings, or words standing alone on a line, as forms of emphasis, or abrupt action, or suspension.

TO A POOR OLD WOMAN: *1*. This is another famous Williams poem. If you read it too quickly, without participating in the feeling, it may strike you as absurd. If you follow what the poet is saying, and share the feeling, you will find it very human and interesting. *2*. The poem is a good demonstration of technique — the effect of breaking a line like 'They taste good to her' at different points. Describe the effect at each break. What is the difference between the fourth line and the final line, although they have exactly the same words?

CONTEMPORANIA: *1*. In the poem, a delightful one written after a rainfall, one seems to be holding one's breath, after the great rain, in the wet garden. But what is the difference between what 'the little leaves' say and the 'green shoots'? Why is there a difference? *2*. Could there be more to this poem than the garden and the rain? Why is it called 'Contemporania'? (Do you see the pun in this?) Williams was aware of a great change coming over poetry, destroying the old metrical rhymed forms and bringing in new forms and new subject matter. How might this idea be contained in a poem about a great rain? Are Williams's own poetic hopes involved?

EDUCATION A FAILURE: *1*. This is the most tricky of Williams's poems included here. What are the 'minor stupidities' that irritate the poet? How are 'heaven and the ideal state' closed? *2*. Describe exactly what the two cats and the bird are doing. Which cat is being watched by the poet? What relation does that cat have to the idea of 'heaven and the ideal state'? Is the bird something remote and impossible to reach? Why is the poet interested in this 'rather' than in heaven? Why is the second cat there? Are there some people who resemble the second cat? *3*. Why is the poem entitled 'Education a Failure'? Is education also affected with 'minor stupidities'? Should education be concerned with 'heaven and the ideal state'? Or with the effort to achieve something difficult in this world – like the cat who is threading the hedge? Why does Williams call education 'a failure'?

Wallace Stevens
pages 111-16

THE EMPEROR OF ICE-CREAM: *1*. In the poem a woman lies dead. What sort of people have come to sit at her funeral? Is it a wealthy home? What food is meant by 'concupiscent curds'? Look up the word *concupiscent*. Which of its meanings fits here? *2*. In line 7, the word 'seem' refers to illusions, self-deceptions, untruth. *Be* is reality, truth. How would you now interpret the line following? (It's a cynical reflection, if that is any help.) *3. Deal* is simply board, or wood. A *fantail* is a pigeon with a fanlike tail. *Horny feet* are, of course, feet with calluses. What emotional response have you to the picture of the dead body presented? Why is the lamp introduced? Would you yourself prefer ice cream? That's what the poet suggests.

THE WORMS AT HEAVEN'S GATE: *1*. The title is a travesty on Shakespeare's line: 'Hark, hark! The lark at heaven's gate sings.' Here, however, a dead princess with a very big name is being carried out of her tomb by little worms. What effect is produced by the contrast with Shakespeare? (The song in Shakespeare has this ending: 'With everything that pretty is, / My lady sweet, arise! / Arise, arise!'). *2*. The name Badroulbadour suggests perhaps a fairy-tale, or an exotic, oriental setting. What does this amusing name do to the feeling of horror we experience? Why do you think the poet writes such a shocking poem? What does it have to do with us?

GUBBINAL: *1*. Here is a dialogue about what life is really like: is it beautiful or ugly? What does the person speaking believe? Test the belief by referring to lines 1, 6, and 9. What does the other person think? (Gubbinal seems to be the name of a simple-minded character, perhaps related to Hobbinol in Spenser's *Shepherd's Calendar*.) Who is supposed to be right? The speaker says he agrees, but does he really? In what sense does he agree when he says 'Have it your way'? *2*. Wallace Stevens really believes that life is what you make it with your imagination; that the ground of reality is nothingness and death, but that imagination creates the 'supreme fictions' that glorify life. Relate his view to the three poems so far read.

ANOTHER WEEPING WOMAN: *1*. What does the title imply? The closing stanza explains the situation. What has happened? *2*. The black blooms of poison grow in the dark of grief. Let us try to see why. The third stanza summarizes Stevens's philosophy: imagination creates everything. But for the woman, what imagination is possible? Does imagination find any nourishment in death and grief? Or is it destroyed by these? What possibility of imagination does the man have? (Check line 11 for the answer.) Examine stanza one again.

TO THE ROARING WIND: *1*. *Vocalissimus* means 'most vocal one'. Where would you locate 'the distances of sleep'? Is someone being kept awake? Possibly. Is there a mystery, for which we are seeking the lost 'syllable'?

TATTOO: *1*. This is a strange poem. But its strangeness can make it fascinating. A spider crawls on a web: what would be the web behind the eyes? Why are there two? *2*. If light travels along the webs of the body — as it does in a sense — then it also travels along lines to reach the eyes. What are these lines or webs called scientifically? Can you imagine a 'crawling' movement of points from which light proceeds to the eye? Can you see these rays as 'filaments of your eyes'? *3*. What does the simile of a spider add to our way of thinking about light? What are the aspects of a spider? *4*. Consider the possible meanings of the title (see your dictionary). Note that the title itself is a metaphor that might suggest another poem.

THE SNOW MAN: *1*. The meaning of the poem is concentrated in the third verse and in the closing line; but notice that the entire poem is one sentence. Try to read this sentence so that it makes sense as a normal English sentence. *2*. Looking at the cold winter, we think of the 'misery' in the sound of the wind. (You may recall Wordsworth in 'Tintern Abbey' hearing in nature 'the still, sad music of humanity'. But here the land is 'full' of the same wind.) What is the view of human life implied? *3*. Can you explain why Stevens thinks that the listener is 'nothing'? (Look at the title!) Does the listener see anything *more* than the barren scene? And, in the final phrase, what does it all amount to? Now, what would you say that the winter and snow represent? Is it perhaps only when looking at winter and snow that the last two lines are true? Or does he mean that this is the ultimate truth? (Discuss.)

FROGS EAT BUTTERFLIES ...: *1.* Here is another strange poem, with a very odd title. It will take some puzzling out. The poem describes a dull, sleepy landscape of rivers, and speaks of a man who built a cabin there. The rivers are compared to swine. Who will eventually swallow these hog-like rivers? (See end of poem.) *2.* Was the man a person of imagination or no imagination? (See line 9.) Why were his days 'arid'? What is it that 'suckled themselves' on him? What animal, in the poem, does suckling suggest? Finally, what swallowed the hours and the arid days? (Something like a sea, into which the hours and the man have disappeared. What is it?) *3.* (*Rattapallax*, by the way, is an invented word for the crash of thunder. Do you like it?) Look at the title. 'Men eat hogs' must mean that men draw into themselves the environment they live in, here the sleepy rivers, which are called 'swine'. Look at the sequence from 'butterflies' to 'hogs'. Where does this put men? What significance have the 'sea-mouths' into which all the rivers of life are swallowed?

BANTAMS IN PINE-WOODS: *1.* Here you have imagination in action, creating a carnival of sound and colour. *Bantams* are a breed of pugnacious domestic fowl. *Henna hackles* are orange-brown neck feathers. A small bantam is calling another one names: the title he gives him in the first line is all out of his head. What puns are involved in the name? *2.* A *blackamoor* here is a coloured slave. What is the small bantam objecting to? What does he assert? *Tangs* are obviously sharp claws. What philosophy toward life is expressed in this nursery-rhyme poem?

Marianne Moore
pages 117-22

POETRY: *1.* Notice how very prose-like the sentences are. Yet there is a great deal of 'form' in this poem. Count the syllables in the last lines of each verse. Marianne Moore constructs a verse that satisfies her, then repeats it by counting syllables, sometimes with minor variations. She employs a very peculiar and strict form.

2. Notice what happens at the ends and beginnings of lines. What effect does the 'it' receive in line 3 by being placed there? What is the effect of the 'a' at the end of verse one? What effect has 'useful' in verse two? And 'baseball fan' in verse three? 3. It is 'useful' to have your hair rise? How? What 'things' are important, as stated in verse four? What two things do we need to have true poetry? What two others prepare the way for it? How important is poetry among the other things mentioned?

THE FISH: 1. Notice the syllabic verse-form again. The title itself gives us the first two words of the poem. The poem is a description of an undersea cliff-side and chasm, with its various sea life in motion. Follow the vivid description closely. 2. The idea of the poem is probably less important than the pictures and the verbal technique. But what is the water doing to the cliff? The light, too, is aggressive (in verses two and three). Yet the rugged cliff persists in being rich with life — fish, crabs, etc. Being repeatedly battered, carved by the sea, it remains alive (despite one dead side), though it doesn't grow any younger. (In fact, the sea grows old.) All this can be taken as a metaphor for human endurance and persistence. Can you think of any examples of such endurance?

BIRD-WITTED: 1. You will want to compare this poem with Williams's 'Education a Failure'. Here three baby mocking-birds are sitting on a low branch of a tree, being fed by their mother. Are they very young? How big? (See verses one and two.) Does the mother have a hard time feeding them? Why? 2. In verse four, the song of the mother bird before the young were born is remembered. Why has her song changed? 3. What motive is attributed to the cat? Are the young birds afraid? 4. 'By hope rewarded — of toil' is a bit difficult. Perhaps it means that in saving her young she is rewarded by the hope of more toil. Is the poem only about birds, or also about people?

E. E. Cummings
pages 123-7

'THE SKY WAS': 1. Can you put the words together and read the poem smoothly? What fairy-tale resembles the description in the first half of the poem? A sophisticated poet, Cummings expresses complex ideas in a style that is childlike in its simplicity. 2. If 'the sky' looked as it is described, how could it be 'under a locomotive'? Something else *looks* like a locomotive. What is he referring to? What looks like 'violets' under it? 3. Is the sky described in the north, south, east, or west? What time of day is it?

'R-P-O-P-H-E-S-S-A-G-R': 1. This is a very popular experimental poem of E. E. Cummings. The subject is of course revealed at the end. What are the letters of the first line? Why should Cummings jumble them up? 2. The parentheses are used here to create shifts of attention, disruptions in vision, such as you might have looking for a grasshopper. So are capitals, exclamation marks, colons, periods, used for their dramatic or descriptive effect, against all the rules. What is the reason, for example, for capitals in line 5? the colon after the letter 'p' in 'leaps'? the capital 'A' in this word? 3. The grasshopper rearranges itself. Can you arrange the words of the poem to make sense? (Note that 'into a The' is Cummings's way of saying that a particular, definite grasshopper appears: The Grasshopper. Also, 'rearrangingly' is a very unorthodox adverb; but everything in the poem is unorthodox.)

'BUFFALO BILL'S DEFUNCT': 1. The poem should be recited by a boy, in real cowboy style. How does the word 'defunct' differ, in feeling, from the word 'dead'? Why are the words in the sixth line compressed together? 2. The word 'Jesus' as used here is a piece of blasphemy. It is not intended to be offensive. What is the effect it produces by being placed where it is? 3. The poem is about a hero who has died. Is 'Mister Death' a 'good guy' or a 'bad guy'? Is he on our side? What is our attitude toward him?

POEM, OR BEAUTY HURTS MR. VINAL: 1. One of E. E. Cummings's best-known satirical poems, this exercise in irony has two subjects. One is current throughout the poem; the other is introduced in lines 15ff. What are these two subjects? (Note that the word 'merde' in line 16, which in English would be an offensive four-letter word, is more readily acceptable in French, with much less vulgar associations – though of course to be avoided in polite conversation.) 2. What does Cummings object to exactly in the things he ridicules? What attitudes does he parody?

Edith Sitwell

pages 128-30

THE MAUVE SUMMER RAIN: *1.* Not the meaning but the music is what matters in the characteristic poems of Edith Sitwell. Study carefully the sound effects and the kinds of pleasure they give. *2.* Is there a rhyme scheme? Where is it abandoned? Is there an emotive reason for breaking the pattern? *3.* Do you find any alliterations? Point them out. What do they do? Where do you find four and even five stressed syllables in succession? What do they imitate?

SONG OF THE MAN FROM A FAR COUNTRY: *1.* Another song, and therefore we must particularly attend to the music. What do the rhyme-words in the first stanza evoke — what picture of Rose and Alice do you see? Is this real or idealistic? What makes it so? *2.* What is the contrast between the appearance of the man and the girls? What will he do to make up for the contrast? What do the birds in the trees represent?

Hart Crane

pages 131-4

'THE NASAL WHINE OF POWER . . .': *1.* This is an extract from a long poem taking inspiration from the machine age, just as poetry once grew out of man-made inventions like castles and palaces, the sword and the plough. How does the sound of the passage correspond to the energy of machinery and power? Study the rhythms, the alliterations, and the choice of words for these effects. *2.* What are 'spouting pillars'? What are the 'new verities'? The 'new universe' of machinery is being related to the cosmos, 'the stars'. (Note that the word 'parts' in line 10 is a verb.) What is the meaning of the question 'Towards what?' What kind of answer is given in the lines that follow? What makes the answer very ambiguous?

VAN WINKLE: *1. Far Rockaway* is on Long Island, New York; the *Golden Gate Bridge* crosses San Francisco Bay. *Macadam* is a special kind of road-paving, here simply an asphalt highway. While America rushes forward, spanning a continent, an old man who sweeps a tenement is shown going on his way to work, remembering his childhood. The problem, unsolved, is to relate the morning of childhood to America and the machine age. Can this be done? Discuss the problem. *2. Pizarro* and *Cortez* are characters from history books, discoverers of the New World. Pizarro conquered Peru, while Cortez opened up Mexico. *Priscilla* and *Captain Smith* belong to early United States history and fable. Captain John Smith was president of Virginia colony. Priscilla occurs in Longfellow's *Courtship of Miles Standish*. What is the relation of all these to the theme of this poem? And why is the story of Rip Van Winkle especially relevant? *3.* Consider the personal memories presented. What makes them so vivid and moving? What is the emotion created by these memories, and by the reference to the 'nickel for car-change' — against the background of continental expansion?

VIRGINIA: *1.* This poem is a love-song, a lyrical vision of young love in modern America. Where is the young man in stanza one? Where in stanza two? How has the weather changed? What season is it? *2. Prince Street* and *Bleecker* are streets in New York's lower East Side. He sees his girl-friend in the window of a tall building. Can you guess what building this is? *3. Virginia* simply means virginal (the state was named for the virgin Queen, Elizabeth I.) Also, the Virgin Mary's colour is blue, hence the girl is 'blue-eyed'. This association, together with the colony of Virginia, makes the poem a fresh beginning. What is the relation here to the two preceding poems?

John Crowe Ransom
pages 135-7

BLUE GIRLS: *1.* Why should not the girls believe their teachers? How are the teachers very different from the girls? *2.* In verse three, why can we not 'establish' beauty? (*Publish* of course simply means affirm.) *3.* In verse four, what is the special sense of 'fallen from'? What is the point of the example given in the verse? Summarize in your own words the thought expressed in this poem.

JANET WAKING: *1.* Notice carefully how the story is told. After three delightful verses you reach the last line of verse four. How does this line change from all that preceded it? *2.* What is the effect of the word 'transmogrifying'? What is the meaning of 'rigor'? What effect is produced by the touches of humour in stanzas three and four? Is there any humour in the last two lines of the poem? How would you summarize the meaning of the poem? Why is a little girl the subject?

Archibald MacLeish
page 138

PSYCHE WITH THE CANDLE: *1.* In the story of Cupid and Psyche, Psyche was not permitted to see Cupid, her lover. (In Greek the word *psuché* means soul.) While he was asleep, she looked at him by the light of a candle, but a drop of wax awakened him — with the result that he vanished, never to return. Relate this story to the title and to the meaning of MacLeish's poem. *2.* In a sentence or two, tell what MacLeish believes to be the 'mystery' of love. Explain fully the 'bird in a fist' metaphor as a means of conveying that 'mystery' and its answer. *3.* What features of sound and rhythm help convey the effect and meaning of the passage 'Either you keep ... in song vanish'?

Robert Graves
pages 139-40

A SLICE OF WEDDING CAKE: *1.* The poem seems to be directed against men. What are the bad qualities in men on which Graves heaps his scorn? What would 'missionary endeavour' signify? *2.* What is the ironic effect of the last sentence in the poem? What must we conclude, if it is true that he does overvalue women? *3.* This piece of wit is called 'a slice of wedding cake'. Why?

Louis MacNeice
pages 141-4

THE DAILY NEWS: *1.* In your own words, state the basic idea expressed in the first six lines. Why should the news to which the author refers seem 'frivolous, if not farcical, without dignity'? What meaning does the passage take on because of the use of the verb 'seems'? *2.* Note four examples of the contrast between the appearance of things and the reality that MacNeice uses in the rest of the poem. Show the relation between these and the first six lines. *3.* There is a metaphor of the stage used throughout the poem.

Study each of these references. What types of plays are contrasted? To what are these compared?

MORNING SUN: *1.* A vivid city poem, describing the effects of sun, and the dullness when the sun disappears behind a cloud. In verse two, what happens to the sun on the streets? What happens to chromium? How does the sun appear in mist? What is the meaning of 'reticulated'? *2.* Is the day calm or windy? What is compared to 'whistling bars of music'? What is like swordplay? Notice the sudden abundance of metaphors at the end of verse three. This is emotional and climactic. *3.* Why is the simile in the last two lines so apt?

SUNDAY MORNING: *1.* In the first ten lines the pleasures of sense experience seem so perfect they are like 'a small eternity'. What is the exact meaning of line *5* that makes this possible? *2.* Everything seems to be spoiled by the ringing of the bells. Why? What do they remind us of? Why is 'skull's mouths' a good metaphor for church bells? *3.* Would we have expected the poet to say this of church bells on Sunday morning? Is the reversal typical of modern life? How?

SNOW: *1.* Describe the position of the window, the snow, and the roses in relation to one another, in verse one. How does the sudden combination of incompatible things strike the poet? *2.* What is unexpected about the phrase 'spiteful and gay'? Does MacNeice still like it? What kind of experience especially does he relish? (See line 11.) Yet he finds 'more than glass' between the incompatibles. What more could there be?

W. H. Auden
pages 145-57

'SAY THIS CITY HAS TEN MILLION SOULS': *1.* The poem is a record of the 1930s and the period of the Second World War when Naźi persecution of the Jews ravaged Europe. The refugees and hunted people are the subject of the poem. Why is the ballad a suitable form for this? *2.* What is the situation described in stanza six? What is the feeling created by the refrain as the poem gathers momentum?

SCHOOLCHILDREN: *1*. Education is for ever a tug-of-war between the impulses of the young, which would burst out and expand in all directions, and the will of adults, which wants to shape these impulses in the patterns prescribed by society, for the general good. Which side is Auden taking in this conflict? Trace his use of the prison metaphor in detail. In verse two, what is wrong with the rebellion of the young? To whom are the young bound with 'bars of love'? *2*. To see an angel of illusion only is to deceive oneself. Why can't the young see a real vision of freedom and self-realization? 'The beast of vocation' is of course the tyranny of future occupations, professions, waiting for the young. Why is the beast afraid? *3*. 'The professor's dream' would be a perfectly obedient child. Why is it not true? And why is tyranny, on the part of adults, 'easy'? Why is Auden dissatisfied with the forms of rebellion described in the final stanza?

THE UNKNOWN CITIZEN: *1*. Unlike the schoolchildren in the preceding poem, this citizen was *perfectly* obedient, 'a saint'. Was this good? Why should not a citizen serve 'the Greater Community'? Why are all the virtues listed in this poem somehow unsatisfactory? *2*. What sort of person is represented in the speaker of the poem? What is his tone of voice? What is his relation to 'the Greater Community'? *3*. What do the last two lines tell us?

WHO'S WHO: *1*. This sonnet presents two sides of an imaginary great man's life. What does the first section, the octet, describe? What is the subject of the sestet? *2*. A *Who's Who* presents the cold facts of biography. How would you describe the tone and attitude of the narrator to the great man in question? Yet, if there is feeling concealed behind the tone, what would the feeling be? How would the great man's life have been made more perfect and happy? What criticism is implied of the fate that usually befalls those who become famous and great?

LAW LIKE LOVE: *1*. The poem gives a series of definitions for 'Law' – the law that we should live by. Go over each definition and consider what idea about law or duty it contains. *2*. In what part of the poem do we find the familiar idea that 'everything is relative'? Why is it ironic that scholars are law-abiding? What does the definition of 'the soft idiot' mean? *3*. Why is making a definition an attempt to 'slip ... into an unconcerned condition'? How does it take you out of your own particular 'position'? *4*. If law resembles love, is there a possible link between the two? (See 'the bars of love' in the poem 'Schoolchildren'.)

MUNDUS ET INFANS: *1*. The title means 'World and Infant'. To what do the first two lines refer? What is the metaphor contained in 'the New Order' — i.e., what two things are being compared? Why is the child an 'ogre'? Is it true that the infant 'resists tyranny'? How is he a 'pantheist' — that is, one who believes that the whole universe is God? *2*. In verse four, explain carefully the difference and the similarity between the saint and the infant. How are 'we' related to these two? *3*. In verse five, the baby is simply helpless and that's that. We, however, always blame our troubles on something else, and promise to overcome them. In the last verse, the ideas become very quick and complicated, a speed-up like violins finishing a string quartet. Adults do not cry before others, they go upstairs. One example of why we cry is that we 'distinguish between hunger and love'. Why should that bring unhappiness? Do we suffer from both? Suppose they were indistinguishable?

IN MEMORY OF W. B. YEATS: *1*. In this elegy for the poet W. B. Yeats, what is the metaphor contained in the third stanza? Once the man of flesh and blood is dead, how is he 'scattered among a hundred cities'? *2*. 'You were silly like us' alludes to such things as Yeats's odd beliefs in supernaturalism, his 'reactionary' political views (he admired aristocracy and peasantry, despised the middle class), and perhaps his romantic love of Maud Gonne. Would you agree that 'poetry makes nothing happen'? (The statement is highly controversial, contradicted even by Auden's own practice as a socialist poet in the 1930s.) *3*. In the third part of the elegy, what is the effect of the change in poetic form? What are the permanent virtues for which Yeats is praised? (Kipling is pardoned for strong Imperialist views and notions of white superiority; Claudel, a Roman Catholic poet, had to be 'pardoned' for his doctrine of submission, it would seem, toward evil.) Is Auden satisfied here with purely aesthetic values, or is a moral concern still part of his conception of poetry?

Stephen Spender
pages 158-62

'MY PARENTS KEPT ME ...': *1*. To what social class does Spender belong, as shown in this autobiographical poem? *2*. As an adult who remembers his boyhood, what are his attitudes now? What is he trying to understand? Why?

THE PYLONS: *1.* Two things are opposed in the poem. What are they? On which side does Spender's sympathy lie through the first four stanzas? How has his position changed in the final stanza? *2.* What quality in the last two lines tells you how he feels about the future? Do you think his prophecy will prove true?

THE EXPRESS: *1.* In this poem about a railway express, the issue between pastoral nature and the new industrial life is again resolved in a vision of beauty. Consider the associations of the first metaphor. At line 11 a second metaphor appears. Is the express being compared to a musical song or a poem? (Look for evidence in the lines that follow.) *2.* In the final seven lines, why does the train's destination seem something vaster than any particular town or city? How is such largeness suggested? And why is the comparison in the last two lines significant?

'HE WILL WATCH THE HAWK ...': *1.* This poem about an airman deals with man's conquest of the air. At the beginning, there is no shadow over man's victory over nature. At what point in the poem does a doubt appear? *2.* Notice the odd mixture of tenses in the poem. Explain why the future tense is used at first and the present tense in the last line. (The past-perfect is used in relation to this present.) What is the real sequence of events? *3.* Bring out all the implications that are involved in the image of Icarus.

'I THINK CONTINUALLY ...': *1.* Read the poem slowly to gather in most of its meaning. Of the great men of this kind, one example that Spender may have had in mind is Beethoven. Can you think of others? *2.* Two aspects of the kind of greatness Spender is thinking of are referred to, both in stanza one. What are they? What is opposed to these?

Robinson Jeffers

pages 163-7

THE ANSWER: *1.* Do you know any evidence from recent history and the newspapers to support what Jeffers says about vio-

lence? Can you point to 'dreams of universal justice or happiness'?
2. To what does Jeffers attribute man's recurring failure? What would you say is the question to which the poem gives 'The Answer'?

SHINE, PERISHING REPUBLIC: *1.* What is the tone or feeling of the first stanza? How does the second differ? Why? How does this explain the paradox in the title? *2.* There is terrible irony in the last two lines. In what way do they suggest blasphemy? Use the preceding poem, 'The Answer', to interpret the meaning of these lines. Why is love, or attachment to man, not enough for Jeffers? Does his meaning really apply to Jesus? (These two lines are a kind of hyperbole directed against man's obsession with himself – even in the form of humanitarian love. 'They say' could imply that any view of Christ's teaching as entirely man-centred is a misinterpretation; or it could imply outright scepticism.)

TRIAD: *1.* Enlarge on the two ideas expressed in line 2. *2.* Jeffers says that science fails to understand the nature of things. He refers to the failure of science to achieve a coherent total explanation of reality, of good and evil, of mind and matter, of the relation between the atomic, the astronomic, and the human worlds. What is the 'trap' into which Russia has fallen? *3.* What three things 'feed the future ... serve God'? (Note the title.) At what moments of history does God appear as 'hardly a friend of humanity'? What events in the Bible can you remember that might be related to this view?

BLIND HORSES: *1.* The meaning of the poem will be fairly clear if you have read the poems preceding. How do the blind horses 'tread their own hoofmarks'? *2.* Is the last question rhetorical? Or could there be an answer? Would the great mystery still remain?

NATURAL MUSIC: *1.* What are 'those voices' in line 8? To what other voices are they compared? *2.* How could these voices be similar? Refer to the preceding poems by Robinson Jeffers before answering the question. Is this view in the end affirmative or negative? What paradox is involved?

FIRE ON THE HILLS: *1.* In a poem of this kind, first one studies the literal image in detail, then interpretation may follow. What has happened in the poem? Why is the eagle then depicted as 'insolent' and 'merciless'? Why are the sky and the hills described as 'merciless'? 2. In the interpretation, first try to turn the particulars into *general* ideas about the nature of life; then look for other concrete examples of this general pattern. In the poems you have read by Jeffers, where is destruction described? Was innocent suffering involved? Beauty? What does 'heaven' have to do with it?

Dylan Thomas
pages 168-73

FERN HILL: *1.* Dylan Thomas here evokes in ecstatic terms the time of youth and his first discovery of the world. Notice his coupling of unusual words — lilting house, apple towns, windfall light, etc. What is the effect of such surprising use of language? Is the feeling or the thought of the first stanza original or fairly familiar? Suppose it were couched in ordinary language, or in clichés? *2.* Do you recognize religious associations in stanza two? Is there a feeling of coming troubles, or is happiness still perfect? *3.* In stanza four, what is the interpretation of the entire poem implied by the line 'Shining, it was Adam and maiden'? *4.* In stanza five, after 'nothing I cared', what is the knowledge about 'time' that he then ignored? What are the 'chains' in the closing line? What does the comparison 'like the sea' add to the image?

THIS BREAD I BREAK: *1.* What does 'bread and wine' immediately suggest? What attitude does this association bring to the poem? *2.* At what point is joy suggested? at what point pain? The second verse restates the idea of the first. In what detail does it differ? *3.* The author speaks of himself in the third stanza, referring to his own blood and flesh. What is the obvious allusion? What is he offering to us that is analogous to bread and wine?

IN MY CRAFT OR SULLEN ART: *1.* In trying to make a work of art, why should one find that art is 'sullen'? In what sense is the light 'singing'? What three things are referred to in lines 7, 8, and 9? *2.* *Spindrift* is blown sea-spray. Who are 'the towering dead'? The lovers in their 'secret heart' would of course acknowledge the truth he writes down. What two aspects of human life, then, are commemorated in this art?

338

AMONG THOSE KILLED IN THE DAWN RAID ...: *1.* The first two lines put the case with utter simplicity. What follows is visionary, or surrealist, in its method. What 'locks' are referred to in line 3? Why is the pavement stone 'burst'? (What is the allusion here?) Similarly, why is the street 'on its back'? In lines 6 to 8 something tremendous has occurred in the man's death. What might this be? Why are keys shot from locks? *2.* The morning, at the end, shines in glory because of this man, and the sun rises triumphant. What do 'storks' represent here? Why are the bones not for the common burial cart?

AND DEATH SHALL HAVE NO DOMINION: *1.* What spiritual reality is referred to in line 3? (This way of expressing it is merely exaggerating the 'anthropomorphic' conception of the hereafter. But clearly the view in this poem is not anthropomorphic.) The poem, then, affirms immortality. *2.* In verse two, whatever their bodies suffer after death, the dead remain whole and entire. What they have formerly believed in may also break up, but they are immortal. In stanza three they no longer know the sounds of nature; yet even though they died mad and are dead, they are resurrected. How? What is the dual nature of immortality suggested in the poem? *3.* The poet here is not expounding a religious system. He is, however, using ideas of a religious nature. Do these ideas seem to be a part of any particular religion or school of thought? (Discuss.)

Karl Shapiro

pages 174-7

THE FLY: *1.* We must be prepared for some disgusting images when the subject is such as that considered here. (One of the tenets of modern art is that there is no subject that is forbidden to art, since all reality demands our understanding.) Duncan Phyfe was a nineteenth-century cabinet-maker who carved elegant furniture. What is the effect of this image? Incidentally, are the stanzas of the poem well-constructed? Note the rhyme scheme and the metrics. *2.* Which of the images are especially apt and amusing? What effect does the comic mood have in relation to the subject? *3.* What is the contrast repeated in stanza three? (Note the literary allusions in the final stanza as a hint.) How is the contrast varied in stanza five? What makes this stanza outstanding? *4.* Note that a great deal of wit is expended in the poem on what is really a minor domestic scene. Such treatment is called 'mock heroic', because methods of epic poetry are applied to trivial subject matter. How does the poem differ radically from Dylan Thomas's 'Fern Hill'?

THE DIRTY WORD: *1.* 'The Pondicherry vulture' is the name of a species of this bird. (Pondicherry is a place in India.) Explain why the simile is apt. What does hiding the bird in the 'dark closet' mean literally? What does 'flaps its wings savagely' and 'trying to escape' mean? Does a dirty word in the mind create nasty by-products? *2.* The boy in this particular poem is Hebrew and the poem is autobiographical. How does the 'rabbi' — or in other religions the priest or minister — eventually 'free' the bird? *3.* Does the poet, the 'I' in the poem, differ in this from most men? Does the dirty word remain a live vulture in the minds of most men? Is this good or bad? Why are poems referred to as 'elegies'? What does a poet often commemorate with cold detachment and self-knowledge? (For example, see Dylan Thomas's 'Fern Hill', or Ransom's 'Blue Girls'.)

Richard Wilbur
pages 178-80

THE BEAUTIFUL CHANGES: *1.* You probably know the wild-flower called Queen Anne's Lace. Lake Lucerne is in Switzerland. In stanza one, what does the loved one do to the mind of the lover? *2.* 'Changes' in stanza two is a verb expressing action upon other things: that is, the beautiful thing 'changes' the objects around it. Follow the idea in the examples given. *3.* In stanza three, what are the roses a part of, if they are 'not only yours'? (No specific answer here; just think of it.) To 'sunder / Things and Things' selves' means to separate from the particular thing itself that something which is more general, mysterious, still uncomprehended. In the last line, how does this involve a 'losing' and a returning 'back'?

JUGGLER: *1.* What keeps the ball from bouncing for ever? In stanza one this is identified with decreasing vitality, loss of 'brilliance' and imagination as we grow older. What does the juggler do to us? What is the double meaning of 'gravity' in stanza two? *2.* Why do you think that such escape from gravity is called 'a small heaven'? Why 'small'? What is the allusion and reversal of ideas contained in 'earth regained'? *3*. What is the point of saying that this heaven is 'made of nothing at all'? *4*. In stanza three, why is 'reels' a good word? What is the metaphor? How is it continued in the next few words? *5*. In the final stanza, what aspect of 'broom', 'table', and 'plate' is being underlined? Which of the words do this? Why do we applaud the juggler? Could the juggler himself be a metaphor?

Robert Lowell
pages 181-3

OUR LADY OF WALSINGHAM: *1*. The poem is one section from a sequence of seven entitled *The Quaker Graveyard in Nantucket*. *Walsingham* is a shrine of the Virgin in England. In ancient Jerusalem there was a pool at Shiloah just outside the wall of the city (see John ix. 7-11). *Sion* is a poetical name for Jerusalem, and here of course it is equated with the shrine itself. The Latin quotation is from the Vulgate text of the Bible (Isaiah liii.2), a prophetic passage taken in the Christian interpretation to refer to the Messiah: 'he hath no form nor comeliness' reads the King James version of this phrase. Here it is applied to the Virgin, as expressing the nature of God, a transhuman reality. (The author has said of the poem that 'The Virgin is a symbol of contemplation'.) The entire Quaker Graveyard poem is dedicated to 'Warren Winslow, dead at sea', and other sections deal with a drowned sailor; hence the 'sailor' in this section. Show how the past is being depicted in the poem and contrast this to references to the present. Why does the vision of the poem go 'past' Sion, and Calvary, and Bethlehem? Does this help interpret the closing line?

COLLOQUY IN BLACK ROCK: *1*. Hugh B. Staples, in his book on Robert Lowell's poetry, notes: 'Black Rock is a section of Bridgeport, Connecticut, and it is so named because of a geological formation that juts out into Long Island Sound. Bridgeport has a large Hungarian population, many of whom worship at St. Stephen's Roman Catholic Church, located a mile or so from the Black Rock district. It is a national parish, named for the patron saint of Hungary. From the vicinity of the church it is possible to look across the black mud flats, which are used as a municipal dump, to the small harbour and Black Rock peninsula beyond.' The poem was written in 1944, during the Second World War, and the Hungarians referred to were working at defence plants near by. In the poem, 'Black Mud' refers to the dumping-ground. Note how these various elements of reality are described. *2*. Who, or what, is being addressed in this colloquy? What is the relation between the 'heart' in stanza one, and 'death' in stanza two? How does 'mud' in the third stanza relate to these? What is meant by 'house'? *3*. The poem is written on Corpus Christi Day. The 'martyre Stephen' in the poem is St. Stephen, the first Christian martyr; the patron saint of Hungary, Stephen I, is a different saint, yet the two seem to be equally present in the poem because the church of St. Stephen is near by. *Kingfisher* is a bird symbolic of Christ. *Stupor Mundi* means 'the astonishment of the world'. Relate the meaning of Corpus Christi, and the image of Christ in the closing stanza, to the ideas contained in the poem, of death, mud, and the beating heart.

David Gascoyne
pages 184-6

ECCE HOMO: *1*. If a sense of horror is given to the crucifixion, this is a tradition that goes back to the Middle Ages. But here the horror is contemporary. The Christ pictured here is called a 'mortal enemy'. Whose? Why are we 'callous contemporaries'? What do 'black shirts' refer to? What other details confirm this? *2*. Notice the shocking reversal of verse six, which prevents this from being a poem of conventional piety. What are the present-day facts referred to in stanzas seven and eight? *3*. There is a prophecy in stanzas ten and eleven. What two words are understood before the word 'wrought' in the last line of stanza ten? *4*. The closing verse is a prayer. Explain it in your own words. How are 'Poetry' and 'Revolution' associated with this concept of Christ?

Alex Comfort
pages 187-8

NOTES FOR MY SON: *1*. This is a section from a longer poem, *The Song of Lazarus*. The opening lines do not mean that every appeal in the cause of freedom is evil, or that freedom is not desirable. For example, the abortive Hungarian Revolution was fought in behalf of freedom. To what kind of 'freedom talk' is Alex

Comfort referring? *2.* What is the observation about the nature of evil in the sixth and seventh couplets? *3.* Would you agree that the eighth and ninth stanzas are better poetry than the final stanza? Why do you think the poet has lost control?

Allen Ginsberg
pages 189-91

A SUPERMARKET IN CALIFORNIA: *1.* Walt Whitman here is the poet who chanted the promise of democratic America in grand idealistic terms. The supermarket is the actual America that has developed instead. Discuss the two sides of this contrast to show what the ideal demands, and what the reality seems to lack. *2.* Why is the poet thinking of 'the store detective'? Why does he never pass the cashier? What relation does this position of the poet have to the central theme? *3.* Where does the humour of the poem approach mere farce? At what point does it take up the serious note? Which is finally significant, humour or dead seriousness? Why is 'Lethe', the river of forgetfulness, mentioned at the end?

Lawrence Ferlinghetti
pages 192-3

'CONSTANTLY RISKING ABSURDITY ...': *1.* How does the form of this extract correspond to the subject described? *2.* What does it mean to be 'above the heads' of the audience? What would 'the other side of day' signify? *3.* The poet does not 'mistake any thing for what it may not be'. Yet how is his truth more than just realism? Is beauty related to truth? Why is the poet merely a 'charleychaplin man' in this feat?

E. J. Pratt
pages 199-203

THE CHILD AND THE WREN: *1.* To make the sense clear, the word 'might' should be understood before 'molest'. The rest of the poem is quite straightforward. *2.* Why does friendship with a bird make us feel delight in the poem? What is the significance of our emotion?

CHERRIES: *1.* A charming love-story. The poetic fiction in the last stanza merits 'suspension of disbelief'. Are you willing to believe it? What is the principle that makes us accept this fiction? *2.* What is Pratt's feeling toward young lovers?

THE DYING EAGLE: *1.* What associations are suggested by 're-connoitre'? Find three other words with the same implications in the lines that follow. What aspects of the eagle are being emphasized? *2.* What is the 'silver flash' that the eagle sees in line 23? What is the 'thunder' in line 59? What are the 'whirling eyes' in line 52? *3.* In E. J. Pratt's poetry, the conflict between the creatures is related to primitive bloodthirst in nature. Find the lines of the poem where this idea appears. *4.* *Vitriol* is sulphuric acid. What purpose does the adjective serve in line 48? (Think of the familiar romantic view of the benevolence of nature.) *5.* Compare the poem with Stephen Spender's 'He will watch the hawk'. What word here is the exact counterpart of Spender's 'indifferent eye'? What does the eagle represent, more generally, in this poem?

Emile Nelligan
pages 204-5

LE VAISSEAU D'OR: *1.* The poem is an extended metaphor which the poet makes explicit at the end. What does the great ship represent? What is meant by calling it a ship ... great ... golden ... sailing unknown seas ... with the goddess of love on its prow? *2.* What is meant by the shipwreck? What relation do 'Dégoût, Haine, et Névrose' have to this?

F. R. Scott
pages 206-9

OLD SONG: *1.* A very clear Laurentian stream is the subject. How does the form of the poem correspond to the subject? What features — at least three — imitate a clear transparent flow? *2.* What does the poet hear behind him, on the hillside? What do these sounds represent, in contrast to what he hears in the stream? *3.* The stream is associated in stanzas three and four with a stage of earth history and of the history of life. Is a scientific or a religious view of ultimate nature implied? What is the significance of the line 'of no mind'?

TOURIST TIME: *1.* Here is satire with an unkind cut. Since the speaker is a Canadian, where does our national modesty appear in this poem? *2.* Why is 'rapid transit' referred to? Does progress have its penalties? What is the poet's real objection to the lady in question? (Surely not her overweight condition!) What class or level of culture is the butt of the satire?

SUMMER CAMP: *1.* Here Scott appears as a social and political satirist. What sort of person is supposed to be speaking in the poem? Examine in detail. *2.* Of what is this person blindly unaware? If the person became aware, what would he or she do? What kind of political policies would such a person approve? Here is the whole point of the poem.

CHRISTMAS SHOPPING: *1.* How does the observation in the poem contrast with the meaning of Christmas? *2.* What would need to be changed to make it consistent with Christmas? Would the stores just close earlier? Or is more required? *3.* Scott implies, in poems of this kind, that a changed society is necessary — a welfare or a socialist society — in which the condition of all the underprivileged would be improved. In his implication, which English poets in this anthology does he resemble?

CONFLICT: *1.* In this war poem, dealing with the Second World War, is the poet taking sides in the conflict? Since the war was fought against Nazi Germany, and we know that the author is a convinced democrat, opposed to Nazism, how do you explain his detachment? Is the poem better, or truer, for this? *2.* What is the contrast between 'bond' and 'beast' in stanza three? Why are 'prison' and 'ghetto' introduced in the stanza? *3.* In the last verse, why is the sacrifice 'narrow'? What does the author desire?

A. J. M. Smith
pages 210-12

THE LONELY LAND: *1.* Do you know the paintings of the Group of Seven in Canada? Several of these artists — especially A. Y. Jackson and F. H. Varley — have painted landscapes in northern Ontario that correspond to this poem. What are the features of this scenery that make it different from landscape outside Canada? *2.* Is there any gentleness or tenderness in the landscape?

345

Where does the theme of love, as a subject, appear in the poem? What does the poem say about it? *3*. What qualities of *human* character does the poem define, in terms of landscape? Do you think these are truly Canadian?

NEWS OF THE PHOENIX: *1*. The *phoenix* is a fabulous bird that dies every 500 years: building itself a funeral pile, it perishes in the flames, then rises again from the ashes. In retelling this ancient myth, what new setting does the poet give to it? From the language and tone, what is the historical period, ancient or modern? What would this signify? *2*. If the phoenix stands for something, in such a setting, what kinds of things could you equate with it? What is 'dying'? What does the official part of society refuse to admit? (Several possibilities are open, but one is especially relevant for a poet.) *3*. What seems to be the author's opinion? Is the phoenix dead for good, or will it rise again? The poem provided the title for A. J. M. Smith's first book. Is this significant?

BESIDE ONE DEAD: *1*. In this poem of death, two preparatory metaphors lead to a third and final one. Take note of these metaphors. How does the first contrast strongly with the last? Can there possibly be a reason? How does the second metaphor already suggest the final one? *2*. In the metaphor of Christ's tomb, what is being equated with 'the Lord'? In what sense was it 'broken'?

A. M. Klein

pages 213-15

THE ROCKING CHAIR: *1*. What is the ambiguity in the word 'seconds'? To what three things is the rocking chair compared in stanza one? *2*. In stanza two, why is the chair 'dangerous' to the toddler? What are the 'white haloes'? In stanza three, what is the historical allusion in 'St. Malo'? *3*. Is 'static folk' an offensive term in the context of the final stanza? Do you know of any reason why the phrase now seems dated, no longer true? What are the feeling and attitude towards French Canada evoked by the last four lines?

LOOKOUT: MOUNT ROYAL: *1*. The pronoun 'it' in the opening line refers to boyhood. Note the several experiences that recall boyhood to the adult. What are the 'white ... mustaches' of the tap? *2*. In stanza two, the past is seen again as 'motion forever stopped'. To what is the eye being compared? Why is the phrase 'tops of f's' particularly effective? _3_. The 'parapet' in stanza three refers to the lookout on Mount Royal, from which at first trees — 'the green marine' — and then the city below and the river are visible. What is it the boy is looking for as he discovers various places in the scene below? Try to describe in your own words the feeling about the past conveyed in the last stanza.

Saint-Denys Garneau
pages 216-21

CAGE D'OISEAU: _1_. Why is 'death', in the cage of the human body, audible 'when nothing is happening'? _2_. The bird will escape when he has 'eaten' all that is within the cage. How do you understand the meaning of 'eaten' here? How does death 'eat' the life within us? _3_. It is a serious and moving poem, perhaps because most of us avoid thinking of death. But it is not a poem of bitterness or despair. By considering the entire image and its conclusion can you explain why?

ACCOMPAGNEMENT: _1_. In the poem, the poet feels that the joy of living, of which he is capable, is somehow impossible for him to attain. Yet he imagines that one day he will make that joy a part of his life. At the beginning, he is a double. At what point does he begin the plan to become one with his joy? Is it a difficult thing for him? _2_. Who is it, then, that walks away once he himself is 'transposed'?

PORTRAIT: _1_. In this portrait of a boy, what predominant quality of his character is being described? Why is the comparison with a bird exactly suitable? But how can 'snail' be reconciled with this? _2_. Why do you 'see' him when he is coming toward you? Why does he seem to vanish when he comes near? What does this mean in reality? _3_. How does the line 'Il ne regarde que pour vous embrasser' fit with the psychological sketch?

P. K. Page
pages 222-4

THE BANDS AND THE BEAUTIFUL CHILDREN: _1_. Note how the band, in the distance, makes a 'tunnel'; and when we see it, it becomes 'high'. Do you see how this corresponds to actual experience? Do you see how drums can make a 'dome'? Imagine yourself in an auditorium: would cornets be like 'windows'? *2.* What is the contrast between the children and the old people? As the children become disillusioned, in strophe three, which side of the contrast begins to win out? What is the 'home' of the children? Is it real? What is the feeling produced by this realization?

THE PERMANENT TOURISTS: *1.* How are the tourists 'somnolent through landscapes'? Why are the words 'alter' and 'enter' well chosen? *2.* In stanza two, what would an 'entire event' be like? (Construe what follows thus: 'they are never as dogs ... perfectly within their climate.') What does 'lock themselves' refer to? What are the tourists 'now incapable of feeling'? Why? *3.* In stanza five, why are the tourists described as 'nude'? How is the 'bill of fare' a *history*? How do 'philosophies' bloom at the table? *4.* How does the poet's attitude in the final stanza change toward the tourists? What meaning would you attach to 'classic' here? (This is a difficult question, with no easy or final answer, but it invites you to search for deeper meanings: for example, why are the columns 'ruined'; and why are the tourists 'permanent'?)

Anne Wilkinson
pages 225-7

ALLELUIA: *1.* What moment in the cycle of the year is described in the first eight lines? What is the warning about? *2.* Why is 'Passion' capitalized? Why 'Soil'? From your answer to these questions, trace the same associations throughout the rest of the poem and in the title. What stage of the 'Passion' is being described?

ON A BENCH IN A PARK: *1.* The sadness of this poem consists in looking at the negative and disillusioning side of the best that life has to offer. We had better face it. Why is love a loss, to the girl? Why is it a loss and a failure to the man? Is there something more we desire? *2.* What are the complaints of the speaker, the older person, in the poem? How do they differ from the complaints of the young lovers? Why do the lovers 'yawn'? How do the last three lines fit with the rest of the poem?

I AM SO TIRED: *1.* What is referred to in 'two eternal yards'? Why 'eternal'? A restless sleep is suggested. How long will it last? *2.* To what span of time do 'night' and 'winter', then, refer?

Earle Birney
pages 228-39

DAVID: Some of the specialized words in this poem require explanation: an *arête* is a sharp mountain spur or ridge; *pika* are a species of hare found in the Rockies; *trilobites* are fossils of early geological ages, the Cambrian and Ordovician; a *col* is a gap or pass; *seracs* are angular, tower-like segments of glacier; a *cirque* is a circular valley; the *bergschrund* is a crevasse in a snow-field at the head of a glacier; *névé* is consolidated snow. *1.* Earle Birney has said that this poem deals with 'the duality of human experience as symbolized by mountain-climbing — the hair's breadth between, on the one hand, beauty, and the exhilaration of being alive, and, on the other, fear and nightmare and death and the static dumb hostility of the non-human world'. To understand further the moral drama of the poem, interpret the meaning of the incident of the robin in Section V. How does it relate to David's accident later on? *2.* Is David consistent in his moral philosophy? What is this philosophy? Does Bobbie share in David's ideal? How far is Bobbie capable of following his hero? At what points does he fail? What is the conflict in his mind? *3.* How does the work at the Survey camp contrast with the exploits of mountain-climbing? Show this in detail. *4.* In the conclusion of the poem, how is the moral drama resolved? How does the meaning of the poem relate to 'the wide indifferent sky' mentioned in Section VIII?

STATUS QUO: *1.* This is a critical poem directed against the evils of society and a world at war. Who is being 'sprayed' by the syllables? How is this related to 'private gain'? The war is referred to in the fourth line. What attitude is expressed in the words? *2.* 'The atom's rage' refers to what? Why are the eyes 'charming'? *3.* What social evils are described in stanza three? What are 'steel-pelted . . . elephants'? How are these two things related? *4.* Why is the heart 'wrinkled' by boundaries? What kind of great 'plan' does the poet have in mind? *5.* The 'slumgirl' and others cannot develop into 'gallant growth'. Why? What do 'Belsen' and 'town of bone' recall?

TIME-BOMB: *1.* This poem was written in a military hospital in England during the Second World War. What is 'the grizzly' in a friend's face? How is it related to war? *2.* *Firedrakes* are fire-breathing dragons. What is referred to? Why is 'blood' rising in wheat? Where does it come from? *3.* What is the time-bomb in our ribs? What qualities are implied in the word 'mankind'?

FOR GEORGE LAMMING: *1.* George Lamming is a West Indian novelist, the author of an autobiography, *In the Castle of My Skin*, which tells of his early years in Barbados. How is this fact alluded to in the poem? *2.* The poet recalls a party among coloured people on his visit to the West Indies. What moment does he recall especially? What is the significance of this memory? *3.* Why does he say there is a 'risk' in speaking about this? How could 'less / and worse' appear in the words? Contrast what this poem conveys to an attitude of race prejudice. How is the beauty of skin colour conveyed in the poem? How are grace, energy, and happiness also suggested?

Roy Daniells
pages 240-1

PSALM 23: *1.* Look up this psalm in the Bible. What has Roy Daniells changed by re-telling it in his own way? *2.* Who is 'the landlord' in this poem? Is the speaker vengeful toward his 'enemies'? Is he a pious man, do you think?

ALL THROUGH THE 'THIRTIES: *1.* The 1930s were not only the period of the Great Depression in industry, they were also hungry drought years in the Prairie Provinces. The poem describes that period. Why was the lamp lit at noon? What is the 'top' on a blade of wheat? What are 'tumbleweeds'? *2.* How did the war take them both away? Why does the last couplet close on a comic double rhyme, or rhyme of several syllables?

Margaret Avison
pages 242-3

HIATUS: *1.* The poem is about moving into a new house or apartment. What is the action described in the first eight lines? Explain each part of it. *2.* What does the person do next? *3.* Do you think the 'you' in the poem is actually the writer of the poem? Give evidence. *4.* The title applies to the state of mind described in the poem. Explain what it means. *5*. God is referred to in philosophy as the 'Unmoved Mover' or 'First Mover' of the universe. How does this term, used as a pun, apply to the speaker of the poem? How is she 'Unmoved'?

John Glassco
pages 244-5

QUEBEC FARMHOUSE: *1*. Recalling your Canadian history, tell why the farmhouse is associated with a 'feudal souvenir'? Why is it a 'fortress of itself' and not of something else? What does 'desertion' refer to in our history? *2*. Why does the poet find the inside 'dark' and 'airless'? What does the farmhouse represent? What is ironic about the phrase 'puffing its soul'? *3*. In the third verse, what positive element is introduced? What is the paradox in stanza four, line 2? Why do the sisters walk 'leglessly'? What are 'beads'? *4*. Is Glassco's analysis entirely objective? Is the presentation sympathetic, cruel, critical, satirical ? What does the poet really desire for French Canada?

R. G. Everson
pages 246-7

GREEKS HAD NOTHING ELSE TO DO: *1*. What is the basic contrast between ancient Greek and modern man? What does the poet object to in modern living? *2*. To what does the 'state of Persian pomp' refer? With what does it contrast? *3*. What is the tone of this poem? Is the poet strongly affected by the problem described, or is he detached? Is his attitude good in poetry? Evaluate.

CREDO: *1*. What four things are opposed and contrasted to 'power and vanity'? Is science associated with either side of this opposition? *2*. With what is science made parallel? Discuss the parallel. What are the qualities of St. Paul implied here? What is the pun in 'suns'? *3*. Why is the page a 'blotpage'? What are the 'nine lines'? How do they fit into the opposition described above? Why is this a 'credo'?

Ralph Gustafson

pages 248-9

IN THE VALLEY OF THE WENKCHEMNA: *1*. The subject of the poem is alluded to at the beginning, and stated finally at the end. What is the point of keeping it vague so long? Do you like this effect? *2*. Examine the telescoped words (eight of them). Why is the first one especially effective? What similar word or words does 'darkwork' suggest? 'Rottenstone' actually describes very well the look of rocks in the Canadian Rockies — close up, they seem to be decayed, rotten. *3*. The poet is travelling here in the Rockies as a sightseer. As a tourist, how does he compare with the lady in F. R. Scott's 'Tourist Time'?

Irving Layton

pages 250-2

FIRST SNOW: LAKE ACHIGAN: *1*. Why are there no boats on the water? 'Ecstasy of hands' no doubt refers to lovers holding hands. Why is the air 'inextricable' (i.e., it cannot be cleared of perplexities). What would the 'lone drummer' be announcing? *2*. What associations exist in 'transaction'? 'Unwinters' is not in the dictionary. Is it a good coinage? *3*. *God's angry man* is a phrase sometimes applied to the prophet Ezekiel. *Thundering Paul* is Saint Paul, powerful preacher and moral voice. Both these suggest the poet's habitual role as violent critic of man and society. The next reference is to Cato the Elder, who ended every speech in the Roman Senate with the words 'Carthage must be destroyed'. What is the contrast between Cato on the one hand and Ezekiel and Paul on the other? What does Cato represent?

FROM COLONY TO NATION: *1*. The title is taken from the history of Canada by A. R. M. Lower. Why are Canadians being called 'dull'? Can you think of activities that might be called 'childish games'? What is being contrasted to the dull people? *2*. Does the poet favour 'a priest's voice'? What is his attitude? *3*. Do you agree with this poem? State your case.

ANGLO-CANADIAN: *1*. Kingston here represents English-Protestant Loyalist traditions. How does the person described here differ from many other Canadians? What does the maple-leaf comparison add? *2.* What happened to the Canadian in Oxford? How was this brought about? Why does the poet Layton object?

Raymond Souster
pages 253-6

I WATCHED A BIRD: *1.* The bird is at the same time frail and helpless, at the mercy of the winds, and serene, in tune with the elements. Point out the words that describe this double aspect. *2.* In the second stanza, is the bird right not to resist or protest? Why? What do you understand by 'boundless air' and 'great mystery'?

THE LILAC POEM: *1.* This poem is specifically about lilacs, but the poet makes clear that lilacs stand for a good many other 'little things'. What quality of these things is shown in stanza one? Why is the young girl's promise an apt comparison? *2.* To what does 'both' refer in stanza two? Does the thought apply to both in the same way? What judgment about values in life does the poem contain?

LAGOONS, HANLAN'S POINT: *1.* The first section describes the lagoons in early morning. Note the details. Then follow two separate pictures of places explored. These represent different parts of 'the antechamber / of a waking world'. What do you understand by this closing phrase? *2.* How do the two places explored differ? Why is the word 'strange' repeated in the second? Why do you think the poet returns to this experience in his past?

THE PENNY FLUTE: *1.* How is the man with the penny flute contrasted with his environment? What kinds of people in the life of a big city does he represent, in general? *2.* Does the speaker in the poem show sympathy? What judgment is the speaker making of himself? Is the reader involved in such a judgment? If so, with whom would the reader be identified?

THE MAN WHO FINDS HIS SON HAS BECOME A THIEF: *1.* Would you say it is true to life that the father does not believe in the guilt of his son? In any case, this father refuses to believe in the existence of 'evil' in his child. Note how the realization is gradually forced upon him. *2.* Why does the father feel 'sick and alone and afraid'? The word 'fear' is repeated later. Of what might he be afraid? *3.* The two closing lines can mean either that this is

353

the way it must have happened, or that this experience in life is inevitable, one cannot escape it. Discuss these alternatives.

Louis Dudek
pages 257-9

TREE IN A STREET: *1.* From the first line, what is the attitude of the speaker toward the tree? What is the implied real opinion behind this attitude? *2.* What do you think the tree, more generally, represents? What is the feeling communicated by lines 2 to 5? *3.* 'Bloomers and bustles' refers to feminine attire at the end of the Victorian age. What feeling and attitude does the mention of them convey? A *cliché* is a hackneyed expression. What do these touches of ridicule do to the subject? Why is the feminine imagery used in the poem?

MIDNIGHT TRAIN: *1.* The interior of the train is contrasted to the night, the nightmare, outside. What do these two things represent? What is the attitude of the poet toward them? What is the intention of the word 'seem' in line 7? What other words confirm this point? *2.* In the last five lines, the subject is neither the train nor the night. What is the relation of this subject to the other two? How does the attitude to this subject differ radically from the attitude to the preceding subjects? *3.* Have you ever seen a 'great horizontal wheel' outside a train window? Explain how such a phenomenon occurs.

IN SPRING: *1.* What is the scientific image contained in the first stanza? In the next verse, is the comparison to 'sweet potatoes' suitable or not? *2.* Why are the fire-escapes a 'wreck'? Why black? Why is the head of the slum child 'shaven'? *3.* What is conveyed by the reference to movie stars (the poem was written when Clark Gable and Lana Turner were top stars)? What are the two conflicting attitudes that run through this poem? Can you discover this conflict in each verse?

NEWS: *1.* The accident is first described. Note that the title is ironic. What makes it so? How is the tragedy ironically played down in the lines that follow 'it comes like that . . .'? *2.* What does the comparison of the ocean add to the idea? How is the ocean used 'for our pleasure'? What does the poem say about triviality and grandeur?

Alain Grandbois

pages 260-5

CE QUI RESTE: *1*. The poet describes the part of day when night is departing, dawn has not yet arrived. The world of nature as well as imaginary 'sleepwalkers' of the city are both in the landscape. Why is this 'the end of the poet's poem'? Why does poetry (so to speak) thrive in the night and vanish in daylight? *2*. How is the judgment of good and evil (line 2) something that belongs to the night? What is the poet's attitude to the night, and to the day (cf. lines 10 and 14-15)? *3*. In stanza three, the waking world reconstructs itself with difficulty. Man, with a 'destiny' in the world of daylight and time, returns, but he has lost some of his self-assurance by being 'drowned' in night. Why?

L'ENFANCE OUBLIEE: *1*. The second line seems to give us the person being addressed, that is, the poet himself as the child he once was. The bells, then, recall childhood. What do you understand by the fifth line? Does the ninth line help to answer the question? Does it explain the paradox of 'torturé d'espoir'? *2*. The same meaning is at last expressed in the image of a violin played for no one. Why is this image fitting?

C'EST A VOUS TOUS ...: *1*. The poet addresses here the faces and figures of his past. What these are will be clearer when the poem as a whole is better understood. At the simplest, they are the faces of people one has known. Why is he sure they will answer if he calls? Why is there a curtain of lead between them? *2*. What is the 'exile' in verse two? If he has abandoned the faces of the past, it was because he entered into a new life. How is this fact alluded to? The 'old scar' is a universal human predicament; we all of us leave the absolute for a life of trouble and confusion. What is the hunger he speaks of, 'cette dure faim'? *3*. Why will their silence be like a cry that fills the night?

Anne Hébert

pages 266-71

NEIGE: *1*. The poet here evokes the beauty of snow and gives it meaning. In the first couplet snow sends us into a dream; in the second it propels us on horseback to imaginary lands. What happens in the third couplet? *2*. In the fourth couplet the 'red eye' of the heart is pierced. Why is red so strongly contrasted to white? In what sense are the 'eye' and the 'snow' opposites? How is the contrast carried through in the final couplet?

UNE PETITE MORTE: *1*. You will understand this poem better if you approach it as you do a fairy-tale, not as a real event. Yet it is serious. Something is represented by the figure of a dead little girl; it may be even an actual girl who died (but certainly not on the doorstep, and she was not left lying there). Suppose it is an actual death; her presence in our minds is expressed in the first eight lines. How does life proceed in the lines that follow? *2*. If the dead girl is, so to speak, in a mirror, and we do not see beyond that, what could be beyond the mirror? The moonlight image expresses how the dead one appears in our imagination. What is the contrast between this and the actuality? Do you feel a shock from the poem?

LA FILLE MAIGRE: *1*. This strange poem affects us even if we do not perfectly understand it. Perhaps the bony girl represents a sense of the body as a living skeleton, reduced to ascetic essentials, the mystery of frail life in the face of death. If so, what does the fourth couplet mean? *2*. She tells us that her lover has no heart; and she will hang herself in that empty place. At the most literal level, this might explain why a particular girl feels thin and dry: she does not feel loved. But the lover here could also represent God, whose 'heart' is at present absent. What would be the sacred object in the casket or reliquary? *3*. Suddenly — 'soudain' — the fancy in verse five is fulfilled, and she addresses the lover as dense space, 'espace comblé'. The universe itself, then, is apparently equated with the lover. Hanging in his breast — 'en ta poitrine, fixée' — what does she dream of as she half opens her eyes?

James Reaney
pages 272-5

THE KATZENJAMMER KIDS: *1*. A famous old comic strip — now less familiar, but still continuing in some newspapers — is the subject of this poem. What emotions does the poet feel for the comics? At what point in the poem does this emotion reach special intensity? *2*. In detail, what are the 'specks' in line 4? What relevance does the phrase 'innocent childish heart' have to the entire poem? What two meanings are contained in the phrase 'that funny paper weather'? Why is the word 'paper' repeated at the end? How does it add pathos to the theme of the poem?

THE SCHOOL GLOBE: *1*. This poem carries on the theme of the preceding poem, but leads to a terrifying conclusion. Poetry is often hyperbolic, an exaggeration, in order to intensify a feeling or idea — here the contrast between the world of harsh experience and the world of early innocence. Discuss such contrast from your own point of view. What do you think of it? *2*. What is the meaning of the word 'pluperfect'? Look up the derivation of the word. How do both the grammatical meaning and the etymology apply here?

Jay Macpherson
pages 276-7

CORAL: *1*. Literally the poem describes a 'tree' of coral under the sea. Are you satisfied with this literal meaning alone, or do you feel that the coral represents something else? Can you give any reasons why you think so? *2*. In verse one, what relation does the coral tree have to normal human pleasures and comforts? In verse two, what happens when it is brought into the human world we know? *3*. If it represents something that is alive, perfect and beautiful — a home for living things, or 'whatever wishes' — somewhere beyond our world — what kind of reality might it represent? (Obviously something unknown, but we might take a few guesses which would all be more or less acceptable.) *4*. Test what happens when you apply your guess to the points raised in question two.

Eli Mandel
pages 278-9

DAY OF ATONEMENT: STANDING: *1*. The poem deals with one of the most solemn holy days of the Hebrew faith, the Yom Kippur or Day of Atonement. It is a day of fasting and prayer. During the service, the believer is required several times to bow, or 'bend', in contrition as the prayer is recited. Does the speaker in this poem find it easy to bend? What is the significance of this? How does 'break' relate to it? *2*. Note the pun on the word 'bare'.

357

When the word is combined with 'tree', what meanings are brought to the poem? *3*. Is this a poem of piety? Answer the question that is posed without a question-mark in the opening line.

THE ANARCHIST-POETS: *1*. What is being referred to as 'bricks' and 'rubble'? In what sense could they be 'weapons'? *2*. Similarly, what is being described metaphorically as 'guerillas' and as 'running havoc'? In what sense did these desire peace, love, etc.? *3*. Although an anarchist political movement actually exists, and is represented in poetry, does the title refer to a particular school? To what, then? What do we learn from this poem about the condition of poetry in our time?

D. G. Jones
page 280

ON THE 24th OF MAY: *1*. In eastern Canadian cities, what does 'driving northward' usually suggest on a day in spring? Why are the cows called 'obsolete structures'? What range of things might be represented by 'cows', and what other things by 'cars'? *2*. Is there humour in the description of the cows? What purpose does it serve? What is the point of saying that the cows are 'profoundly unmoved'? Why 'profoundly'? (Compare this poem with Spender's 'He will watch the hawk', or E. J. Pratt's 'The Dying Eagle'.)

Leonard Cohen
pages 281-3

LES VIEUX: *1*. The *Northeastern* was one of a chain of low-cost cafeterias in Montreal, now no longer in business. Located in the centre of the city, it was frequented by vagrants and unemployed men. What is the irony in the phrase 'public men'? Why do these men tell lies? Why are children introduced into the picture? *2*. Why are the men 'unaware' of the commercial street? What are the 'letters of reference'? What does 'speaking all the languages' bring into the poem?

PRAYER FOR SUNSET: *1*. Read the story of Absalom in 2 Samuel xviii. 1-17. Compare closely the description of sunset in this poem with that story. (Terebinth is a small tree with winged, pinnate leaves.) *2*. What does 'clash' in line 13 suggest? Where is this again mentioned? *3*. The call for Joab suggests retribution. How might this be relevant (note lines 11-13)?

THE BUS: *1*. In what city is the poet riding this bus? What time of day is it? How do these two facts relate to the theme of the poem? *2*. In his fantasy, how far does he travel? Why do you think he indulges in such fantasy? Is there a general significance in this? *3*. What can you observe about the driver of the bus? Is this central or peripheral to the poem? Explain.

Gilles Vigneault
pages 284-90

QUAND VOUS MOURREZ DE NOS AMOURS: *1*. The meaning of a song lyric, unlike other poems, is often either very simple or even empty of rational meaning. It may, nevertheless, contain effective emotional or symbolic content. Love and death are closely linked in the imagination: the ecstasy of love is often considered as a kind of death. In this song, is the idea of death serious? Describe the fantasy of what the poet will do in each verse of the song. *2*. Can we interpret the meaning of each fantasy? (Verses two and three are easiest; they lead to the question of what love-poetry retains when the lovers are dead.) Interpret verses four and five in this sense.

'A DES OISEAUX D'AILLEURS . . .': *1*. *Ma mie* is an old poetic word for 'my love'. This song is almost Provençal in its feeling of old romance. In the first verse the poet asks his love to go and explain his songs to the world of nature. In what sense is time wearing the lovers away? How is the erosion of time made to appear more threatening in verse two? *2*. What should be the effect upon nature of the lover's statement? If this is imaginary, do you think it is justified? Why? What might be the 'secret' alluded to at the end?

SI LES BATEAUX: *1*. This poem is also based on a romantic fantasy that is easily interpreted. What does the building of ships probably mean to the two lovers? One of them is leaving and singing a song of farewell. What does he mean by saying that the imaginary ships they had built might sail before he returned? *2*. The refrain tells us of his love in hyperbolic terms. Why is the remoteness of England especially touching. *Istorlet* is literally the common tern in Acadian and northern Quebec dialect. Starling, which is cognate with this word, has been used as an English poetic equivalent. *3*. What does he encourage his lover to do about their dreams while he is gone (see verse two)? What kind of life is meant by becoming 'facteur ou jardinier'? What proposal from his old love would then be considered 'contrebande'? What experience that she might find elsewhere is described as 'que tu as vu l'Irlande'?

Jean-Guy Pilon
pages 291-5

NOCES: *1*. Jean-Guy Pilon has travelled to many parts of the world. This is a poem of return. What feeling does he record about the world he has seen? What is the poet's relation to this world? Is it clear or difficult for him to determine? *2*. What gives him a sense of direction at the end? What is his purpose in life? How does his affirmation relate to his native soil? What is the meaning of the title?

'L'EXIGENCE DU PAYS! ...': *1*. This selection is from a poem in thirteen sections in which the poet seeks for his true country, the country he needs to love. In the poem it has no name, 'même pas la douceur des syllabes', so that it may be Canada — if that becomes the land to which he can dedicate himself — or another, 'le choix difficile'. The poem is highly significant in Canada's present awakening and its crisis of nationhood. In this section, what geographical land seems to be described? *2*. In a later section the poet says, 'Tu ne seras jamais dans ton pays comme dans ta famille. / Tu accumuleras les échecs, les luttes, les fatigues et les humiliations.' [In your country you will never be at home as in your own family. / You will gather frustrations, quarrels, boredoms and humiliations.] How is this feeling of obstacles and difficulties related here to geographical size? Explain why it is difficult for the poet to call Canada 'my country'.

Alfred Purdy
pages 296-8

NEGROES ON ST. ANTOINE: *1*. The St. Antoine district in Montreal lies in an industrial section of the city, intersected by railways; it is also the Harlem of Montreal. What does the metaphor of 'molars' suggest? *2.* Mr. Kenyatta is the African leader in Kenya. What is the point of the comparison here? What 'century' or 'time' does the boy before the billboard enter when he dances? *3.* Why are the references to Israeli gunners, Spartacus, and Lumumba introduced? What have they in common with the present subject? *4.* How is Mount Royal related to the problem? Place Ville Marie is a new complex of skyscrapers. Why is the 'cruciform' shape mentioned?

SCARCITIES: *1.* In this love poem, the idea of snow is first introduced as a metaphor, affording reticence. *2.* In the last six lines, the metaphor seems to be 'reversed' and we are talking of actual snow. This makes for interesting indirection. How does the title clarify the meaning?

Alden Nowlan
pages 299-301

THE BULL MOOSE: *1.* What is the contrast between the bull moose and the cattle in stanza two? What is the view that the poet takes of the people in stanzas three and four? *2.* What would you say the final roar of the moose conveys to us? Why do the young men 'lean on their ... horns'? What is the feeling you get from this closing picture?

THE EXECUTION: *1.* In wanting to be considered simply as 'Press', what 'attitude' does the speaker want to take to the event? He is unable to take this attitude in the conclusion. Why? In a general way, does this apply to other tragic events in life? Do you see what the poem means? *2.* What does the mistaken identity of 'Padre' bring to the poem? How does it contrast with 'Press'?

Eldon Grier
pages 302-3

'ENGLISH POETRY NEVER WENT CRAZY': *1.* These lines are an extract from a longer poem in several sections. Compare them with the poem by Lawrence Ferlinghetti at the end of the British and American selections. *2.* How do you understand the phrase 'music not meaning'? Are there poems in this book that approach this definition? Which ones? 3. What is the ultimate reality conveyed by such jewelled words? Would you like more of such poetry? If so, your reading begins where this book ends.

Poems for Comparison and Contrast

POEMS ABOUT GOOD AND EVIL

WHITMAN, 'The little one sleeps in its cradle'; YEATS, 'The Second Coming'; SANDBURG, 'Chicago'; MASTERS, 'Seth Compton', 'Minerva Jones', 'Doctor Meyers', 'Daisy Fraser'; POUND, 'What thou lovest well remains . . .'; JEFFERS, 'Shine, Perishing Republic'; GASCOYNE, 'Ecce Homo'; SCOTT, 'Conflict'.

POEMS ABOUT AGE AND DEATH

HOPKINS, 'Spring and Fall'; HOUSMAN, 'To an Athlete Dying Young'; FROST, 'Out, Out — '; ELIOT, 'Death by Water'; WILLIAMS, 'The Act'; STEVENS, 'The Emperor of Ice-Cream', 'The Worms at Heaven's Gate'; CUMMINGS, 'Buffalo Bill's defunct'; RANSOM, 'Blue Girls', 'Janet Waking'; THOMAS, 'And Death shall have no Dominion'; SMITH, 'Beside One Dead'; GARNEAU, 'Cage d'oiseau'; WILKINSON, 'I Am So Tired'; LAYTON, 'First Snow: Lake Achigan'; DUDEK, 'News'; HÉBERT, 'Une Petite Morte'; NOWLAN, 'The Bull Moose'.

ON EDUCATION

MASTERS, 'Emily Sparks', 'Reuben Pantier'; WILLIAMS, 'Education a Failure'; AUDEN, 'Schoolchildren'; COMFORT, 'Notes for My Son'; SOUSTER, 'The Man Who Finds His Son Has Become a Thief'; REANEY, 'The School Globe'.

ON THE NATURE OF BEAUTY

HOPKINS, 'Spring'; DICKINSON, 'I died for beauty'; YEATS, 'Adam's Curse'; POUND, 'The Study in Aesthetics'; ELIOT, 'A Game of Chess'; WILLIAMS, 'The Red Wheelbarrow', 'Contemporania'; CUMMINGS, 'Poem, or Beauty Hurts Mr. Vinal'; MACNEICE, 'Morning Sun', 'Snow'; SPENDER, 'The Pylons'; JEFFERS, 'Natural Music', 'Fire on the Hills'; THOMAS, 'Fern Hill'; WILBUR, 'The Beautiful Changes'; SMITH, 'The Lonely Land'; PAGE, 'The Bands and the Beautiful Children'; DUDEK, 'Tree in a Street'.

ON POETS AND POETRY

YEATS, 'Adam's Curse'; MASTERS, 'Minerva Jones'; FROST, 'The Pasture'; STEVENS, 'Bantams in Pine-Woods'; MOORE, 'Poetry'; AUDEN, 'In Memory of W. B. Yeats'; SPENDER, 'I think continually . . .';

THOMAS, 'This Bread I break', 'In My Craft or Sullen Art'; FERLIN-
GHETTI, 'Constantly risking absurdity . . .'; NELLIGAN, 'Le Vaisseau
d'Or'; SMITH, 'News of the Phoenix'; EVERSON, 'Greeks Had Nothing Else To Do', 'Credo'; MANDEL, 'The Anarchist-Poets'; GRIER,
'English poetry never went crazy'.

POEMS OF LOVE AND SEPARATION

YEATS, 'He Thinks of Those Who Have Spoken Evil of His Beloved', 'Adam's Curse'; SANDBURG, 'Cool Tombs', 'Gone', 'The
Shovel Man'; POUND, 'The River-Merchant's Wife: A Letter';
LAWRENCE, 'A Young Wife'; WILLIAMS, 'Love Song'; CRANE, 'Virginia'; GRAVES, 'A Slice of Wedding Cake'; PRATT, 'Cherries';
VIGNEAULT, 'Quand vous mourrez de nos amours', 'A des oiseaux d'-
ailleurs . . .', 'Si les bateaux'; PURDY, 'Scarcities'.

POEMS OF FAITH AND DOUBT

HOPKINS, 'No worst, there is none'; DICKINSON, 'Some keep the Sab-
bath going to church', 'I taste a liquor never brewed'; HARDY, 'The
Darkling Thrush'; ROBINSON, 'Richard Cory'; YEATS, 'The Second
Coming'; MASTERS, 'Seth Compton'; POUND, 'What thou lovest well
remains . . .'; ELIOT, 'Journey of the Magi', 'Choruses from "The
Rock"'; WILLIAMS, 'Education a Failure'; STEVENS, 'The Emperor
of Ice-Cream', 'The Worms at Heaven's Gate', 'The Snow Man';
CUMMINGS, 'Buffalo Bill's defunct'; MACNEICE, 'Sunday Morning';
JEFFERS, 'The Answer', 'Blind Horses', 'Fire on the Hills'; THOMAS,
'This Bread I break', 'And Death shall have no Dominion';
LOWELL, 'Our Lady of Walsingham'; GASCOYNE, 'Ecce Homo';
SCOTT, 'Christmas Shopping'; DANIELLS, 'Psalm 23'; MANDEL, 'Day of
Atonement: Standing'.

POLITICS AND THE WORLD DISORDER

YEATS, 'On Being Asked for a War Poem'; SANDBURG, 'Chicago';
POUND, 'These fought in any case', 'There died a myriad'; ELIOT, 'A
Game of Chess'; CUMMINGS, 'Poem, or Beauty Hurts Mr. Vinal';
CRANE, 'The nasal whine of power . . .'; MACNEICE, 'The Daily
News'; AUDEN, 'Say this city has ten million souls', 'The Unknown
Citizen'; JEFFERS, 'The Answer', 'Shine, Perishing Republic',
'Triad'; GASCOYNE, 'Ecce Homo'; COMFORT, 'Notes for My Son';
SCOTT, 'Conflict'; BIRNEY, 'Status quo', 'Time-bomb'; LAYTON, 'From
Colony to Nation', 'Anglo-Canadian'; PURDY, 'Negroes on St.
Antoine'.

364

Books on Modern Poetry

COMPREHENSIVE ANTHOLOGIES

Baillargeon, Samuel, *Littérature canadienne-française*, Montreal, Fides, 1957.

Smith, A. J. M., ed., *The Book of Canadian Poetry: A Critical and Historical Anthology*, 3rd edition, Toronto, W. J. Gage Limited, 1957.

Untermeyer, Louis, *Modern American Poetry, Modern British Poetry*, New York, Harcourt, Brace & World, Inc., 1953.

GENERAL

Allen, Donald A., ed., *The New American Poetry: 1945-1960*, New York, Grove Press, 1960 (Toronto, Saunders of Toronto Limited).

Bogan, Louise, *Achievement in American Poetry*, Chicago, Henry Regnery Co., 1951 (Toronto, The Copp Clark Publishing Co., Ltd.).

Brooks, Cleanth, *Modern Poetry and the Tradition*, University of North Carolina Press, 1939 (Toronto, The Ryerson Press).

Deutsch, Babette, *Poetry in Our Time*, New York, Holt, Rinehart & Winston, 1952 (Toronto, Doubleday Publishers).

Durrell, Lawrence, *A Key to Modern British Poetry*, Norman, Oklahoma, University of Oklahoma Press, 1952 (Toronto, Burns & MacEachern Limited).

Fraser, G. S., *The Modern Writer and His World*, New York, Criterion Books, 1955.

Hulme, T. E., *Speculations*, New York, Harcourt, Brace & World, Inc., 1924 (Toronto, Longmans Canada Limited).

MacNeice, Louis, *Modern Poetry*, Oxford, Oxford University Press, 1938 (Toronto, Queenswood House Limited).

O'Connor, Wm. Van, *Sense and Sensibility in Modern Poetry*, Barnes & Noble, 1948 (Toronto, The Ryerson Press).

Rosenthal, M. L., *The Modern Poets: A Critical Introduction*, New York, Oxford University Press, 1960 (Toronto, Oxford University Press).

Spender, Stephen, *The Struggle of the Modern*, London, Hamish Hamilton, 1963 (Toronto, William Collins Sons & Co. Canada Ltd.).

Thorp, Willard, *American Writing in the Twentieth Century*, Cambridge, Mass., Harvard University Press, 1960 (Toronto, Saunders of Toronto Limited).

INDIVIDUAL AUTHORS

W. H. AUDEN

Hoggart, Richard, *Auden: An Introductory Essay*, London, Chatto and Windus Ltd., 1951 (Toronto, Clarke, Irwin and Co. Ltd.).

Spears, Monroe K., *The Poetry of W. H. Auden: The Disenchanted Island*, New York, Oxford University Press, 1963.

T. S. ELIOT

Selected Essays, 1917-1932, New York, Harcourt, Brace & World, Inc., 2nd edition, 1960 (Toronto, Longmans Canada Limited).

Matthiessen, F. O., *The Achievement of T. S. Eliot: An Essay on the Nature of Poetry*, New York, Oxford University Press, 1947.

Unger, Leonard, ed., *T. S. Eliot: A Selected Critique*, New York, University of Minnesota Press, 1961 (Toronto, The Copp Clark Publishing Co.).

ROBINSON JEFFERS

Squires, Radcliffe, *The Loyalties of Robinson Jeffers*, Ann Arbor, University of Michigan Press, 1956 (Toronto, Ambassador Books Ltd.).

EZRA POUND

Selected Essays, New York, New Directions, 1951 (Toronto, McClelland and Stewart Ltd.).

Paige, D. D., ed., *The Letters of Ezra Pound, 1907-1941*, New York, Harcourt, Brace & World, Inc., 1950 (Toronto, Queenswood House Limited).

Rosenthal, M. L., *A Primer of Ezra Pound*, New York, The Macmillan Company, 1960 (Toronto, Collier-Macmillan Canada Ltd.).

CARL SANDBURG

Golden, Harry, *Carl Sandburg*, Cleveland, World Publishing Company, 1961 (Toronto, Nelson, Foster and Scott, Ltd.).

STEPHEN SPENDER

World Within World, London, Hamish Hamilton, 1951 (Toronto, William Collins Sons & Co. Canada Ltd.).

DYLAN THOMAS

Brinnin, John Malcolm, *Dylan Thomas in America: An Intimate Journal*, New York, The Viking Press, 1955 (Toronto, The Macmillan Company of Canada Limited).

Olson, Elder, *The Poetry of Dylan Thomas*, Chicago, University of Chicago Press, 1954 (Toronto, University of Toronto Press).

WALT WHITMAN

Allen, Gay Wilson, *Walt Whitman*, New York, Grove Press, Evergreen Profile Book 19, 1961 (Toronto, Saunders of Toronto Limited).

WILLIAM CARLOS WILLIAMS

The Autobiography of William Carlos Williams, New York, New Directions, 1965 (Toronto, McClelland and Stewart Ltd.).

W. B. YEATS

Hall, James, and Martin Steinmann, eds., *The Permanence of Yeats*, New York, Collier Books, 1961 (Toronto, Collier-Macmillan Canada Ltd.).

Hone, Joseph, *W. B. Yeats, 1865-1939*, London, Macmillan & Co. Ltd., 1942 (Toronto, The Macmillan Company of Canada Limited).

Jeffares, Norman, *W. B. Yeats, Man and Poet*, London, Routledge & Kegan Paul Ltd., 1949.

CANADIAN LITERATURE

Marcotte, Gilles, *Une Littérature qui se fait*, Montreal, les Editions HMH, Ltee, 1962.

Pacey, Desmond, *Creative Writing in Canada: A Short History of English Canadian Literature*, Toronto, The Ryerson Press, 1961.

Pacey, Desmond, *Ten Canadian Poets: A Group of Biographical and Critical Essays*, Toronto, The Ryerson Press, 1958.

Rashley, R. E., *Poetry in Canada: The First Three Steps*, Toronto, The Ryerson Press, 1958.

367

Index of Authors

369